my **revision** notes

AQA A-level
BUSINESS

Neil James

HODDER
EDUCATION
AN HACHETTE UK COMPANY

Hachette UK's policy is to use papers that are natural, renewable and recyclable products and made from wood grown in sustainable forests. The logging and manufacturing processes are expected to conform to the environmental regulations of the country of origin.

Orders: please contact Bookpoint Ltd, 130 Milton Park, Abingdon, Oxon OX14 4SB.
Telephone: (44) 01235 827720.
Fax: (44) 01235 400454.
Email education@bookpoint.co.uk

Lines are open from 9 a.m. to 5 p.m., Monday to Saturday, with a 24-hour message answering service. You can also order through our website: www.hoddereducation.co.uk

ISBN: 978 1 4718 4216 0

First published in 2016 by
Hodder Education,
An Hachette UK Company
Carmelite House
50 Victoria Embankment
London EC4Y 0DZ
www.hoddereducation.co.uk

Impression number   10   9   8   7   6   5   4   3
Year   2020   2019

Cover photo reproduced by permission of peshkov/Fotolia

Typeset in Bembo Std Regular 11/13 pts. by Aptara, Inc.

Printed in India

A catalogue record for this title is available from the British Library.

Get the most from this book

Everyone has to decide his or her own revision strategy, but it is essential to review your work, learn it and test your understanding. These Revision Notes will help you to do that in a planned way, topic by topic. Use this book as the cornerstone of your revision and do not hesitate to write in it — personalise your notes and check your progress by ticking off each section as you revise.

Tick to track your progress

Use the revision planner on pages 4 and 5 to plan your revision, topic by topic. Tick each box when you have:

- revised and understood a topic
- tested yourself
- practised the exam questions and gone online to check your answers and complete the quick quizzes

You can also keep track of your revision by ticking off each topic heading in the book. You may find it helpful to add your own notes as you work through each topic.

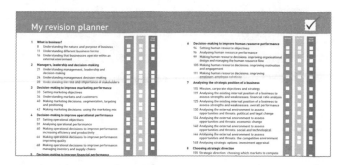

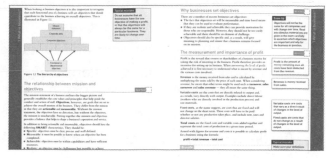

Features to help you succeed

Exam tips

Expert tips are given throughout the book to help you polish your exam technique in order to maximise your chances in the exam.

Typical mistakes

The author identifies the typical mistakes candidates make and explains how you can avoid them.

Now test yourself

These short, knowledge-based questions provide the first step in testing your learning. Answers are at the back of the book.

Definitions and key words

Clear, concise definitions of essential key terms are provided where they first appear.

Key words from the specification are highlighted in bold throughout the book.

Revision activities

These activities will help you to understand each topic in an interactive way.

Exam practice

Practice exam questions are provided for each topic. Use them to consolidate your revision and practise your exam skills.

Summaries

The summaries provide a quick-check bullet list for each topic.

Online

Go online to check your answers to the exam questions and try out the extra quick quizzes at **www.hoddereducation.co.uk/myrevisionnotes**

My revision planner

		REVISED	TESTED	EXAM READY

1 What is business?

7 Understanding the nature and purpose of business ✓ ✓ ☐

10 Understanding different business forms ✓ ✓ ☐

15 Understanding that businesses operate within an external environment ☐ ☐ ☐

2 Managers, leadership and decision-making

20 Understanding management, leadership and decision-making ☐ ☐ ☐

23 Understanding management decision-making ☐ ☐ ☐

27 Understanding the role and importance of stakeholders ☐ ☐ ☐

3 Decision-making to improve marketing performance

32 Setting marketing objectives ☐ ☐ ☐

33 Understanding markets and customers ☐ ☐ ☐

39 Making marketing decisions: segmentation, targeting and positioning ☐ ☐ ☐

41 Making marketing decisions: using the marketing mix ☐ ☐ ☐

4 Decision-making to improve operational performance

56 Setting operational objectives ☐ ☐ ☐

58 Analysing operational performance ☐ ☐ ☐

59 Making operational decisions to improve performance: increasing efficiency and productivity ☐ ☐ ☐

65 Making operational decisions to improve performance: improving quality ☐ ☐ ☐

67 Making operational decisions to improve performance: managing inventory and supply chains ☐ ☐ ☐

5 Decision-making to improve financial performance

72 Setting financial objectives ☐ ☐ ☐

76 Analysing financial performance ☐ ☐ ☐

87 Making financial decisions: sources of finance ☐ ☐ ☐

90 Making financial decisions: improving cash flow and profits ☐ ☐ ☐

6 Decision-making to improve human resource performance

93 Setting human resource objectives ☐ ☐ ☐

95 Analysing human resource performance ☐ ☐ ☐

98 Making human resource decisions: improving organisational design and managing the human resource flow ☐ ☐ ☐

104 Making human resource decisions: improving motivation and engagement ☐ ☐ ☐

110 Making human resource decisions: improving employer–employee relations ☐ ☐ ☐

7 Analysing the strategic position of a business

114 Mission, corporate objectives and strategy

118 Analysing the existing internal position of a business to assess strengths and weaknesses: financial ratio analysis

124 Analysing the existing internal position of a business to assess strengths and weaknesses: overall performance

129 Analysing the external environment to assess opportunities and threats: political and legal change

133 Analysing the external environment to assess opportunities and threats: economic change

139 Analysing the external environment to assess opportunities and threats: social and technological

145 Analysing the external environment to assess opportunities and threats: the competitive environment

147 Analysing strategic options: investment appraisal

8 Choosing strategic direction

154 Strategic direction: choosing which markets to compete in and what products to offer

156 Strategic positioning: choosing how to compete

9 Strategic methods: how to pursue strategies

162 Assessing a change in scale

168 Assessing innovation

171 Assessing internationalisation

176 Assessing greater use of digital technology

10 Managing strategic change

181 Managing change

187 Managing organisational culture

191 Managing strategic implementation

196 Problems with strategy and why strategies fail

202 Now test yourself answers

Exam practice answers and quick quizzes at www.hoddereducation.co.uk/myrevisionnotes

REVISED   TESTED   EXAM READY

Countdown to my exams

6–8 weeks to go

- Start by looking at the specification — make sure you know exactly what material you need to revise and the style of the examination. Use the revision planner on pages 4 and 5 to familiarise yourself with the topics.
- Organise your notes, making sure you have covered everything on the specification. The revision planner will help you to group your notes into topics.
- Work out a realistic revision plan that will allow you time for relaxation. Set aside days and times for all the subjects that you need to study, and stick to your timetable.
- Set yourself sensible targets. Break your revision down into focused sessions of around 40 minutes, divided by breaks. These Revision Notes organise the basic facts into short, memorable sections to make revising easier.

REVISED ☐

4–6 weeks to go

- Read through the relevant sections of this book and refer to the exam tips, summaries, typical mistakes and key terms. Tick off the topics as you feel confident about them. Highlight those topics you find difficult and look at them again in detail.
- Test your understanding of each topic by working through the 'Now test yourself' questions and 'Revision activities' in the book. Look up the answers at the back of the book.
- Make a note of any problem areas as you revise, and ask your teacher to go over these in class.
- Look at past papers. They are one of the best ways to revise and practise your exam skills. Write or prepare planned answers to the exam practice questions provided in this book. Check your answers online and try out the extra quick quizzes at **www.hoddereducation.co.uk/ myrevisionnotes**
- Use the revision activities to try different revision methods. For example, you can make notes using mind maps, spider diagrams or flash cards.
- Track your progress using the revision planner and give yourself a reward when you have achieved your target.

REVISED ☐

One week to go

- Try to fit in at least one more timed practice of an entire past paper and seek feedback from your teacher, comparing your work closely with the mark scheme.
- Check the revision planner to make sure you haven't missed out any topics. Brush up on any areas of difficulty by talking them over with a friend or getting help from your teacher.
- Attend any revision classes put on by your teacher. Remember, he or she is an expert at preparing people for examinations.

REVISED ☐

The day before the examination

- Flick through these Revision Notes for useful reminders, for example the exam tips, summaries, typical mistakes and key terms.
- Check the time and place of your examination.
- Make sure you have everything you need — extra pens and pencils, tissues, a watch, bottled water, sweets.
- Allow some time to relax and have an early night to ensure you are fresh and alert for the examination.

REVISED ☐

My exams

A-level Paper 1: Business 1

Date:...18th March...............................
Time:...9am..
Location:...

A-level Paper 2: Business 2

Date:...25th March.............................
Time:...9am..
Location:...

A-level Paper 3: Business 3

Date:...30th March.............................
Time:...9am..
Location:...

1 What is business?

Understanding the nature and purpose of business

Why businesses exist

Businesses exist in many shapes and sizes and for different purposes. The opportunity for making **profit** is an important reason why they exist, but it is not the only reason. Other reasons are:

- to provide goods and services; this includes public services, such as the NHS and police and fire services
- to develop a good idea (enterprise)
- to provide help and support for others, most notably charities that raise funds in various ways to help and support the lives of others

Mission statements

A business **mission statement**, sometimes called a 'vision statement', defines what an organisation is, why it exists and its reason for being. It is a declaration of its core purpose and focus. Here are two examples:

> A **mission statement** is a declaration of a business's core purpose and focus.

> To passionately create innovation for our stakeholders at the intersection of chemistry, biology and physics. (**The Dow Chemical Company**)

> Bring inspiration and innovation to every athlete in the world. (**NIKE, Inc.**)

The purpose of the mission statement is to help bring focus and meaning to a business and act as a guide when making critical decisions that may affect the direction of a business.

Common business objectives

When looking at the **objectives** of a business, it is important to remember that they are quite complex and will vary according to circumstances and the type of organisation. A charity will have different objectives to a public limited company, but even different public limited companies may have different objectives. Three key objectives of business are:

> An **objective** is a goal to help a business achieve its mission.

- survival
- growth
- profit

Over recent years the global nature of business and the intense competition in many markets has meant that two other objectives have become increasingly important, namely:

- customer service
- corporate social responsibility (CSR)

CSR refers to the commitment of business to behave ethically towards their workforce, the local community and society at large, i.e. companies take responsibility for their impact on society.

When looking at business objectives it is also important to recognise that each functional area of a business will set objectives that should contribute to the business achieving its overall objectives. This is illustrated in Figure 1.1.

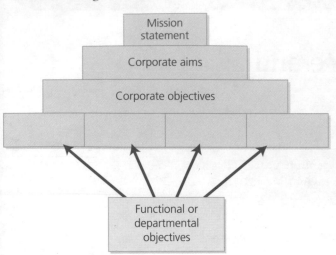

Figure 1.1 The hierarchy of objectives

The relationship between mission and objectives

 REVISED

The mission statement of a business outlines the bigger picture and generally establishes the core values and principles that help guide the conduct and action of staff. **Objectives**, however, are goals that are set to achieve the overall mission of the business. They differ from the mission in that they are **actionable** and **measurable**. Without the mission statement, the objectives have no direction, but without the objectives, the mission is unachievable. Putting together the mission and objectives provides a balance that helps to shape a business's operation and service.

In addition to being actionable and measurable, objectives should have the following **SMART** characteristics. They should be:

- **S**pecific: objectives must be clear, precise and well defined.
- **M**easurable: it must be possible to know when an objective has been completed.
- **A**chievable: objectives must be within capabilities and have sufficient resources.
- **R**ealistic: an objective must be challenging but possible to achieve given the capabilities and resources.
- **T**ime based: there must be a deadline to work to.

As an example, an objective for a new coffee chain entering the UK market might be increasing market share by 2.5% a year for the next 5 years. This is a SMART objective as there is a clearly defined and measurable goal, whereas simply aiming to achieve growth in market share is not.

The relative importance of different objectives is likely to vary over time depending on circumstances. In difficult economic times, survival is likely to be more important than profit or environmental targets, whereas in a booming economy, profit, growth and social issues will take on a far more important role.

Why businesses set objectives

There are a number of reasons why businesses set objectives:
- The fact that objectives set will be measurable and time based means that they can be used to evaluate performance.
- If they are realistic and achievable they can provide motivation for those who are responsible. However, they should not be too easily achievable and there should be an element of challenge.
- Objectives should also be specific and, as a result, will give meaning to planning and ensure that a business remains focused on its mission.

> **Exam tip**
>
> Objectives will not be the same for all companies and will change over time. Read any stimulus material you are given in the exam carefully to ascertain which objectives are important and why for the business in question.

The measurement and importance of profit

Profit is the reward that owners or shareholders of a business receive for taking the risk of investing in the business. Profit therefore provides an incentive for setting up in business. When measuring the level of profit achieved it is first necessary to understand what is meant by revenue and the various costs involved.

Revenue is the money received from sales and is calculated by multiplying the units sold by the price of each unit. When considering revenue, be aware that other terms might be used, such as **turnover**, **sales turnover** and **sales revenue** — they all mean the same thing.

Variable costs are the costs that are directly related to output and, as a result, vary directly with output. Examples include direct labour (workers who are directly involved in the production process) and raw materials.

Fixed costs, as the name suggests, are costs that are fixed and will not change in the short term. These costs will have to be paid whether or not any production takes place, and include rent, rates and director salaries.

Total costs are the fixed costs and variable costs added together and represent the total costs of production in a given time period.

Armed with figures for revenue and costs it is possible to calculate profit for a business using the formula:

> Profit = total revenue – total cost

> **Profit** is the amount of money remaining once all costs have been deducted from the revenue.
>
> **Revenue** is money received from sales.

> **Variable costs** are costs that vary as a direct result of changes in the level of output.
>
> **Fixed costs** are costs that do not change as a result of changes in the level of output.

> **Example**
>
> A business produces 10,000 units which it sells for £5 each. Its variable costs are £25,000 and its fixed costs £10,000.
>
> Profit = total revenue – total costs
>
> Total revenue = 10,000 × £5 = £50,000
>
> Total cost = variable costs + fixed costs = £25,000 + £10,000 = £35,000
>
> Profit = £50,000 – £35,000 = £15,000

> **Typical mistake**
>
> Make sure your definitions are complete and your examples are accurate. When defining variable costs it is not enough to say that they vary with output — they vary *directly* with output. In the same way, it is not labour that is the variable cost but labour *directly* involved with output.

Now test yourself

1 List three reasons why businesses exist.
2 Outline how a mission statement differs from objectives.
3 List five business objectives.
4 Draw up a table to illustrate the likely objectives of the following: a public limited company; a public sector organisation; a charity.
5 Explain briefly why a business would write a mission statement.
6 Outline why it is necessary for any business objective to be SMART.
7 From the figures below, calculate the expected profit of ABC Ltd.
Output: 10,000 units
Price: £5 per unit
Fixed costs: £5,000
Variable costs: £3 per unit

Answers on p. 202

Understanding different business forms

Different forms of business

REVISED

Private sector businesses

Businesses in the **private sector** fall into two broad categories: corporate and non-corporate, as shown in Table 1.1.

> The **private sector** is part of the economy made up of private enterprises — businesses that are owned and controlled by individuals or groups of individuals.

Table 1.1 Types of business

Corporate businesses	Non-corporate businesses
Private limited companies	Sole traders (or sole proprietors)
Public limited companies	Partnerships

Corporate businesses

Corporate businesses have a legal identity that is separate from that of their owners. Their owners benefit from limited liability. **Limited liability** restricts the financial responsibility of shareholders for a company's debts to the amount they have individually invested. It means that a company can sue and be sued and can enter into contracts. Limited liability has an important implication for the owners (shareholders) of corporate businesses because, in the event of such a business failing, the shareholders' private possessions are safe. Their liability is limited to the amount they have invested.

There are two methods by which the liability of shareholders can be limited:

- **By shares.** In this case, a shareholder's liability is limited to the value of the shares that he or she has purchased. There can be no further call on the shareholder's wealth.
- **By guarantee.** Each member's liability is restricted to the amount he/she has agreed to pay in the event of the business being wound up. This is more common with not-for-profit businesses.

> **Corporate businesses** are businesses which have a legal identity that is separate from that of their owners.
>
> **Limited liability** restricts the financial responsibility of shareholders for a company's debts to the amount they have individually invested.

There are two main types of corporate company:
- **Private limited companies.** These are normally much smaller than public limited companies. Share capital must not exceed £50,000 and 'Ltd' must be included after the company's name. The shares of a private limited company cannot be bought and sold without the agreement of other shareholders. The company's shares cannot be sold on the Stock Exchange. Private limited companies are normally relatively small and are often family businesses.
- **Public limited companies.** Their shares can be traded on the Stock Exchange and bought by any business or individual. Public limited companies must have the term 'plc' after their name. They must have a minimum capital of £50,000 by law; in practice, this figure is likely to be far higher. Public limited companies have to publish more details of their financial affairs than do private limited companies.

Those forming a company must send two main documents to the Registrar of Companies:
- **Memorandum of Association.** This sets out details of the company's name and address and its objectives in trading.
- **Articles of Association.** This details the internal arrangements of the company, including frequency of shareholders' meetings.

Once these documents have been approved, the company receives a Certificate of Incorporation and can commence trading.

Non-corporate businesses

Non-corporate businesses and their owners are not treated as separate elements — an owner's private possessions are all at risk in the event of failure. Sole traders and partners are usually said to have unlimited liability. However, since 2000 it has been possible to establish limited liability partnerships (LLPs) which offer partners financial protection.

The different types of non-corporate business are:
- **Sole traders (or proprietors).** These are businesses owned by a single person, although the business may have a number of employees. Such one-person businesses are common in retailing and services, e.g. plumbing and hairdressing.
- **Partnerships.** These comprise between two and 20 people who contribute capital and expertise to a business. A partnership is usually based on a Deed of Partnership, which states how much capital each partner has contributed, the share of profits each shall receive and the rules for electing new partners. Some partners may be 'sleeping partners', contributing capital but taking no active part in the business. Partnerships are common in the professions, e.g. dentists and accountants.

The advantages and disadvantages of the various legal forms of business are shown in Table 1.2.

Not-for-profit businesses

Not all businesses aim to make profits. A **not-for-profit business** is any organisation, such as a charity, that has business objectives other than making a profit. These businesses are also called 'social enterprises'.

Social enterprises trade in a wide range of industries and operate with a number of non-profit objectives:
- **To provide services to local communities.** Some social enterprises may remove graffiti or clean up beaches for the benefit of entire communities.

> **Typical mistake**
>
> Do not propose starting a new business as a public limited company in response to an examination question. The huge costs involved mean that this is most unlikely to happen.

> **Typical mistake**
>
> Many students argue that it is expensive and complicated to set up a private limited company. This is not true and these are not valid reasons to argue against the use of this legal form of business.

> A **not-for-profit business** is an organisation that has business objectives other than making a profit.

- **To give people job-related skills.** The television chef, Jamie Oliver, runs a chain of restaurants (called 'Fifteen') with the prime objective of providing training in a variety of catering skills for young people from disadvantaged backgrounds.
- **Fair-trading activities.** Some businesses import products from less developed countries but pay above the market price for the products. They may also invest in facilities, such as education and healthcare, in the exporting communities.

Mutuals

Mutuals are generally private businesses whose ownership base is made up of their clients and policy holders. They are characterised by the fact they are run for the benefit of their members, e.g. cooperatives. Insurance companies and building societies were traditionally organised in this way, but many of the biggest have changed to become public limited companies.

Table 1.2 The advantages and disadvantages of different legal forms of business

Type of business	Advantages	Disadvantages
Sole trader	<ul><li>Simple and cheap to establish with few legal formalities.</li><li>The owner receives all the profits (if there are any).</li><li>Able to respond quickly to changes in the market.</li><li>Confidentiality is maintained as financial details do not have to be published.</li></ul>	<ul><li>The owner is likely to be short of capital for investment and expansion.</li><li>Few assets for collateral to support applications for loans.</li><li>Unlimited liability.</li><li>It can be difficult for sole traders to take holidays.</li></ul>
Partnership	<ul><li>Between them, partners may have a wide range of skills and knowledge.</li><li>Partners are able to raise greater amounts of capital than sole traders.</li><li>The pressure on owners is reduced as cover is available for holidays and there is support in making decisions.</li></ul>	<ul><li>Control is shared between the partners.</li><li>Arguments are common among partners.</li><li>There is still an absolute shortage of capital — even 20 people can only raise so much.</li><li>Unlimited liability.</li></ul>
Private limited company	<ul><li>Shareholders benefit from limited liability.</li><li>Companies have access to greater amounts of capital.</li><li>Private limited companies are only required to divulge a limited amount of financial information.</li><li>Companies have a separate legal identity.</li></ul>	<ul><li>Private limited companies cannot sell their shares on the Stock Exchange.</li><li>Requiring permission to sell shares limits potential for flexibility and growth.</li><li>Private limited companies have to conform to a number of expensive administrative formalities.</li></ul>
Public limited company	<ul><li>Public limited companies can gain positive publicity as a result of trading on the Stock Exchange.</li><li>Stock Exchange quotation offers access to large amounts of capital.</li><li>Stock Exchange rules are strict and this encourages investors to part with their money.</li><li>Suppliers will be more willing to offer credit to public limited companies.</li></ul>	<ul><li>A Stock Exchange listing means emphasis is placed on short-term financial results, not long-term performance.</li><li>Public limited companies are required to publish a great deal of financial information.</li><li>Trading as a public limited company can result in significant administrative expenses.</li></ul>

Public sector organisations

Some services and business in the UK are controlled and run by the government or local authorities and are referred to as being in the **public sector**. This includes services such as police, fire, the BBC and the NHS as well as local council run services such as rubbish collection. This sector used to include a number of key industries and utilities such as coal, steel, water, telephone etc. that were known as 'nationalised industries'. These have largely been sold off to the private sector through a **privatisation** process.

> The **public sector** is part of the economy that is owned and controlled by the government or local authorities.
>
> **Privatisation** is the process of converting government owned and controlled industries/businesses to the private sector.

Now test yourself TESTED

8 Identify three differences between a corporate business and a non-corporate business.
9 Using examples, define the public sector.
10 List and explain three objectives that a not-for-profit business may have.
11 How does a mutual organisation differ from other incorporated business organisations?

Answers on p. 202

Reasons for choosing different forms of business

 REVISED

The key choice in terms of business structure is between **unincorporated** and **incorporated** status. There are a number of factors that may be considered here:

● **Formalities and expenses.** Sole traders and partnerships are relatively easy to set up with few formalities. This is an ideal form for small businesses such as joiners, electricians and corner shops.
● **Size and risk**. If a business is and intends to remain small and carries little in the way of risk, then a sole trader or partnership may be the most appropriate form of business. This is the reason many corner shops, joiners and electricians remain as sole traders.
● **Objectives of the owners**. If the objectives of the owners involve growth, then forming an incorporated business might be more appropriate. This is likely to give greater access to capital and limited liability would reduce the risks involved for the owners.

Reasons for changing business form

 REVISED

The main reasons for changing business form are as follows:

● **Circumstances.** Due to changing circumstances, such as the growth of a business, the owner/s may wish to become incorporated in order to benefit from limited liability.
● **Capital.** The owner/s of a business may find it easier to raise capital by becoming incorporated or by becoming a public limited company if it is a private limited company.
● **Acquisition or takeover.** This may cause a change of structure, e.g. a private limited company may be taken over by a public limited company.

Although businesses generally change from private limited to public limited, it is also possible to move the other way, i.e. from public to private limited. A business may do this to escape the constant scrutiny of the city and the pressure of short-term shareholder objectives. A good example of this is Richard Branson's Virgin.

Now test yourself questions

TESTED

12 Why are most new businesses set up as sole traders?
13 List three reasons for changing the legal form of a business.

Answers on p. 202

The role of shareholders and why they invest

REVISED

Ordinary share capital is the money invested in a company by **shareholders** entitling them to part ownership of the company. This capital is permanent and will never have to be paid back to the owners by the company. If the owners wish to get their money back, they can sell their shares through the stock market. Private individuals can invest in public limited companies, becoming shareholders and part-owners of the business, but private individuals will only ever own a small fraction of the shares of any one business. By far the biggest shareholders will be financial institutions such as pension funds and insurance companies.

Shareholders have certain rights and a role to play in the running of a business. Major decisions that will have an impact on shareholders are required to be approved by the shareholders at a general meeting called by the directors. The main role of shareholders therefore is to attend this meeting and discuss whatever is on the agenda and to ensure the directors do not go beyond their powers. There are also only certain actions that can be done by shareholders, such as the removal of directors or changing the name of a company.

There are two reasons why private individuals and financial institutions invest in shares:

● **Income.** Shareholders are entitled to a share of company profits known as a **dividend**. The total amount given to shareholders is decided by the board of directors and can vary, but investors hope that the return they get will increase over time.
● **Capital growth.** Shareholders hope that the value of their shares will increase over time.

> **Shareholders** are the owners of a limited company and include any person, company or other institution that owns at least one share.

> A **dividend** is a share of the after-tax profit of a company distributed to its shareholders according to the number of shares held.

> **Typical mistake**
>
> Students often assume that when a shareholder sells shares they are sold back to the company. This is not true. Shares are sold through the Stock Exchange to a new shareholder who wishes to buy. This works in the same way as buying and selling used cars.

Influences on and the significance of share price changes

REVISED

Both the level of dividend and the share price of a company can fluctuate, and it is important to recognise that they can go down in value as well as up. The price of an individual share is determined through the market. If demand is greater than supply the price will go up; if there are more sellers than buyers the price will fall. There are a number of reasons why shares and dividend may fluctuate in value:

● **Performance.** If there are worse than expected profits, e.g. if a retailer reports a poor performance during the Christmas period, a time when traditionally sales are good, shares will go down in value. If profits are higher, then share values will increase.

- **Expectation of better or worse profit performance.** This might be as a result of a new product due to be launched on the market.
- **Changes within the market or competitive environment.** For example, the move of consumers from the mainstream supermarkets such as Tesco to the discounters such as Lidl and Aldi will adversely affect the value of Tesco's shares.
- **World uncertainty.** Conflict in the Middle East, for example, or an economic downturn will cause share prices to fluctuate.

Market capitalisation is calculated by taking the share price and multiplying it by the number of shares issued. This gives a valuation of a company. Changes in the share price will therefore affect the valuation of a business. A falling share price might provide an opportunity for investment or even takeover, or it might be an indication of a business in decline.

> **Exam tip**
>
> An economic downturn may be bad for some businesses, but for others it may be good (Tesco v. Aldi). The same can be said about conflict in the Middle East — this is bad for some businesses, but arms manufacturers are likely to benefit.

> **Market capitalisation** is calculated as follows:
>
> **share price × number of shares issued**

The effects of ownership on mission, objectives, decisions and performance

REVISED

Profit is a key objective of many private sector businesses, and for some this may dominate the decision-making process.

Public limited companies are owned by shareholders who are often driven by profit, which can lead to a short-term approach to business. Decision-making will be made on the basis of achieving profit, and the philosophy outlined in the mission statement may take a back seat. This emphasis on profit has been demonstrated by Tesco. In 2014, Tesco saw falling profits and made mistakes in reporting profits higher than they actually were. These failings led to a big fall in its share price and the resignation of its CEO.

Sole traders and private limited companies, however, will be less affected by this need to achieve profits, and may be able to keep a closer focus on their mission statement and objectives.

Now test yourself

TESTED

14 Briefly give two reasons why people invest in shares.
15 List four reasons why share prices may fluctuate.
16 XYZ plc has a share price of 57p and 2,100 million shares. What is its market capitalisation?

Answers on p. 202

Understanding that businesses operate within an external environment

The world businesses operate in is both unpredictable and uncertain, and changes in this external environment will have an impact on the demand for goods and services, costs and the way a business operates generally.

How the external environment can affect costs and demand

The external environment refers to aspects that are out of the control of the business and include competition, market conditions, economic factors (such as incomes and interest rates), social and environmental issues and demographic factors. These factors not only affect demand for a product or service and the costs of operating a business, but also impact on its ability to achieve its strategic goals and objectives. Some of these influences may be predictable in that trends can be spotted in a particular market, but others, such as the recession of 2008, are less predictable. Whether predictable or not, a business is likely to have to take action to prepare for or respond to the changing circumstances.

> **Exam tip**
>
> Do not always assume that any change in the external environment will be negative. Sometimes changes can be positive for a business, and what is negative for one might be positive for another.

Competition

Almost all businesses operate within a competitive environment, competing against other businesses that offer the same or similar goods. The strategies adopted by competitor firms will therefore have an impact on a business. For example, we have seen the impact of competition on the grocery industry with the big four of Tesco, Asda, Sainsbury's and Morrisons all suffering lower demand as a result of the discount retailers Aldi and Lidl. It is important, therefore, that a business tries to differentiate its own products or services in order to encourage consumers to purchase its products or services.

Furthermore, sometimes a competitor will come up with an innovative product or service, such as Apple with the iPod and iPhone, which have had huge impact on the markets they operate in. Some businesses have also been quicker to use technology in their operations and have benefited, whereas others, such as Morrisons, were slow to adopt internet selling and suffered as a result. HMV did not anticipate the rise in downloading of music, films and books and almost went out of business.

Not only can competition have an impact on demand, but it can also have an impact on costs. In a competitive environment, firms are likely to compete on price, and this is likely to lead to pressure on costs with individual firms looking to reduce costs wherever possible.

Market conditions

Market conditions refer to the characteristics of a particular market and might include its size, growth rate, any barriers to entry, seasonal factors and the amount and intensity of competition. All these factors will have an impact on a business in terms of demand and costs. For instance, a market with high market growth and a low intensity of competitiveness is likely to present greater opportunities for higher demand than the opposite. A market with high barriers to entry, such as the aeronautical engine market, will protect operators in this market from new entrants.

Economic factors

Economic factors include the stage of the economic cycle, interest rates, inflation, and exchange rates. It is, however, interest rates and incomes that are the focus of the AS specification.

Interest rates

Changes in interest rates can have a big impact on both the demand for goods and services provided by a business and its cost. This impact may be positive for some businesses but negative for others. Rising interest rates generally result in lower demand, as consumers are likely to have less disposable income due to higher borrowing costs for loans and mortgages. Other consumers might also be encouraged to save more as a result of rising interest rates. Not all businesses will be affected negatively though — discount retailers might actually benefit as consumers switch from traditional grocery stores such as Tesco to ones such as Lidl. It has also been shown that restaurants, such as Pizza Hut, have gained as consumers have cut back on spending.

Costs will also be affected by changes in interest rates. A business with high levels of borrowing will be faced by higher costs when interest rates rise. This, coupled with any fall in demand, can be crippling for some businesses. Again, not all businesses will be affected in the same way — those with little in the way of borrowing will be less affected by interest rate rises. Should interest rates fall it is likely to have the opposite effect on both demand and costs.

Interest rates can also affect a business in terms of decision-making: high or rising interest rates may lead to a business postponing new capital investment due to the costs involved. Low or falling interest rates will be more conducive to capital investment. Finally, if a business has large cash reserves, it could benefit from rising interest rates due to the higher interest received.

Incomes

Demand in the economy will also be affected by the level of incomes. Falling incomes, as in the recession of 2008, saw falling demand, whereas as the economy has picked up and income has risen, demand has increased. It should, however be recognised that not all businesses will be affected to the same extent — demand for necessities will be less affected by changes in income than demand for luxuries. This is discussed in more detail in the section on income elasticity on pp. 38–39.

Demographic factors

Demography is the study of human populations and includes factors such as the age, gender, income and occupation of the population as well as the birth and death rates, the level of public health and immigration. In the UK, not only is the population growing with immigration making a large contribution to this growth, it is also an ageing population. These factors affect the level of demand and the nature of the goods and services purchased. They also affect the structure of the working population itself. As a result, workers are now facing the prospect of working longer before they receive the state pension. Some businesses, such as B&Q, actively seek to recruit older workers, and the demand for holidays such as cruises has increased over recent years. It is therefore important for businesses to recognise and anticipate the demographic changes taking place.

Environmental issues and fair trade

Businesses ignore environmental issues today at their peril. The influence of the media and social media means that any misdemeanour in terms of pollution and exploitation of people in less developed countries is quickly brought to light. This can then have an impact on reputation, the sales and the costs of a business.

In the UK, successive governments have introduced legislation to help protect the environment from pollution. As a result, businesses have to spend large amounts on measures to ensure that water, air and the surrounding countryside are kept free of pollution. Some businesses have

> **Exam tip**
>
> When looking at interest rates and income, be aware of the interrelationship between them. A rise in interest rates will indirectly cause a fall in the income available to consumers to spend (disposable income), whereas a fall will have the opposite effect.

located themselves overseas where legislation is less stringent, but even there they are not always free from the public gaze.

Concern for the environment is being driven by factors such as global warming. It is believed that carbon emissions are the major contributing factor to global warming and that not just businesses but governments should be doing more to cut these emissions. Sustainable development has also become an issue due to the worry that certain resources are running out and that we should try and conserve and sustain them wherever possible, e.g. the fishing industry is subject to quotas and some paper manufacturers now say they plant one new tree for every one cut down.

Fair trade has also become a concern. This is about achieving better prices, decent working conditions and fair terms of trade for farmers and workers in less developed countries. This is likely to mean higher costs for a business, but could also lead to greater demand, better reputation and could act as a selling point.

These external factors (see Figure 1.2) can have a significant impact on the demand for products and services provided, the costs incurred and profit. Although a business might sometimes be caught out by sudden changes in the external environment (e.g. the recession of 2008 and its depth), it should be able to anticipate and plan for some changes. For instance, demographic changes can be identified, changes in interest rates anticipated and new products and services provided in order to stay ahead of competitors. As a result, any negative impact on cost and demand may be minimised and any positive impact maximised.

> **Exam tip**
>
> The external factors affecting a business can be easily recalled using the acronym PESTLE: **P**olitical, **E**conomic, **S**ocial, **T**echnological, **L**egal and **E**nvironmental.

POLITICS	• Government type and policy • Funding, grants and initiatives
ECONOMY	• Inflation and interest rates • Labour and energy costs
SOCIAL	• Population, education, media • Lifestyle, fashion, culture
TECHNOLOGY	• Emerging technologies, web • Information and communication
LEGAL	• Regulations and standards • Employment law
ENVIRONMENT	• Weather, green and ethical issues • Pollution, waste, recycling

Figure 1.2 External factors affecting businesses

Now test yourself

TESTED

17 Briefly explain why it is important for a business to differentiate its product or service in a competitive market.
18 How might a manufacturer of luxury products be affected by a rise in interest rates?
19 List three reasons why a study of demographics might be important to a business.
20 What do you understand by the term 'fair trade'?

Answers on pp. 202–203

Exam practice

XYZ plc

When XYZ plc converted to a public limited company, everything seemed rosy. It had a mission of being the best in the business and objectives of both market growth and growth of market share. Three years on and things seemed very different: customer complaints had increased and the company had failed to hit its targets for market growth and share. Understandably, shareholders were very unhappy with the steadily declining share price and lack of dividends. Although its problems had for the most part been caused by the changing external environment with rising interest rates and an increasingly competitive market, it was also clear XYZ plc was inadequately prepared for the change to public status.

Key data of XYZ plc

	At flotation	Present
Sales	£25m	£27.5m
Market share	5.3%	5.2%
Share price	50p	35p
Number of shares	100m	100m

Questions

a Calculate the change in market capitalisation of XYZ plc. [4]

b Explain why although sales have increased, XYZ plc market share has decreased. [6]

c Analyse the factors shareholders may have considered before investing in XYZ plc. [9]

d To what extent do you believe XYZ plc was correct in its decision to convert to a public limited company? [16]

Answers and quick quiz 1 online

ONLINE

Summary

You should now have an understanding of all the points below.

Understanding the nature and purpose of business

- why businesses exist
- common business objectives and their purpose
- the relationship between mission and objectives
- the measurement and importance of profit covering revenue, fixed costs, variable costs and total costs

Understanding the different forms of business

- the reasons for choosing different forms of business and for changing business form including sole traders, private and public limited companies, non-profit organisations as well as public sector organisations
- limited and unlimited liability
- ordinary share capital, market capitalisation and dividends
- the role of shareholders and why they invest
- influences on share price and the significance of share price changes
- the effects of ownership on mission, objectives, decisions and performance

Understanding that businesses operate within an external environment

- how the following external factors affect costs and demand: competition, market conditions, incomes, interest rates, demographic factors, environmental issues and fair trade

2 Managers, leadership and decision-making

Understanding management, leadership and decision-making

What managers do

Peter Drucker, who some look upon as the creator of the modern study of management, outlined five basic tasks of a manager:

1 **Set objectives.** The manager sets goals for a group and decides what work needs to be done.
2 **Organise.** The manager divides the work into manageable activities and selects the people to undertake them.
3 **Motivate and communicate.** The manager creates a team that works together.
4 **Measure.** The manager not only sets targets but analyses and appraises performance.
5 **Develop people.** It is up to the manager to develop people, who may be looked upon as the most important asset of a business.

Henri Fayol also outlined five elements of management: planning, organising, commanding, coordinating and controlling.

The role of a manager then is varied, but can be summed up in four key tasks: they **plan**, **organise**, **direct** and **control**.

Types of management and leadership styles

Leadership style is the way in which a leader approaches his/her role of planning, organising, directing and controlling. There are three basic styles of leadership:

- **Autocratic leaders**, who make decisions without consulting others.
- **Democratic leaders**, who make the final decision but include others in the process.
- **Laissez-faire leaders**, who allow team members freedom if they do their work and meet deadlines.

Other styles of leadership include **charismatic leaders**, who believe they can do no wrong, **paternalistic leaders**, who consult and try to make decisions in the best interest of all, and **bureaucratic leaders**, who do everything exactly by the rules.

This range of leadership styles is illustrated by the Tannenbaum and Schmidt continuum (see Figure 2.1). This classifies the style according to how much a leader tells or listens to his/her staff.

The figure shows the relationship between the level of freedom in decision-making a manager gives to a team of workers and the level of authority retained by the manager. As the workers' freedom increases, so the manager's authority decreases.

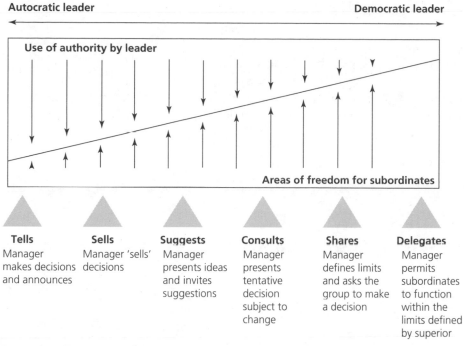

Figure 2.1 Tannenbaum and Schmidt's continuum of leadership behaviour

A further study of leadership by Blake and Mouton portrays leadership through a grid depicting concern for people on the y axis and concern for production on the x axis with each dimension ranging from 1 to 9. This results in five leadership styles as shown in Figure 2.2 and outlined below.

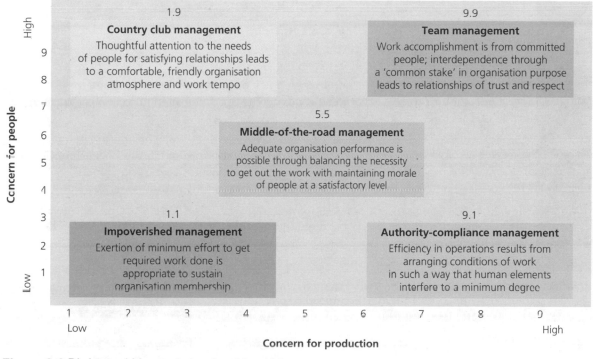

Figure 2.2 Blake and Mouton's leadership grid

- **Country club management.** The emphasis is on people, with little concern for the task. This style may hamper production as it relies on workers being motivated.

2 Managers, leadership and decision-making

- **Authority–compliance management.** Leadership here is autocratic with a clear emphasis on the task and little concern for people. It may increase production, but employees are likely to be unhappy.
- **Impoverished management (produce or perish).** Leadership will be ineffective with little concern for either the task or the people.
- **Middle-of-the-road management.** There is a compromise here with some focus on people and some on the task, but it is likely to lead to average performance.
- **Team management.** This style focuses on both the task and the people. It is likely to be the most effective, with emphasis on empowerment, trust and team working.

The effectiveness of different styles of leadership and management and influences on these

REVISED

The effectiveness of different styles of leadership is summarised in Table 2.1.

Table 2.1 Leadership styles

	Democratic	Authoritarian	Laissez-faire
Description	Democratic leadership entails running a business on the basis of decisions agreed by the majority.	An authoritarian leadership style keeps information and decision-making among the senior managers.	Laissez-faire leadership means the leader has a peripheral role, leaving staff to manage the business.
Key features	Encourages participation and makes use of delegation.	Sets objectives and allocates tasks. Leader retains control throughout.	Leader evades duties of management and uncoordinated delegation occurs.
Communication	Extensive, two-way. Encourages contributions from subordinates.	One-way communications downwards from leader to subordinates.	Mainly horizontal communication, though little communication occurs.
Uses	When complex decisions are made requiring a range of specialist skills.	Useful when quick decisions are required.	Can encourage production of highly creative work by subordinates.
Advantages	Commitment to business, satisfaction and quality of work may all improve.	Decisions and direction of business will be consistent. May project image of confident, well-managed business.	May bring the best out of highly professional or creative groups.
Disadvantages	Slow decision-making and need for consensus may avoid taking 'best' decisions.	Lack of information, so subordinates are highly dependent on leaders; supervision needed.	May not be deliberate, but bad management — staff lack of focus and sense of direction. Much dissatisfaction.

Different leaders adopt different styles of leadership and the style adopted will vary according to the individual and the circumstances involved. Key influences might be:

- **The individual.** Some leaders feel they always have to be in control and may lean more towards an autocratic approach, whereas others may feel more comfortable discussing decisions and will be more democratic in their approach. In other words, the style adopted will depend on the leader's personality and skills.
- **Nature of the industry.** Some industries require a high degree of creativity, whereas with others safety might be paramount.

Typical mistake

Do not assume that a democratic style of leadership is always the best style to adopt — it will depend on the circumstances of the individual business.

The leadership style adopted is likely to reflect this with a more laissez-faire approach adopted where creativity is needed and a more autocratic approach where safety is of concern.

● **Business culture.** If a business has a tradition of doing things in a particular way, then this might determine the style adopted. It may have always operated with a more laissez-faire or autocratic approach that might prove difficult to change.

> **Exam tip**
>
> Do not assume that there is one best style of leadership, as the style adopted is likely to depend on and evolve with the circumstances a business finds itself in.

TESTED

Now test yourself

1 Identify four key aspects of a leader's role.
2 State three influences on leadership style.
3 Identify one key feature of a democratic leader and one key feature of a laissez-faire leader.
4 How are leaders classified in the Tannenbaum and Schmidt continuum?

Answers on p. 203

Understanding management decision-making

The value of decision-making based on data (scientific decision-making) and on intuition

REVISED

Scientific decision-making is the systematic approach of collecting facts and applying logical decision-making techniques, such as decision trees, to the decision-making process. The alternative to this approach is trial and error and intuition (gut feeling).

> **Scientific decision-making** is decision-making based on data that uses a logical and rational approach.

In business there are uncertainties involved with any decision. These may stem from the market, the economy, the consumer, competitors and even how the various functional areas within a business will react to a decision. When making decisions, managers do so in the expectation that there will be some reward in terms of achieving objectives. Any decision made, however, will involve some risk, and it is for this reason that a scientific approach to decision-making may be adopted — to reduce risk. This involves the collection and analysis of data and the use of analytical tools in the forming of decisions. Examples of analytical tools include the Boston matrix, product life cycle, investment appraisal and ratio analysis as well as decision trees, which are investigated below.

Opportunity cost

Managers may also consider the **opportunity cost** when making a decision. This is the cost of the next best alternative that will be missed by making a particular decision. Business resources, particularly finance, are limited and, as a result, a business will not be able to undertake everything it would like: it will have to make a choice. For example, by investing in a new fleet of vehicles it may miss out on a new computer system — the computer system represents the opportunity cost.

> **Opportunity cost** — the next best alternative forgone.

Intuition

Intuition refers to decisions that are made on a gut feeling rather than based on evidence and rational processes. Data are not always correct. For example, the decision by Coca-Cola to change its recipe in response

> **Intuition** is making decisions based on gut feeling rather than data and rational analysis.

to taste tests proved to be a marketing disaster. For other innovative products it may be impossible to judge consumer reaction if they have never seen the product. If an analytical approach had been adopted, the Sony Walkman and probably the MP3 player would never have been introduced to the market. Intuition then will always be an important factor in decision-making.

The use and value of decision trees in decision-making

Decision trees are tree-like diagrams that can be used to determine the optimum course of action in situations where several possible alternatives with uncertain outcomes exist. They are a visual representation of the various risks, rewards and potential value of each option.

> **Decision trees** are tree-like diagrams showing various options, their probabilities and financial outcomes.

Drawing and evaluating a decision tree

Every decision tree begins with a square. This represents the decision to be made:

At least two lines will come out of the square representing the possible options. There will often be a third line — the do-nothing option:

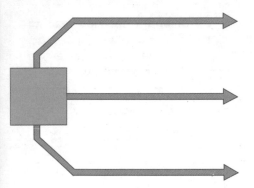

Taking each line in turn it is now necessary to decide whether it is a result, uncertain or another decision has to be made.

For a result there is no more to do, uncertain is represented by a circle and a decision by another square. The do-nothing line is a result and for our purposes we will assume there are no further decisions (note more complicated decision trees are likely to have further decisions). The resulting decision tree will be as follows:

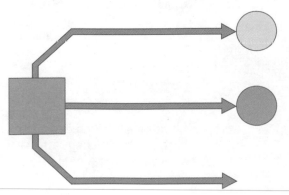

From each circle, lines will be drawn showing the possible outcomes:

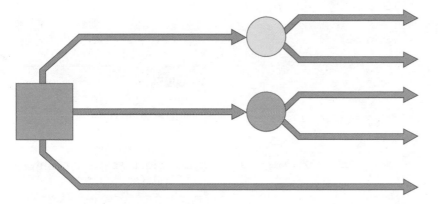

In order to evaluate the decision tree, all lines need to be fully labelled. This means indicating the following information on the decision tree:

● the cost of each option
● the potential outcomes
● the probabilities

This is shown in Figure 2.3. XYZ plc is considering whether to relaunch an existing product that has been failing or whether to undertake the development and launch of a completely new product. The data in Table 2.2 relates to each.

Table 2.2 XYZ plc relaunch and new product data

	Relaunch existing product	New product
Cost	£2.5m	£6m
Outcome success	£8.5m	£12m
Outcome failure	£0.5m	£2m
Probability success	0.7	0.6
Probability failure	0.3	0.4

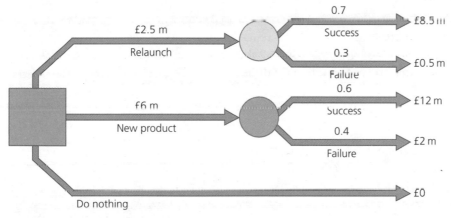

Figure 2.3 Decision tree for XYZ plc

Finally, it is necessary to calculate the expected values.

For each circle the outcomes are multiplied with the probabilities and added together. The cost of that option is then subtracted. Each option can then be compared to see which provides the highest return.

In the example above the calculation is as follows:

Relaunch

(£8.5m × 0.7 + £0.5m × 0.3) – £2.5m

£5.95 + £0.15 – £2.5m = **£3.6m**

New product

(£12m × 0.6 + £2m × 0.4) – £6m

£7.2m + £0.8m – £6m = **£2m**

From these calculations relaunch would be the most lucrative option.

Decision trees can be a useful analytical tool as they make managers think and quantify decisions rather than just go by intuition. They do, however, have limitations as managers may be influenced by their own bias towards one decision rather than another. In other words, they may make the returns for their favoured approach more attractive and thereby justify their decision. There is also the problem with establishing probabilities: it may be possible to base these on past experience, but even so they are likely to be just guesstimates.

> **Exam tip**
>
> Although the AQA specification does not require students to construct decision trees, an ability to do so will certainly aid understanding.

Now test yourself

TESTED

5 Identify three key pieces of information required for a decision tree.
6 Briefly outline the benefits and drawbacks of decision trees.

Answers on p. 203

Influences on decision-making

REVISED

There are a number of influences on decision-making as outlined below.

Mission and objectives

The mission of a business is its essential purpose and, to some extent, a business will be guided in its decision-making by its mission and the objectives it sets. For example, decision-making at Poundland will be influenced by its pricing policy.

Ethics

Ethics is about making decisions that are morally correct. The growth in fair trade products such as chocolate and coffee illustrates how some businesses have been influenced by this in their decision-making.

External environment

The external environment may have a big impact on decision-making. A downturn in the economy or rise in interest rates could see decisions being postponed or even totally abandoned, whereas an expanding economy or fall in interest rates might see decisions being brought forward. Decision-making will also be influenced by changing demographics, (e.g. the growing elderly population), increased environmental awareness and by changes in the law.

Competition

All business operates within a competitive environment and decisions will be influenced by this. Some business decision-making will be aimed at first-mover advantage and getting ahead of competition, whereas other decision-making will simply be responding to the action of competitors. The major supermarket chains, for example, have all been forced to respond to the actions of the discount retailers such as Aldi and Lidl.

Resource constraints

A business will only be able to do what it is physically possible to do. Production capacity, skills of the workforce and financial resources will, in the short term, limit what a business can do. In the long term, it may be possible to overcome these constraints, but a business needs to be certain about any decision being made.

> **Exam tip**
>
> In making a decision a business is likely to consider the opportunity cost and will be limited by the resources available.

Now test yourself

TESTED ☐

7 Briefly outline how the external environment may impact on decision-making.
8 List four other influences on decision-making.

Answers on p. 203

Understanding the role and importance of stakeholders

The need to consider stakeholder needs when making decisions

REVISED ☐

The various **stakeholders** and their interests are outlined below:
- **employees:** job security, good working conditions and pay
- **customers:** good customer service and value for money
- **shareholders:** capital growth and dividends
- **suppliers:** regular orders and on-time payment
- **local communities:** avoidance of pollution and congestion, employment
- **government:** employment, payment of taxes

> A **stakeholder** is any individual or group who has an interest in the activities and performance of a business.

Decisions taken by business will have an impact on the various stakeholders so it is important to consider and manage these needs.

Stakeholder mapping

Stakeholder analysis and management is important in decision-making and to this end A. Mendelow drew up the matrix shown in Figure 2.4.

In this matrix (or stakeholder map), stakeholders are categorised according to the amount of power they have and their level of interest. Those with high power and high interest are key players, and management needs to keep this group happy, perhaps by involving them in the decision-making process.

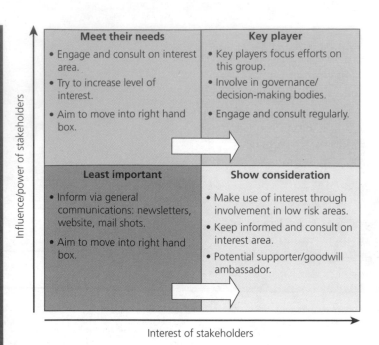

Figure 2.4 Mendelow's matrix

Those with low power and interest require minimal effort, perhaps simply keeping them up to date with what is happening. Those with high power and little interest need to be consulted and, if possible, have their level of interest increased in order to avoid potential conflicts at a later date. Those with high interest and little power need to be kept informed and up to date in order to avoid potential conflicts and enhance the reputation of the business as a considerate business.

Stakeholder needs and the possible overlap and conflict of these needs

REVISED

The potential overlap and conflict of stakeholder interests are illustrated in Table 2.3 below.

Table 2.3 Potential overlap and conflict of stakeholder interests

Decision	Overlap	Conflict
Relocate overseas	• **Shareholders:** potential for lower costs and increased profit. • **Management:** achieve objectives in terms of costs and profit.	• **Local community:** impact on local economy. • **Employees:** lost jobs. • **Government:** less tax.
Introduce new technology	• **Shareholders and management:** lower costs and potential profit. • **Consumer:** may result in better quality and reliability.	• **Employees:** may lose jobs. • **Less employment:** could impact on local community.
Expand production	• **Shareholders:** higher sales and profit. • **Employees:** job opportunities. • **Customers:** greater availability. • **Suppliers:** more orders. • **Government:** tax. • **Community:** greater production.	• **Local community:** greater congestion and pollution.

Decision	Overlap	Conflict
Increase price	• **Shareholders:** potential profit increase. • **Management:** improved performance. • **Government:** more tax.	• **Customers:** cost more.
Cut costs	• **Shareholders:** potential profit. • **Management:** achieving objectives.	• **Employees:** potential job loss. • **Customers:** quality might be affected. • **Suppliers:** pressure on prices.
Enter new markets/products	• **Shareholders:** potential profit. • **Employees:** job security. • **Suppliers:** increased orders. • **Community:** greater employment.	• **Local community:** pollution due to increased production.

Influences on the relationship with stakeholders

There are a number of influences on the relationship with stakeholders, one of which is the power and interest of individual stakeholders as illustrated by stakeholder mapping. Other influences include:

- **Leadership styles.** The style of leadership may have an impact: an authoritarian leader may have little concern for individual stakeholder groups and would be unlikely to consult them. A more democratic leader, however, would be more likely to consult individual stakeholders when making decisions.
- **Business objectives.** Some businesses may be committed to an ethical approach in their decision-making whilst others may be less concerned. For example, The Body Shop is committed to not testing on animals and therefore attracts less attention from pressure groups.
- **Government.** Legislation introduced by the government (or EU) can affect relationships with stakeholders. Examples include legislation regarding employment, the environment or safety.
- **State of economy.** When economic and market conditions are booming, it is easier for a business to address issues related to stakeholders. In these circumstances there is likely to be greater access to finance to improve working conditions and environmental aspects. The opposite is the case when the economy or market is in decline.

How to manage the relationship with different stakeholders

Although there is always potential for conflict between stakeholders, this can be significantly reduced if managed correctly. Stakeholder mapping gives an indication of how this might be managed in terms of recognising those stakeholders with the greatest power and interest in a decision. Key to the management, however, is good communication, involvement and participation in any decisions being made. If there is a culture of good communication and consultation of stakeholder groups in decisions, the likelihood of conflict can be minimised. Careful planning and introduction of decisions may reduce the impact on individual groups. For instance, it might be possible to phase in new technology, which might avoid the need for redundancies.

> **Exam tip**
>
> When evaluating the conflict of interest between stakeholder groups a short- versus long-term approach is often useful.

Now test yourself

9 Draw up a table to show four stakeholder groups and their interest in a manufacturing business.
10 How does Mendelow categorise stakeholders in his matrix?
11 Besides the power and interest of individual stakeholders, identify four other influences on the relationship with stakeholders.
12 Briefly outline the key to managing stakeholder relations.

Answers on p. 203

Exam practice

McTavish's shortbread

Hamish McTavish was used to getting his own way, and as the majority shareholder in the family business, this had been easy to achieve. His latest idea, however, was rather more controversial and was likely to split the board of directors unless he could convince them otherwise. He had been very successful in developing the shortbread biscuit business and establishing a highly respected brand name within Scotland. He wanted to diversify into other biscuits and cakes, but the other directors wanted to expand the core area throughout the UK. In order to support his case, he adopted a scientific decision-making approach and drew up the decision tree below.

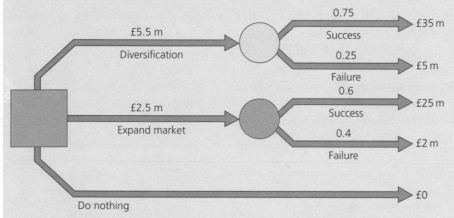

Would this be enough to convince the other directors or would Hamish just have to follow his intuition and force this through anyway?

Questions

a How does intuition differ from scientific decision-making? [4]
b Using the decision tree above calculate the difference in outcome between expansion and diversification. [6]
c Analyse the potential problems Hamish might face in forcing through the decision of diversification. [9]
d Evaluate the extent to which using the scientific approach to decision-making is the right approach for Hamish to take. [16]

Answers and quick quiz 2 online

Summary

You should now have an understanding of all the points below.

Understanding management, leadership and decision-making

- the role of managers including objective setting, analysing, leading, making decisions and reviewing
- types of management and leadership styles, their effectiveness and influences on them
- theories of management including the Tannenbaum Schmidt continuum and the Blake Mouton grid

Understanding management decision-making

- the risks, rewards, uncertainty and opportunity costs involved in decision-making
- the distinction between scientific decision-making and intuition
- the use and value of decision trees, including the ability to interpret and calculate expected values and net gains
- influences on decision-making: mission, objectives, ethics, external environment and resource constraints

Understanding the role and importance of stakeholders

- the consideration of stakeholder needs in decision-making and stakeholder mapping
- the possible overlap and conflict of stakeholder needs
- influences on and management of stakeholder relations

3 Decision-making to improve marketing performance

Marketing is the business function that provides the link between the business and the consumer. The Chartered Institute of Marketing defines marketing as 'the process responsible for identifying, anticipating and satisfying customer requirements profitably'.

Setting marketing objectives

Marketing objectives should be a part of the overall corporate business objectives and sit within the overall business plan and strategy. Objectives might include:

- **Sales volume and sales value.** Sales volume is the number of units sold and sales value is how much the sales are worth, e.g. in pounds sterling.
- **Market size.** In itself this is difficult to use as an objective, but a knowledge of market size will give an indication of the potential market. This would enable realistic targets to be set for sales, growth, and share.
- **Market and sales growth.** This would involve targeting an increase in overall sales in order to either maintain market share (in a growing market) or improve it.
- **Market share.** This is the proportion of a particular market that is controlled by an individual business. Increasing **market share** is likely to bring benefits for a business, such as brand loyalty and greater revenue.
- **Brand loyalty.** Achieving sales is one thing, but what businesses want is for customers to come back time after time. In other words, businesses want to achieve **brand loyalty**.

> **Typical mistake**
>
> Students sometimes assume that just because sales may be growing, market share automatically increases. This is not always the case, as in a growing market an individual business's sales may be increasing at a slower rate than others in the market.

> **Market share** is the percentage of a market's total sales that is earned by a particular company over a specified time period.
>
> **Brand loyalty** is when consumers become committed to a particular brand and make repeat purchases over time.

The value of setting marketing objectives

REVISED

The value of setting objectives might include the following:

- **Target setting.** This gives the business a focus and sense of direction.
- **Motivation.** Objectives can be motivating for those responsible.
- **Evaluation of performance.** As with all objectives, they need to be SMART: **S**pecific, **M**easurable, **A**chievable, **R**ealistic and **T**ime based. All of the marketing objectives outlined above are quantifiable and therefore measurable. As a result, they can be used to judge performance.

Possible calculations

- **Market share:** sales of firm/total market sales × 100
- **Sales growth:** difference in sales/earliest year × 100
- **Market growth:** difference in sales/earliest year × 100
- **Market size:** (sales/market share) × 100

> **Exam tip**
>
> The calculations you will be asked to perform in examinations are normally straightforward provided you have learned the formula and practised them regularly.

External and internal influences on marketing objectives and decisions

REVISED

External influences include:

- **Market and competition.** Marketing objectives are likely to vary according to whether the market is growing or static, and depending on the actions of competitors.

- **Economic factors.** Factors such as the stage of the economic cycle and interest rates will influence objectives as they will affect consumer spending.
- **Social factors.** Over time, consumer tastes and fashion change and this needs to be reflected in marketing objectives.
- **Ethics.** Since consumers are more aware of ethical issues, many businesses have reviewed their marketing objectives to reflect this. This can be seen in the move to promote fair trade products and the fact they do not exploit workers in sweat shops.
- **Technology.** This has had a big impact on the way businesses both produce and sell their goods and services. Growth of online sales and the facility for consumers to design their own products (mass customisation) have had a major impact on marketing objectives.

Internal influences include:
- **Finance available.** All marketing functions need to operate within the budget allocated, although a business whose finances are in a healthy state will be able to allocate larger amounts to marketing.
- **Production capacity.** The marketing function must liaise with the operations function in order to ensure that is it physically possible to achieve any targets set for sales growth.
- **Human resources.** Objectives set must also take into account the size and capabilities of the workforce. Increasing market share might be difficult without further recruitment and training.
- **Nature of product.** Any objectives set need to reflect the nature of the product. Innovative products might have considerable scope for growth, whereas products such as bread and fuel will have little scope.

Now test yourself

1 Briefly outline the difference between sales volume and sales value.
2 How is it possible for sales to increase but market share to fall?
3 Why would a business wish to achieve brand loyalty?
4 Identify three internal and three external influences on marketing objectives.
5 If XYZ plc market share is 5% and its sales are £30m, what is the total market size?

Answers on pp. 203–204

Understanding markets and customers

The value of primary and secondary marketing research

A market is a place where buyers and sellers come together. All businesses will sell their product or service within the relevant market. This might be direct to the consumer, online or to distributors and retailers. It is very important that a business fully understands the market in which it operates and to help with this, **market research** will be undertaken. This may involve one or more of the following:
- study of market trends and characteristics
- analysis of market shares and potential of existing products

> **Market research** is the process of gathering data on potential customers.

- sales forecasting for products
- analysis and forecasting sales of new products

Market research is separated into **primary** and **secondary research**.

Primary research

Also known as 'field research', **primary research** involves the collection of information for the first time directly by or for a business to answer specific issues or questions. Examples include:

- **Surveys:** conducting questionnaires face to face, by post, telephone or online.
- **Observation:** watching people, reactions to displays or counting footfall.
- **Focus groups:** using small groups of people to determine consumer attitudes and opinions.
- **Test marketing:** trying out products on a small group prior to a full-scale launch.

The main advantage of primary research is that it is directly related to the specific needs of a business, but it can be expensive to undertake.

> **Primary research** is the collection of information for the first time for specific purposes.

Secondary research

This is second-hand research involving the collection of data that already exists. Examples include:

- **Published reports.** These might be reports published by trade associations and journals, which may contain valuable information on markets and trends.
- **Government and other agencies.** A great deal of information is available. A key publication is the *Annual Abstract of Statistics*.
- **Internet.** Again, a great deal of information is widely available regarding markets and consumer behaviour.

Market research can also be separated into **qualitative** and **quantitative research**.

> **Secondary research** is the collection of data that already exists and has been used for other purposes.

Qualitative market research

The aim of **qualitative market research** is to find out about attitudes and opinions of consumers. It is collected from small groups of consumers such as focus groups. It can reveal consumer reactions to the:

- product
- pricing
- packaging
- branding

This might enable a business to design products that are more appealing to consumers.

> **Qualitative market research** is research into the attitudes and opinions of consumers that influence their purchasing behaviour.

Quantitative market research

Quantitative market research is the collection of information on consumer views that can be analysed statistically. It can be represented in easy-to-read charts and graphs showing:

- sales and potential sales
- size of the market
- prices consumers are prepared to pay

> **Quantitative market research** is the collection of information on consumer views and behaviour that can be analysed statistically.

Market mapping

Market mapping can enable a business to identify the position of its product in the market relative to others. Two key features of a product or service are identified, e.g. price and quality. A grid can then be established and each brand in that market can be placed on the grid according to the quality, high or low and price, high or low. Figure 3.1 is a market map of the supermarket industry. Supermarkets are placed according to price (low or high) and quality (low or high).

Figure 3.1 Market map of the UK supermarket industry

Such an approach enables a business to see where competition is most concentrated and may reveal potential gaps in the market.

The value of sampling

REVISED

A business will not collect information from all its potential consumers: this would be too expensive and time consuming. Firms need to select a sample that is representative of the whole target market (called 'the population'). **Sampling** is the selection of a representative group of consumers from a larger population. The general principle is that the larger the sample, the more accurate the results are likely to be.

There are a number of ways in which samples can be collected:

- **Random sampling.** This is when each member of the population has an equal chance of being included. This is appropriate when a firm is researching a product aimed at a large target group. Computers are often used to select people randomly.
- **Stratified random sampling.** This separates the population into segments or strata. This approach can avoid bias by ensuring that the composition of the sample reflects accurately that of the entire population.
- **Quota sampling.** This splits the population into a number of groups, each sharing common characteristics. For example, a survey might be conducted on the views of women about a new product, and the number of interviewees in each age category could be clearly set out. This saves money by limiting the number of respondents.

Exam tip

It is not enough to know the various methods of market research. You need to be able to make some assessment of their value in particular circumstances.

Factors influencing choice of sampling methods

The most obvious factor affecting the choice of sampling method is the amount of finance available. Businesses with larger marketing budgets will spend more and conduct research using larger samples.

Market research involves a fundamental trade-off between cost and accuracy. Firms require accurate information on which to base marketing decisions, such as:
- pricing policies
- product design
- types of promotion
- target customers

The greater the amount of information collected, the more reliable it should be, but the greater the cost to the firm. Many newly established businesses have limited budgets, yet accurate market research is invaluable in aiding decision-making. Firms face a further dilemma. Even extensive and costly market research cannot guarantee unbiased data. Respondents do not always tell the truth and samples do not always reflect the entire population accurately.

Exam tip

When assessing a business's methods of sampling, consider the costs of the chosen approach against the expected financial benefits.

Now test yourself

TESTED ☐

6 List three ways primary market research differs from secondary market research.
7 Explain the difference between qualitative and quantitative market research. Support your answer with examples of situations in which they may be appropriate.
8 Briefly outline the value of sampling.

Answers on p. 204

The interpretation of marketing data

REVISED ☐

Marketing data can be interpreted using various statistical tools, including correlation, confidence intervals and extrapolation.

Correlation

Correlation occurs when there is a direct relationship between one factor and another. This relationship might be positive or negative, e.g. a price increase may lead to a fall in demand, which is a negative correlation, but a price decrease might lead to a rise in demand, which is a positive correlation. Knowledge of correlation might therefore help in decision-making, e.g. knowing that there is a positive correlation between rising incomes and sales might enable a business to more accurately forecast sales. Figures 3.2(a) and (b) illustrate positive and negative correlations.

Correlation is a statistical technique used to establish the extent of a relationship between two variables such as the level of sales and advertising.

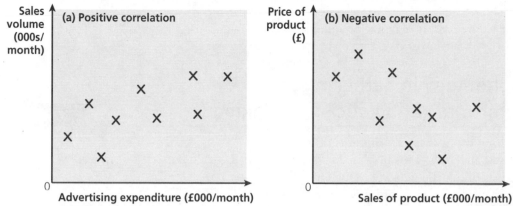

Figure 3.2 Positive and negative correlations

Figure 3.2(a) shows a positive correlation between sales and advertising expenditure and 3.2(b) a negative correlation between price and sales. Results of correlation should be treated with caution as correlation only shows a relationship between two variables. Sales might appear to rise with increased advertising, but it might be due to a competitor raising its prices rather than the increased advertising.

Confidence intervals

Since a business cannot be 100% certain in market research findings, **confidence intervals** may be used to help evaluate the reliability of any estimate. This is the **margin of error** that a researcher would experience if he/she asked a particular question to a sample group and expected to get the same answer back. For instance, if a researcher used a confidence interval of 5, and 70% of respondents gave a particular answer, then he/she could be sure that between 65% and 75% of the whole population would give the same answer.

The confidence interval used is likely to be affected by the sample size — the smaller the sample, the greater the margin for error and therefore the greater the confidence interval.

A **confidence level**, on the other hand, is an expression of how confident that researcher is in data collected. A confidence level is expressed as a percentage and indicates how frequently that percentage of the population would give an answer that would lie within the confidence interval. The most commonly used confidence level is 95%.

Extrapolation

Extrapolation uses known data to predict future data. By looking at past sales figures it may be possible to predict future sales by extending a **trend** line on a chart or graph (see Figure 3.3).

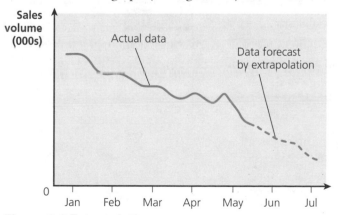

Actual data

Data forecast by extrapolation

Figure 3.3 Extrapolation

Exam tip

Be careful with correlation. For example, just because US suicides correlate with US spending on science space and technology does not mean that there is a positive correlation.

Confidence interval or **margin of error** is the plus or minus figure used to show the accuracy of results arising from sampling.

Confidence level is the probability that research findings are correct.

Extrapolation analyses past performance of a variable, such as sales, and extends the trend into the future.

A **trend** is an underlying pattern of growth or decline in a series of data.

Extrapolation, however, should be treated with caution as it assumes that the future will be similar to the past. It may not be suitable for industries subject to rapid change such as fashion and technology.

The value of technology in gathering and analysing data for marketing decision-making

REVISED

Developments in technology mean that vast amounts of information can be collected, stored and analysed. This may enable a firm to gain a much greater understanding about the person buying a product and, as a result, firms such as Amazon can make recommendations to individual customers based on past buying habits.

Technology can provide faster communication, make forecasting easier, and enable targeted sales messages, but a business must have the right data in the first place.

Now test yourself

TESTED

9 Distinguish between correlation and extrapolation.
10 In market research 60% of respondents preferred a particular soap brand. What does a 5% confidence interval tell analysts about this result?

Answers on p. 204

> **Exam tip**
>
> It is important to always look critically at marketing data. At first sight it may seem reliable, but you should question whether it has been influenced by any other factors, e.g. seasonality or problems experienced by a competitor.

The interpretation of price and income elasticity of demand data

REVISED

Elasticity refers to the responsiveness of demand to a change in a variable such as price or income. The AQA specification does not require students to be able to calculate elasticity, but knowing how it is calculated can aid understanding and interpretation. The calculation for price and income elasticity are as follows:

$$\text{price elasticity of demand} = \frac{\text{percentage change in demand}}{\text{percentage change in price}}$$

$$\text{income elasticity of demand} = \frac{\text{percentage change in demand}}{\text{percentage change in income}}$$

> **Elasticity** is a measure of the responsiveness of demand to a change in a variable, e.g. price or income.

When analysing elasticity, a marketing manager will be interested in whether demand for the product or service is elastic or inelastic.

An answer greater than 1, i.e. the percentage change in demand is greater than the percentage change in the variable, indicates elastic demand. An answer less than 1, i.e. the percentage change in demand is less than the percentage change in the variable, indicates an inelastic demand.

A knowledge of elasticity can be useful in decision-making as not all products will be affected in the same way by changes in variables. Some products, e.g. bread, fuel and salt, will be relatively inelastic in that demand will change very little when price or income change, whereas others, e.g. cars and television, will be relatively elastic.

> **Exam tip**
>
> When looking at a figure for elasticity, if the answer is greater than 1 demand is elastic. If it is less than 1 it is inelastic.

The value of the concepts of price and income elasticity of demand to marketing decision-makers

REVISED

Both price and income elasticity can be useful tools in marketing decision-making. They can be used to evaluate the impact of changes in prices and incomes on sales (volume and value). The effect of changes in price is summarised in Table 3.1.

Table 3.1 The effect of changes in price

	Price rise	Price fall
Elastic demand	Total revenue falls.	Total revenue rises.
Inelastic demand	Total revenue rises.	Total revenue falls.

The impact of changes in income will vary according to the type of product. Demand for luxuries tends to be elastic, whereas demand for necessities tends to be inelastic. The demand for new cars (luxury) tends to increase with rising incomes and decrease with falling incomes, whereas the demand for fuel (necessity) is likely to be less influenced by changes in income.

Although elasticity can be a useful tool, marketing decisions should not be based on this alone. Other factors that should be considered include:
- brand loyalty
- competitor actions
- consumer tastes and fashion
- availability of substitutes

> **Exam tip**
>
> Elasticity changes over time, and it is important in decision-making to use the most up-to-date figures. A figure that is even one year old may be out of date as the market may have changed or competitors introduced new products.

The use of data in marketing decision-making and planning

REVISED

Marketing managers want to reduce risk and uncertainty in decision-making, and the analysis of all available data makes a good starting point for this. Data may also create a much better understanding of the market, environment and consumers, and so is likely to improve the quality of decision-making.

Now test yourself

TESTED

11 A business has calculated the price elasticity of its product at −2.3. What would be the impact on revenue of a price increase?
12 Briefly outline why demand for a luxury product is likely to be income elastic.

Answers on p. 204

Making marketing decisions: segmentation, targeting and positioning

Market segmentation is the process of dividing a market into distinct groups. Those customers within the same segment will share common characteristics that can help a business to target them and market to them effectively.

> **Market segmentation** is dividing the market into identifiable sub-markets, each with its own customer characteristics.

Market targeting is when a business targets its marketing at a specific market segment (or target market). Identifying the target market is an essential step in the development of a marketing plan.

Market positioning refers to how a consumer views an individual brand relative to that of competing brands. The objective of a marketing strategy may therefore be to achieve a clear, unique and therefore advantageous position in consumers' minds.

> **Market targeting** is deciding which segment a business wants to operate in.

> **Market positioning** is where a particular brand stands in relation to other brands in the market.

The process and value of segmentation, targeting and positioning

REVISED

From the above it is evident that segmentation, targeting and positioning are linked:

Segmentation Targeting Positioning

The process of segmentation breaks the market into clearly definable groups. This might be by age, gender, income, social class or geographical area. Once the market has been segmented it is then possible to determine at which groups a particular product or service will be aimed. Next, a business will consider how it wants to position its product or service within the target market. How does it want the product to be perceived by consumers? This might be in terms of its pricing, quality and overall brand image.

There are a number of benefits of the above process:
- Marketing will be more effective as it can be directed specifically at the target group and convey a clear message relative to the positioning of the product or service.
- Resources will be used more effectively as a result of the targeted marketing approach.
- Sales and market share may increase as a result of the clear focus of marketing.

This approach may have its drawbacks, however:
- By targeting particular segments of the market, a business may overlook a potentially profitable segment.
- It is also possible that any changes in taste and fashion could be overlooked.

> **Exam tip**
>
> There is a link between market positioning and market mapping — a business might use market mapping to determine the position of its product or service in the market.

Influences on choosing a target market and positioning

REVISED

There are a number of influences on the target market and positioning:
- **The nature of the product.** This might be the actual qualities of the product that help differentiate it or what the product may be used for.
- **Competition.** A business may want to avoid areas of the market that are highly competitive.
- **The consumer.** Products might be developed specifically to suit consumer needs.

One decision a business is likely to make is whether it should target a niche market or a mass market.

Niche marketing is when businesses identify and satisfy the demands of small segments of a larger market. An example is the radio station Classic

> **Niche marketing** is when businesses identify and satisfy the demands of small segments of a larger market.

FM which serves the niche of people who wish to listen to popular classical music.

The **advantages** of niche marketing are:
- The first company to identify a niche market can often gain a dominant market position as consumers become loyal to the product, even if its price is higher.
- Niche markets can be highly profitable, as companies operating in them often have the opportunity to charge premium prices.

The **disadvantages** of niche marketing are:
- Because sales may be relatively low, firms operating in niche markets may not be able to spread fixed overheads over sufficient sales to attain acceptable profit margins.
- If a niche market proves to be profitable, it is likely to attract new competition, making it less attractive to the companies that first discovered the market.

Mass marketing occurs when businesses aim their products at most of the available market. Many small and medium-sized businesses sell in mass markets.

> **Mass marketing** is when businesses aim their products at most of the available market.

Businesses must be able to produce on a large scale if they are to sell successfully in a mass market. This may mean that the firm has to invest heavily in resources such as buildings, machinery and vehicles. Often, firms have to be price competitive to flourish in mass markets, or have a unique selling point (USP) that makes the company and its products distinctive.

Now test yourself

TESTED

13 Briefly outline the benefits and potential drawbacks of market targeting.
14 Distinguish between a niche and a mass market.

Answers on p. 204

Making marketing decisions: using the marketing mix

The elements of the marketing mix (7Ps)

The **marketing mix** is the combination of marketing activities that an organisation engages in so as to best meet the needs of its targeted market. The marketing mix was first developed for fast-moving consumer goods and consisted of the 4Ps of **Price, Product, Place** and **Promotion**. As the service sector has grown in importance, the mix has been expanded to include **People, Process** and **Physical environment**. It is, however, likely that all businesses will give some consideration to the three additional Ps. Figure 3.4 illustrates the mix and the aspects involved with each of the 7Ps.

> **Marketing mix** — the main variables comprising a firm's marketing strategy.

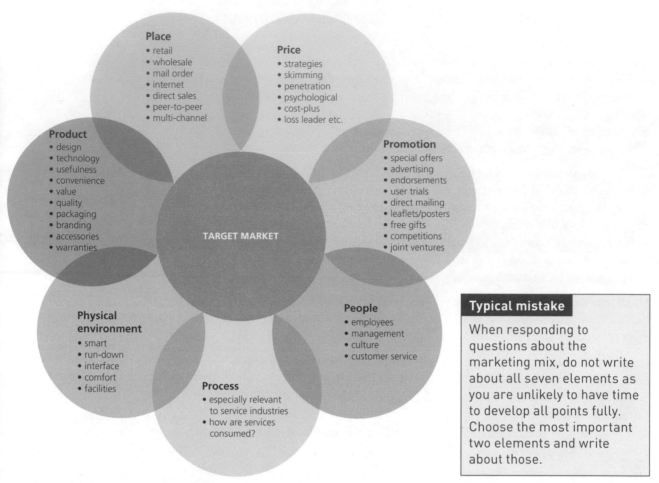

Figure 3.4 The seven Ps of marketing

Typical mistake

When responding to questions about the marketing mix, do not write about all seven elements as you are unlikely to have time to develop all points fully. Choose the most important two elements and write about those.

The influences on and the effects of changes in the elements of the marketing mix

REVISED

Managers take a range of factors into account when designing the marketing mix for a product (see Figure 3.5).

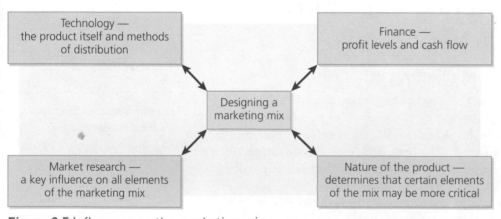

Figure 3.5 Influences on the marketing mix

Finance

The level of profits that a business earns can impact on the price that it charges. A profitable business is able to cut prices significantly, at least in the short term. Its financial reserves also enable it to engage in extensive promotional campaigns.

Another aspect of finance that affects the marketing mix is that a business with a healthy cash flow will be able to extend the range of outlets it uses by offering favourable trade credit terms.

The nature of the product

The type of product can influence which elements of the mix are emphasised. An insurance firm may spend heavily on advertising to generate large numbers of enquiries to win an acceptable number of customers. In contrast, a portrait painter may rely on the quality of the product and word-of-mouth promotion to achieve sales.

Technology

Some products that possess the latest technology may use advertising to inform potential customers of their existence and benefits. They will have high prices to maximise short-term profits and cover the costs of research and development. Technology has also affected the place element of the marketing mix. Developments have allowed publishers of music and books to distribute their products using internet downloads.

Market research

Primary market research may be the most importance influence in designing a marketing mix. Its findings may provide information to help to make judgements on the form, functions and design of the product. The research may uncover information on prices that consumers will be willing to pay and the type of purchasers. Market research may also determine pricing strategies.

Now test yourself

TESTED

15 For what reason has the marketing mix been extended from 4Ps to 7Ps?
16 Briefly explain two factors a marketing manager will take into consideration when designing a marketing mix.

Answers on p. 204

Product decisions

REVISED

Influences on and the value of new product development

A number of factors have an effect upon the development of new goods and services:

- **Technology.** Developments in technology are at the heart of many of the new products that come on to the market. For example, advances in battery technology have helped to generate a range of more efficient electric cars. Firms use these technological advances as the basis for the development of new products that meet the needs of consumers more fully.
- **Competitors' actions.** A competitor producing a new product can be a spur to a rival to produce something that is at least as good, if not better. Hotels, for example, have improved their services by offering guests a choice of different types of pillow to enhance comfort.

● **The entrepreneurial skills of managers and owners.** One of the talents of successful entrepreneurs is creativity. The skill of being able to think up new ideas for goods and services that fit with customer needs leads to the development of many new products.

The importance of unique selling points

Businesses commonly add value by creating a **unique selling point or proposition (USP)** for their products. A USP allows a business to differentiate its products from others in the market. This can help the business in a number of ways:

● The business can base its advertising campaigns around the (real or perceived) difference between its product and those of its rivals.
● Having a USP assists in encouraging brand loyalty, as it gives customers a reason to continue to buy that particular business's product.
● A USP commonly allows the firm to charge a premium price for the product.

> **Exam tip**
>
> You will be better prepared for questions on this area if you try to think about the factors that influence the development of new products by small and medium-sized businesses.

> A **unique selling point or proposition (USP)** allows a business to differentiate its products from others in the market.

The product life cycle

The product life cycle is the theory that all products follow a similar pattern throughout their life. Products take varying amounts of time to pass through these stages. The Mars Bar was launched in the 1920s and is still going strong. In contrast, modern motor cars are expected to have a life cycle of about 10 years. The stages are outlined below and illustrated in Figure 3.6.

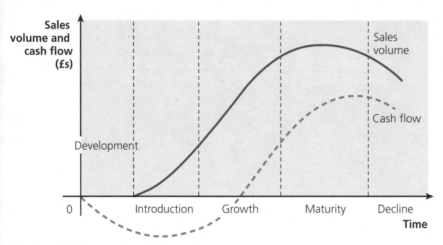

Figure 3.6 The product life cycle

1 **Development.** Firms undertake research and development to create new products that will be their future best sellers. Many products fall by the wayside, as they do not meet the demands of consumers. This can be a very expensive stage and cash flow is expected to be negative.

2 **Introduction.** This stage commences with the product's initial appearance on the market. At this time, sales are zero and the product has a negative cash flow. Sales should begin to rise, providing the company with some revenue. However, costs will remain high. The failure rate for new products is high — 60% to 90%. Promotion can be expensive and cash flow will remain negative. The price may have to be high to recoup the high initial launch costs.

3 **Growth.** During the growth stage, sales rise rapidly and a firm's cash flow can improve considerably. The business's profits per unit sold are likely to be at a maximum. This is because firms tend to charge a high price at this stage, particularly if the product is innovatory. Firms with a technically superior good may well engage in price skimming (see p. 47). The growth stage is critical to a product's survival. The product's success will depend on how competitors react to it.

4 **Maturity.** During the maturity stage, the sales curve peaks and begins to decline. Both cash flow and profits also decline. This stage is characterised by intense competition with other brands. Competitors emphasise improvements and differences in their versions of the product. At this stage, consumers of the product know a lot about it and require specialist deals to attract their interest.

5 **Decline.** During the decline stage, sales fall rapidly. New technology or a new product change may cause product sales to decline sharply. When this happens, marketing managers consider eliminating unprofitable products. At this stage, promotional efforts will be cut too.

Extension strategies

Firms may attempt to prolong the life of a product as it enters the decline stage by implementing extension strategies. They may use techniques such as the following:

● **Finding new markets for existing products.** Some companies selling baby milk have targeted less economically developed countries.
● **Changing the appearance or packaging.** Some motor manufacturers have produced old models of cars with new colours or other features to extend the lives of their products.

The product mix

A well-organised business will plan its product range so that it has products in each of the major stages of the life cycle: as one product reaches decline, replacements are entering the growth and maturity stages of their lives (see Figure 3.7). This means that there will be a constant flow of income from products in the mature phase of their lives to finance the development of new products.

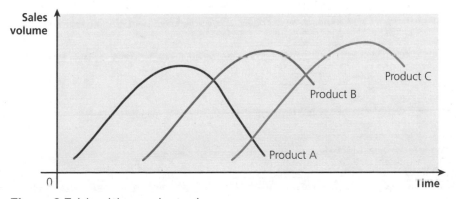

Figure 3.7 A healthy product mix

The Boston matrix

The Boston matrix was developed by the Boston Consulting Group. The matrix allows businesses to undertake product portfolio analysis based on the product's market growth rate and its market share.

> **Exam tip**
>
> For all major theories, such as the product life cycle, you should be able to give some assessment of the theory's strengths and weaknesses. This will help you to write evaluatively as well as confirming your understanding.

The matrix, as shown in Figures 3.8 and 3.9, places products into four categories:

- **Star products** have a dominant share of the market and good prospects for growth.
- **Cash cows** are products with a dominant share of the market but low prospects for growth.
- **Dogs** have a low share of the market and no prospects for growth.
- **Problem children** are products that have a small share of a growing market.

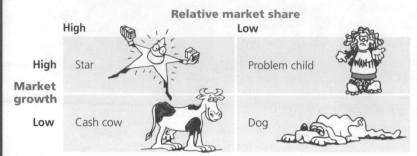

Figure 3.8 The Boston matrix

A number of conclusions can be drawn from the Boston matrix:

- Firms should avoid having too many products in any single category. Obviously, firms do not want lots of dogs, but they also need to avoid having too many stars and problem children.
- Products in the top half of the chart are in the early stages of their life cycle and are in growing markets, but the cost of developing and promoting them will not have been recovered.
- Continuing production of cash cows will provide the necessary cash to develop the newer products.
- Firms need problem child products as they may become tomorrow's cash cows.

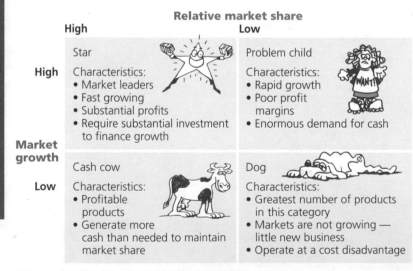

Figure 3.9 Features of the components of the marketing mix

Now test yourself

17 Briefly explain the difference between the Boston matrix and product life cycle and suggest how managers might use them to make decisions about the portfolio of products being sold.

18 Explain the difference between a cash cow and problem child in the Boston matrix.

Answers on p. 204

Pricing decisions

The pricing strategies used by businesses

The **price of a product** is simply the amount that a business expects a customer to pay to purchase the good or service.

Pricing strategies are the medium- to long-term pricing plans that a business adopts. There are four principal pricing strategies:

1 **Price skimming.** This is often used when a new, innovative product is launched. It is unlikely that this product will face direct competition immediately. By setting a high price, the business will achieve limited sales but with a high profit margin on each. This allows the firm to recoup some of the product's development costs. The price is lowered when competitors enter the market.

2 **Penetration pricing.** Firms entering a market with products similar to those already available may use penetration pricing. The price is set deliberately low to gain a foothold in the market. The expectation is that, once the product is established, the price will be increased to boost profit margins.

3 **Price leadership.** Price leadership is used for established products with strong brand images. The firm adopting this strategy will probably dominate the market and other businesses will usually follow their lead.

4 **Price taking.** Price takers set their prices equal to the 'going rate' or the established market price. This is a common pricing strategy for small and medium-sized businesses. Price takers have no influence over the market price, as they are normally one of many smallish firms competing for business.

Once a business has determined its pricing strategy, it may employ a number of pricing tactics. Pricing tactics are a series of pricing techniques that are normally used only over the short term to achieve specific goals. They include:

● **Loss leaders.** This entails setting prices very low (often below the cost of production) to attract customers. Businesses using this tactic hope that customers will purchase other (full-price) products while purchasing the loss leader.

● **Special-offer pricing.** This approach involves reduced prices for a limited period of time or offers such as 'three for the price of two'.

Influences on pricing decisions

There is a range of factors that might influence a firm in its pricing decisions. A firm is more likely to select strategies and tactics that result in low prices if it is seeking to expand its market share. This type of approach may also be more popular with businesses that are in a financially strong position. In contrast, a business that is selling a product that is highly differentiated or facing increasing popularity may opt for higher price levels.

Price elasticity of demand

One key factor influencing managers in their pricing decisions is price elasticity of demand. **Price elasticity of demand** measures the extent to which the level of demand for a product is sensitive to price changes. An increase in price is almost certain to reduce demand, while a price reduction can be expected to increase the level of demand. However,

Price of a product — the amount that a business expects a customer to pay to purchase the good or service.

Pricing strategies — the medium- to long-term pricing plans that a business adopts.

Typical mistake

Some students write about pricing tactics when the question asks about pricing strategies. If a question asks about strategies, you must write about relevant pricing actions that a business can take in the long term, and not short-term tactical decisions.

Price elasticity of demand is the extent to which the level of demand for a product is sensitive to price changes.

the extent to which demand changes following a given price change is less predictable.

Demand is said to be price elastic if it is sensitive to price changes. So, an increase in price will result in a significant lowering of demand and a fall in the firm's revenue. Products with a lot of competition are price elastic, as an increase in price will result in substantial loss of sales.

Price inelastic demand exists when price changes have relatively little effect on the level of demand. Examples of products with price inelastic demand are petrol and other essentials. Price elasticity of demand (PED) is calculated by the formula:

$$\text{price elasticity of demand} = \frac{\text{percentage change in quantity demanded}}{\text{percentage change in price}}$$

Firms would prefer to sell products with demand that is price inelastic, as this gives greater freedom in selecting a pricing strategy and more opportunity to raise prices, total revenue and profits.

Businesses can adopt a number of techniques to make demand for their products more price inelastic:
- **Differentiating products from those of competitors.** Making a product significantly different from those of competitors can increase brand loyalty. Consumers are more likely to continue to purchase a product when its price rises if it has unique characteristics.
- **Reducing competition through takeovers and mergers.** In recent years, many markets have seen fewer, but larger firms competing with each other. This process results in fewer products being available to the consumer and may mean that demand will be less responsive to price.

Now test yourself

TESTED

19 Using examples, explain the difference between a pricing strategy and a pricing tactic.
20 Outline the circumstances in which a business might decide to use a strategy of price skimming.

Answers on p. 204

Decisions about the promotional mix

REVISED

What is promotion?

Promotion is bringing consumers' attention to a product or business. Promotion aims to achieve targets including:
- to attract new customers and retain existing customers
- to improve the position of the business in the market
- to ensure the survival and growth of the business
- to increase awareness of a product

> **Promotion** is bringing consumers' attention to a product or business.

Exam tip

It is easy to think that promotion just means advertising. Figure 3.10 emphasises that this is not the case. Strong answers to examination questions on this topic will demonstrate awareness of the circumstances in which each of the elements of the promotional mix might be appropriate.

The elements of the promotional mix

The **promotional mix** is the combination of methods used by businesses to communicate with prospective customers to inform them of their products and to persuade them to buy these products.

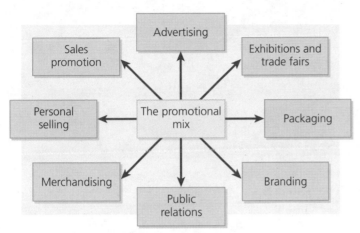

Figure 3.10 The promotional mix

Advertising

Advertising is a paid form of non-personal communication using mass media to change the attitudes and buying behaviour of consumers. Advertising can be separated into two types:

- **Informative advertising.** This is designed to increase consumer awareness of a product by providing consumers with factual information. Such adverts centre on the prices and features of the products being advertised.
- **Persuasive advertising.** This attempts to get consumers to purchase a particular product by, for example, claiming that the product is better than the competition.

Sales promotions and merchandising

Merchandising is in-store promotional activity by manufacturers or retailers at the point of sale. Merchandising can be important when consumers make purchasing decisions at the point of sale and a variety of rival products are on display in stores — confectionery is an example.

Other forms of sales promotion include:
- special offers and competitions
- in-store demonstrations
- coupons, vouchers and free gifts

These forms of promotion may be used when rival businesses wish to avoid starting a price war, which they might not win. Merchandising can be relatively cheap, but is not good at targeting specific groups of consumers.

Packaging

Packaging emphasises the attractiveness of the product and informs consumers of its features, functions and contents. Packaging also protects the good during its distribution to ensure that it reaches the consumer in perfect condition.

Exhibitions and trade fairs

These are events staged to attract all those people involved in a particular market, both sellers and buyers. An example is the Motor Show held in Birmingham each year.

Branding

This establishes an identity for a product that distinguishes it from the competition. Successful branding allows higher prices to be charged and can extend the product's life cycle by creating customer loyalty. Brand loyalty occurs when consumers regularly purchase particular products and it can allow firms to charge higher prices.

Personal selling

Personal selling involves visits by a firm's sales representatives to prospective customers. This may be used more in business-to-business selling, or in selling expensive products such as double glazing. Personal selling is a relatively expensive method of raising public awareness of a product.

Public relations (PR)

PR is promoting the company's image to establish a favourable public attitude towards the company. It aims to improve the image of a business and its products in the expectation of increasing sales through sponsoring sporting or cultural activities or making donations to worthwhile causes.

Influences on the choice of promotional mix

Managers will take into account a range of factors when deciding on the precise promotional mix to be deployed:

- **The product's position in its life cycle.** A newly launched product is likely to need heavy advertising to inform customers of its existence and the benefits it provides. An established product may use sales promotions to persuade customers to buy it.
- **The type of product.** Expensive products and those where design is a major element will make greater use of exhibitions and trade fairs in the promotional mix. This element of the mix is important, for example, to firms selling homes and fashion products.
- **The finance available to the business.** Firms with larger budgets may engage more in public relations and personal selling, as these methods of promotion are expensive.
- **Where consumers make purchasing decisions.** For businesses that sell products that are purchased on impulse, often at the point of sale, merchandising and packaging may be particularly important. The attractiveness of the wrappers and the positioning of the product within shops may be vital.
- **Competitors' actions.** If a business's rivals are engaging in heavy advertising or extensive sales promotions, it is likely that the business will respond similarly. This is more likely if the business trades in a market where there is relatively little product differentiation.

> **Typical mistake**
>
> Many students respond to questions about the promotional mix by writing about the marketing mix. Do not confuse these two concepts.

Now test yourself

TESTED

21 State four elements of the promotional mix.
22 Explain two influences on the promotional mix of a newly opened restaurant.

Answers on pp. 204–205

Distribution (place) decisions

The **distribution of a product** refers to the range of activities necessary to make the product available to customers.

Choosing appropriate outlets and distributors

The choice of an outlet or a distributor to supply the products to outlets must fit with the rest of the product's marketing mix. For example, it is vital that if the product is to be sold cheaply, possibly to increase market share, then suitable outlets are chosen. In this situation, a cost-cutting retail outlet might be appropriate, so that the benefit of low prices is passed on to the final customer.

Other factors that a business might take into account when choosing outlets and distributors include:

- **Location.** Businesses will seek outlets and distributors in areas where their target customers live and where few competitors operate.
- **Credit terms.** A newly established or struggling enterprise might opt for outlets or distributors that do not request long periods of trade credit. This can help to protect a business's cash flow.
- **Willingness to display products in prominent positions.** For some products (e.g. foods and confectionery), a good position in a retail outlet is an essential part of successful distribution.

The types of distribution channel that exist

There are a number of different forms of distribution. The three main channels are illustrated in Figure 3.11.

- **Traditional.** Many small retailers buy stock from wholesalers, as they do not purchase sufficient quantities to buy directly from producers. Wholesalers offer other benefits besides small quantities, such as advice, credit and delivery, although they can be expensive.
- **Modern.** Major retailers such as Marks and Spencer purchase directly from manufacturers and arrange their own distribution. They can do this because they buy huge quantities of products and are able to negotiate large discounts that more than cover the costs of distribution. As a consequence, they can offer discounts to consumers, enhancing their market position.
- **Direct.** This is a rapidly growing channel of distribution. It is attractive to many firms because it lowers the prices at which they can sell products to the consumer. Many small businesses have started to sell their products directly to customers using the internet.

> **Distribution of a product** involves the range of activities necessary to make the product available to customers.

> **Typical mistake**
>
> Do not ignore place or distribution. It is sometimes called 'the forgotten P' and students often respond poorly to questions that are set on it. You should know the different distribution methods and which are appropriate in different circumstances.

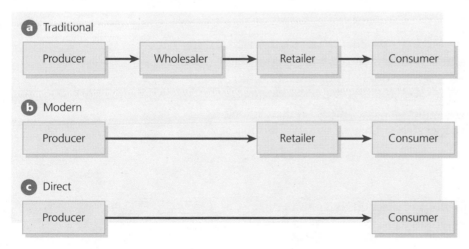

Figure 3.11 The channels of distribution

The choice of a distribution channel will be influenced by a number of factors:

- **The type of product.** Products that are difficult to transport because of their bulk, fragility or perishable nature are more likely to be distributed direct to avoid incurring additional costs. Producers selling large amounts of relatively low-priced products are more likely to use a wholesaler as it is expensive to store this type of product.
- **The nature of the market.** Businesses selling in dispersed markets usually require the services of wholesalers as they have the resources to supply in these circumstances.
- **The technical complexity of the product.** Technically complex products (such as laptops) are better distributed when the customer and the producer can easily contact each other to solve problems of installation or operation.

Multi-channel distribution

Consumers today expect to be able to access products in a variety of ways: in shops, online and click and collect. As a result many businesses now offer **multi-channel distribution**.

> **Multi-channel distribution** — where firms use more then one type of distribution channel.

Now test yourself

TESTED ☐

23 Tesco uses a multi-channel distribution strategy. Briefly outline the different channels it uses.

Answer on p. 205

Decisions relating to other elements of the marketing mix: people, process and physical environment

REVISED ☐

People

The people involved with selling a service or a product are crucial and can make or break a sale. A customer's first impressions of a business are important and it is essential that the people offering advice or delivering the service are interested, helpful and polite. It is therefore important that employees are well trained and motivated, as good customer service can enhance a business's reputation, sometimes providing a USP and increased brand loyalty.

Process

This relates to the whole process of buying a product or service, from first entering a business premises or going on a website to the delivery of the product or service and the after-sales service offered. For instance, with online sales, is the website easy to use? Are products delivered on time? Or for a fast food restaurant, do consumers have to queue? Is there a long wait for food? The efficiency of the service can have a significant impact on the level of sales.

Physical environment

It is important a business gives the right impression to consumers. The premises of a business selling a luxury product should be located in a more up-market area and the decor should reflect the nature of the product.

Now test yourself

TESTED

24 Briefly explain why people and process are just as important when selling products as they are for selling services.

Answer on p. 205

The importance of and the influences on an integrated marketing mix

REVISED

The importance of an integrated marketing mix

An integrated marketing mix is one that fits together. If a business is selling a premium product, the entire mix should support this. The elements might be constructed as follows:

- **Product.** This should be high quality in terms of design, innovativeness, features or functions.
- **Price.** The price is likely to be high (skimming) to reflect the premium nature of the product.
- **Place.** The business would seek outlets that reflect the quality or exclusivity of the product.
- **Promotion.** This would be targeted at the people who are likely to purchase the product.
- **Physical environment** should reflect the premium nature of the product. **People** should be well trained and motivated in order to deliver the customer service necessary for a more exclusive premium product. Consumers should find the whole **process** from first deciding to purchase to the delivery of the product or service first rate.

If the marketing mix is inconsistent, consumers may be deterred from purchasing the product, thereby depressing sales and profits. In the case of a premium product, a low price might be a mistake as it may lead some consumers to think that the product is not premium quality.

> **Exam tip**
>
> Remember that marketing mixes can be integrated in different ways depending on factors such as price and the target audience. For example, easyJet and Rolls Royce have markedly different marketing mixes, but both are integrated.

Influences on an integrated marketing mix

There are a number of influences on an integrated marketing mix:

- **Position in the product life cycle**. A product in the growth stage will need a different mix to one in the maturity or decline stage.
- **Boston matrix.** A cash cow will require a very different mix to a problem child.
- **Type of product.** The type of product and where it is sold, for example a product that is sold business to business (B2B), will require a different mix to one that is sold business to consumer (B2C).
- **Marketing objectives.** The mix is likely to change with changes in marketing objectives. For example if an objective of growth is introduced this might require additional promotion and adjustments to place.
- **Target market.** The mix should reflect the target market. For example, younger buyers may be more in tune with online sales than older buyers.

- **Competition.** Businesses should be looking to stay ahead of competitors; reviewing and changing the mix may enable them to achieve this.
- **Positioning.** The mix should reflect the positioning in the market, for instance whether it is a convenience or a luxury good.

Now test yourself

TESTED

25 Briefly explain how positioning and product life cycle might affect the marketing mix.

Answer on p. 205

Understanding the value of digital marketing and e-commerce

REVISED

Developments in technology have had a significant impact on the business marketing function. Benefits include:

- Businesses can gather more detailed information about consumers and build relationships with them. This is illustrated by the way in which Amazon continuously recommends products based on past shopping purchases.
- There is greater contact between consumer and business, allowing consumers to build their own products and give reviews of products or services purchased.
- Social media has also become very important and cannot be underestimated from a business point of view. If a business can tap into this with its marketing it can be a very cost-effective way of boosting sales.
- Digital marketing makes it easy for any business to set up and sell almost anywhere in the world.

Exam tip

Although there are many positives associated with digital marketing it is important to remember there are some negatives. Reputations can be destroyed through online reviews and social media. Consumers are free to write reviews on products and services which may not always be a true reflection of the product or service offered.

Now test yourself

TESTED

26 Briefly explain how digital marketing has benefited businesses.

Answer on p. 205

Exam practice

JJ's plc

JJ's plc is a manufacturer of a range of soft drinks targeted at a variety of markets and age groups within the mass market. Its latest product, branded JJ's Fitness Fuel, failed to generate forecast target sales. This was despite extensive primary market research, which included both qualitative and quantitative research. The qualitative research in particular indicated that consumers liked the product. Market mapping also indicated a gap in the market for an essentially healthy fitness drink. Jim Jones, managing director, was unsure of the next move. What he did know, however, was that his business needed a new rising star in its product portfolio and not a dog.

The latest brainstorming session about the product raised the following questions:
● Had JJ's put too much emphasis on product in the marketing mix?
● Is it targeting the wrong market?

Fit people tend to be healthy, so the product might not appeal. Should JJ's target a wider market and reposition the product? Should it change the marketing mix, particularly price, which was set slightly higher, and should it aim for a much wider distribution?

Questions

a What do you understand by the terms rising star and dog in the Boston matrix? [4]

b Explain the various forms of qualitative market research JJ's might have used. [6]

c Analyse the possible drawbacks to JJ's of targeting a narrow market segment. [9]

d To what extent do you believe JJ's may have put too much emphasis on product in its marketing mix? [16]

Answers and quick quiz 3 online

ONLINE

Summary

You should now have an understanding of all the points below.

Setting marketing objectives
● the value of setting and the internal and external influences on marketing objectives

Understanding markets and customers
● the value of primary (including sampling) and secondary market research
● the calculation of market and sales growth, market share and size
● the interpretation of marketing data including correlation and extrapolation
● the value and interpretation of price and income elasticity
● the use of data in marketing decision-making and the value of technology in this

Making marketing decisions: segmentation, targeting and positioning
● the process and value of segmentation, targeting and positioning

● influences on choosing a target market and positioning including niche and mass marketing

Making marketing decisions: using the marketing mix
● the 7Ps of the marketing mix, influences on and effects of changes in them
● product decisions including Boston matrix, product life cycle and new product development
● pricing decisions including penetration and skimming
● promotional mix decisions
● decisions related to people, process and physical environment
● the importance of an integrated marketing mix
● value of digital marketing and e-commerce

4 Decision-making to improve operational performance

The operations function of a business is the function that is responsible for the actual production of a good or service. It involves managing the process of transforming inputs into outputs. An important concept in this process is that of **added value**. This means the value of the final output, product or service, will be greater than the value of all the inputs added together. Adding value therefore enables a profit to be made and is likely to be an operational target.

> **Added value** is an amount added to the value of a product or service, equal to the difference between its cost and the amount received when it is sold.

> **Exam tip**
>
> It is not only the operations process that can add value. Marketing can also create greater brand awareness and a USP, which will add value in terms of a higher selling price.

Setting operational objectives

The value of setting operational objectives

REVISED

Besides added value, operational objectives might include the following:
- **Costs.** Anything a business can do to lower costs is likely to improve competitiveness. In terms of operations management objectives this will relate to unit costs of production. These might be reduced by achieving greater capacity utilisation or improved productivity, or by negotiating better terms with suppliers.
- **Quality.** If a business can consistently provide a quality product or service, this is likely to lead to a competitive advantage. Quality, however, is more than just the final product or service. It involves the whole process of operations. Targets in quality could therefore be set for any of the following: wastage, returns, number of complaints and reliability.
- **Speed of response and flexibility.** This is the time taken for a customer need to be fulfilled, e.g. the time taken from ordering a meal in a restaurant to receiving it or from ordering a product online to receiving it. The time taken will impact on the customer's perception of a business and in turn on reputation and sales. It is therefore important that if any targets are set in this respect they are met.
- **Dependability.** This relates to the reliability of a business in terms of product and service. Is a product reliable? Is quality consistent? Does a business do what it says it will do, e.g. is first class post delivered the next day? Failure in this objective is likely to damage a business's reputation and lead to a loss of sales.
- **Environmental objectives.** With greater consumer awareness, environmental objectives have taken on a much greater importance over recent years. Examples in this area could relate to pollution, minimising waste, the amount of packaging used, recycling and sustainability.

Whatever the operational objectives, they must fit with the overall corporate objectives and, as with all objectives, they must be SMART. By being SMART they can be used to evaluate and judge the overall performance of operations management.

External and internal influences on operational objectives

Like other functional areas, the operations function does not operate in isolation. Internally, any decision made will have implications for the other functional areas in a business, and externally the environment a business operates in will be changing all the time.

External influences

Operational decisions will be affected by the following external influences:

- **Political or legal influences.** Businesses always have to be aware of the legal environment and potential changes in legislation both from government and, in the case of EU, countries from the EU. This is illustrated by the greater awareness in recent years of health and safety and environmental issues, which has brought increasing amounts of legislation.
- **Economic influences.** The operations function needs to be both prepared for and respond to changes in the economy as demand will fluctuate according to the stage of the **economic cycle**. In addition, due to the global nature of the economy, resources can be sourced from anywhere in the world and it is possible to undertake production from anywhere, both factors that may be considered by the operations function.
- **Technological influences.** Technology has had a significant impact on the operations function both in terms of production and the way consumers purchase goods and services. The introduction of computer aided design (CAD) and computer aided manufacture (CAM) has resulted in speedier innovation and production and better quality. The advent of the internet means that consumers are more aware and demanding in terms of price, quality and customer service. Newspapers can be read online and books, films and music can be simply downloaded by consumers. There are apps for just about anything, and the growth of social media has an influence on operational objectives.
- **Competitive influences.** Markets have become increasingly competitive with competition both at home and from overseas. As a result, there is increasing pressure on businesses in terms of costs, quality and price. Added to this is a greater awareness amongst consumers resulting in increasing pressure on the operations function to play its part in maintaining consumer loyalty.

> The **economic cycle** is the natural fluctuation of the economy between periods of expansion (growth) and contraction (recession).

Internal influences

- **Finance.** The availability of finance will determine the extent of any operational decision-making, e.g. investment in new production technology.
- **Marketing.** It is likely that the marketing function will determine both what has to be produced and the quantities, so the operations department will have to liaise closely with the marketing department.
- **Human resources.** The skills of the workforce determine both what can be produced and its quality.

The above illustrates the integrated nature of a business, and the operations manager needs to analyse the impact of any decision on each functional area. Added to this will be the awareness of the overall corporate objectives as these are likely to be the drivers of decision-making.

> **Exam tip**
>
> When analysing and evaluating the influences on decision-making, your aim should be to identify which factors are most important and why for the business in the question.

Analysing operational performance

Included under the heading of operations data are four main areas:

- capacity
- capacity utilisation
- labour productivity
- unit costs

A business is likely to set targets in each of these areas. Any targets set will be SMART and can be used to identify trends and judge performance.

Calculation of operations data

REVISED

Capacity

When referring to the capacity of a business we are referring to the total or maximum amount a business can produce in a given time period if it is working flat out.

Capacity utilisation

Capacity utilisation refers to the actual production of a business in a given time period as a percentage of the maximum capacity and is calculated as follows:

$$\frac{\text{actual output in time period}}{\text{maximum possible output per period}} \times 100$$

For example, if a business has a maximum capacity of 10,000 units and is producing 7,500 units, its capacity utilisation is 75%:

$$\frac{7,500}{10,000} \times 100 = 75\%$$

> **Capacity utilisation** measures the extent to which a business uses its production potential. It is usually expressed as a percentage.

Labour productivity

Labour productivity relates to the efficiency of individual workers and is of interest to human resources as well as operational managers. Put simply, it is a measure of the output per worker in a given time period. It is calculated as follows:

$$\text{Labour productivity} = \frac{\text{output per time period}}{\text{number of employees}}$$

If in the example above the business employed 75 workers, the labour productivity would be 100 units per worker:

$$\frac{7,500}{75} = 100 \text{ units per worker}$$

> **Labour productivity** measures the output per worker in a given time period.

Unit cost

This is sometimes referred to as the 'average cost of production' and is the cost of producing one unit of output. It is calculated as follows:

$$\frac{\text{total cost}}{\text{units of output}}$$

Using the example above, again if total costs were £150,000, **unit costs** would be £20:

$$\frac{£150,000}{7,500} = £20$$

> **Unit cost** is the cost of producing one unit (item) of a good or service.

The interpretation and use of data in operational decision-making and planning

There are a number of points to note from looking at data in operational decision-making and planning. If capacity utilisation goes up, labour productivity will rise (assuming the number employed remains the same). In addition, unit cost of production will be reduced, as the fixed costs will be spread over more units of output. If capacity utilisation decreases, the opposite will occur — labour productivity will decline (assuming the number employed remains the same) and unit costs will increase, as fixed costs are now spread over fewer units of output.

A change in the number employed will also impact on productivity. If a business can maintain a certain level of output with fewer employees, the productivity of the remainder will rise. Employing more workers without increasing output would lead to a decline in productivity.

A knowledge of operational data is therefore key when making operational decisions and planning.

Now test yourself

3 Distinguish between capacity and capacity utilisation.
4 A business has a maximum capacity of 25,000 units and currently produces 20,000 units with 75 employees. Total costs of production are £1m. Calculate capacity utilisation, labour productivity and unit costs of production.
5 Explain why unit costs of production will decline when capacity utilisation and labour productivity increase.

Answers on p. 205

Making operational decisions to improve performance: increasing efficiency and productivity

Increasing operational efficiency is all about getting more output from a given level of resources. If this can be achieved, then unit costs will fall, enabling a business to charge more competitive prices. There are a number of aspects related to improving efficiency and these are investigated below.

The importance of capacity

Capacity and the level of capacity utilisation are very important to operational efficiency. We have already seen that unit costs decline as capacity utilisation increases. It is therefore important that a business does not have too much spare or **excess capacity**. Operating at 60% capacity utilisation results in 40% spare or excess capacity, which means that resources in terms of factory space, equipment and possibly labour are not being used efficiently. On the other hand, operating at maximum capacity would create its own problems as this would reduce flexibility in terms of new orders. It might also put undue pressure on workers and machinery if proper maintenance could not be undertaken. It is therefore important that a business operates at an **optimal level of capacity**, i.e. as close to 100% as possible, whilst leaving sufficient spare capacity to cope with new orders. In a growing market this would need to be planned carefully.

> **Excess capacity** occurs where actual production falls below maximum potential production.

> **Exam tip**
>
> When making a judgement about an individual business's capacity utilisation, it is important to compare with both capacity utilisation in previous years and the average for that industry.

The importance of efficiency and labour productivity

Labour productivity is a measure of output per worker in a given time period. An increase in labour productivity is likely to lead to a reduction in the unit costs of production and therefore could lead to a business being more competitive in terms of price.

How to increase efficiency and labour productivity

The following methods might be used to increase efficiency and labour productivity:

- **Investment in technology.** Such investment may both improve the quality and reliability of a product and result in greater output from fewer employees.
- **Improvements in training and motivation.** The aim of training is to improve the skills of the workforce, which is likely to lead to greater output. In addition, if as a result of training employees feel more involved in the process, this could lead to greater motivation and further improvements in both quality and output.
- **Job redesign.** This involves changing the content of a job in terms of duties and responsibilities and may be executed in such a way as to improve the overall performance of the employee in question.
- **Reduction in the labour force.** A reduction of the labour force will automatically improve productivity if the same level of output can be maintained. This might be achieved through investment in technology or better training.

For more on job design, training and motivation see the human resources section on pp. 98–110.

> **Exam tip**
>
> It is important to recognise that improvements in productivity should come without any reduction in quality or dependability of service.

The benefits and difficulties of lean production

Lean production is all about getting more from less. It is a Japanese approach to management that focuses on cutting out waste in terms of time, space and resources. Features of lean production include just-in-time (JIT) management, Kaizen, total quality management (TQM) and quality circles, and it is the first of these that is included in the AQA AS specification.

Just-in-time management (JIT)

Just-in-time management is an inventory (stock) strategy companies employ to increase efficiency and decrease waste by receiving goods only when they are needed in the production process. The benefits of such a system is that it reduces waste in terms of damaged stock or stock going out of date, and reduces the amount of space needed as there is no requirement for storage warehouses. It may also save time and reduce the number of employees required as the stock will be delivered directly to the production line. Less waste, space, time and employees will result in lower costs and help to improve the competitiveness of a business.

Further benefits might be greater flexibility as a business may be able to respond more quickly to changing customer tastes and needs. Additionally, there may be a reduced likelihood of being left with outdated, unsold stock. JIT also requires a much greater involvement from the workforce in terms of ensuring production continues uninterrupted, leading to greater responsibility and potential improvements in motivation.

For more on employee engagement see pp. 104–110.

Despite the many benefits, JIT does have a number of **drawbacks**:
- **Running out of stock.** JIT relies on the supplier delivering on time. Any transport problems due to weather or industrial action could halt production. In addition, if supplier firms are struck by disaster, as happened in Japan with the earthquake and tsunami in 2011, production can be interrupted for months.
- **Opportunities for bulk purchase.** Supplies will be purchased in smaller quantities and only when needed, and this may limit the opportunity for bulk purchase discounts.
- **Trust.** Such a system is dependent on the relationship between the company and its supplier. A company must have complete trust in the supplier to provide the necessary quality required as components will be going straight onto the production line.

> **Just-in-time management (JIT)** is an inventory strategy companies employ to increase efficiency and decrease waste by receiving goods only as they are needed for production.

> **Typical mistake**
>
> Although it is possible that the opportunity to benefit from bulk purchase discounts may be lost when using a JIT strategy, a business may be able to negotiate a special price for buying on-going supplies over a period of time. This is because the supplier will also save costs due to the reduced requirement for storage and themselves undertaking JIT production.

> **Now test yourself** TESTED
>
> 6 Briefly outline two advantages and two disadvantages of JIT production.
>
> Answer on p. 205

Difficulties of increasing efficiency and labour productivity

REVISED

The difficulties of increasing efficiency and labour productivity include:
- **Cost.** Any improvement in labour productivity is likely to come with a cost. New technology is expensive, and workers who have been trained and acquired new skills may demand higher pay. However,

improvements in productivity may lead to greater competitiveness and greater sales, which in the long run may more than cover the original costs.

- **Quality.** When looking to improve labour productivity, a business needs to make sure this is not achieved at the expense of lower quality. This can be the case when workers are encouraged to produce more through financial incentives, e.g. working on a piece-rate system.
- **Resistance of employees.** Sometimes employees can be resistant to change, especially where job losses are concerned and job security is threatened. The introduction of technology into the production process often brings with it job losses, and a business would need to consider carefully how it is introduced.

> **Exam tip**
>
> Whether to adopt a long- or a short-term approach to improving labour productivity lends itself to evaluation.

Now test yourself

TESTED

7 Draw up a table to show the benefits and drawbacks of investing in improving labour productivity.

Answer on p. 205

How to choose the optimal mix of resources

REVISED

Resources are the factors of production:

- **land:** physical land and the natural resources, e.g. oil and iron ore
- **labour:** the workers employed by a business
- **capital:** the machines and equipment used in a business
- **enterprise:** the skill of combining the other factors of production

The requirements for these resources will vary from one business to another and will depend on the nature of the business and what it can afford. A business operating in the service sector, for instance, will have different requirements to one operating in manufacturing.

In addition, what might be an optimal mix for one business might be different for another even though they are operating in the same industry. For instance, some businesses may employ a **capital-intensive** approach to production where there is a high level of capital equipment used and a lower emphasis on labour. Other businesses might be more **labour intensive**, placing a greater emphasis on labour and less on capital equipment. A capital-intensive approach to manufacturing might be employed in countries where labour is expensive, and a labour-intensive approach where labour is relatively cheap. It is also the case that some industries, such as oil refineries and chemical plants, by their very nature are likely to be capital intensive, whereas others, such as hotels or restaurants, are more likely to be labour intensive.

> **Capital intensive** describes those businesses requiring a large amount of capital relative to labour.
>
> **Labour intensive** describes those businesses requiring a large proportion of labour relative to capital.

Now test yourself

TESTED

8 Explain the likely benefits to a company manufacturing in the UK of a capital-intensive approach to production.

Answer on p. 205

How to utilise capacity efficiently

Achieving the optimum level of capacity utilisation is very important. In order to overcome situations of excess or spare capacity a business might consider the following:

- **Increase sales.** This might be achieved by undertaking a new marketing campaign or introducing extension strategies to find new uses or markets for a product.
- **Reduce capacity.** If a low level of capacity utilisation is expected to continue far into the future, it might be advisable to rationalise production and sell off some capacity. Such a decision should not be taken lightly as once done it cannot be reversed.
- **Alternative uses.** It may be possible to find alternative uses for the capacity, such as the introduction of new products or leasing it to other businesses.

If demand is so high that a business is facing the problem of lack of capacity it might consider the following:

- **Outsourcing.** This involves transferring portions of work to outside suppliers.
- **Investment.** This involves investment into the permanent establishment of new capacity, but should only be undertaken if high levels of demand are expected to continue well into the future.
- **Reducing demand.** This might be achieved by increasing price. The use of **dynamic pricing** has enabled businesses, such as airlines and hotels, to control more effectively the level of demand.

> **Dynamic pricing** is a pricing strategy where businesses set highly flexible prices for products or services based on the market demand at a particular time.

Now test yourself

9 Distinguish between a situation of excess production capacity and a lack of production capacity.
10 Briefly explain two methods of improving capacity utilisation.

Answers on p. 205

How to use technology to improve operational efficiency

Types of technology used in operations

Technology is changing quickly and affects how businesses produce goods and services as well as the products themselves. Technological developments that may affect production include:

- **More advanced computer systems**, for example enabling automated stock control systems and electronic data interchange.
- The **internet**, which enhances a business's ability to promote and sell products and its ability to communicate with customers.
- **Computer-aided manufacture (CAM)**, where manufacturers use robots as an integral part of the production process.
- **Computer-aided design (CAD)**, which can be linked to CAM systems.

Even small businesses can benefit from developments in stock control and design technology to improve the quality of their product or service. Such improvements will enable them to compete with larger-scale competitors.

The development of CAD has made the design of new products easier to carry out, store and alter. Modern software can also be used to estimate the cost of newly designed products. Technology has revolutionised manufacturing too. Computer-aided manufacturing is used by manufacturing firms of all sizes. Computers control the machines on the production line, saving labour and costs, and CAM systems can be linked to CAD technology to transform the entire process.

Benefits of new and updated technology

New technology offers businesses and consumers a range of benefits:
- It reduces unit costs of production, enhancing the competitiveness of the business concerned. For example, it allows publishers to send books electronically to be printed overseas, where costs are lower.
- For high-technology products, such as games consoles, it offers the opportunity to charge a premium price until the competition catches up. Such price skimming is likely to boost profits.
- A consistent standard of quality can be guaranteed through the use of CAM.
- Using technology efficiently may enable employees to work more efficiently. For example, electronic point of sale (EPOS) systems record information on sales and prices, and can be operated by the checkout operator in a shop as a routine part of work. EPOS automatically adjusts stock levels and reorders stock automatically as well as providing data to calculate sales revenue figures.
- It may allow access to new markets: for example, the internet allows potteries to sell worldwide.
- The use of technology can reduce waste, e.g. water control systems in commercial buildings recycle rainwater and other water for reuse within the business.

Costs of new and updated technology

New technology also poses difficulties for many businesses:
- It can be a drain on an organisation's capital. Firms may experience difficulty in raising the funds required to install high-technology equipment or to research a new product.
- It almost inevitably requires training of the existing workforce and perhaps recruitment of new employees. Both actions can create considerable costs for businesses.
- Its introduction may be met with opposition from existing employees, especially if job security is threatened. This may lead to industrial relations problems.

Now test yourself

TESTED

11 Technology is a topic with links to many other areas of the specification. Divide a sheet of paper into four sections and label these as (i) marketing, (ii) finance, (iii) operations management and (iv) people in business. In each of the four sections compile a list of the implications for that function of the business of a decision to use new technology in producing a product or in the product itself.

Answer on p. 206

Making operational decisions to improve performance: improving quality

A quality product will satisfy customer needs and can be a major determinant of a business's competitiveness.

The importance of quality REVISED

Quality can be important to a business because it can:
- provide a USP, and give consumers a reason to buy the product
- allow a business to charge higher prices, increasing profit margins
- enable a business to increase its sales
- enhance reputation and brand loyalty

Methods of improving quality REVISED

When a business considers quality, it should not just be the end product or service that is considered: it should be the whole process of production from the acquisition of resources through to the final purchase and use of a product or service by the consumer. There are a number of ways this might be improved, as outlined below.

Quality assurance

Quality assurance refers to the mechanisms put in place to ensure that the entire operations process meets the required standards. With quality assurance it is the responsibility of all workers throughout the production process to make sure that each stage meets the required standard. As a result, employees have a greater responsibility and may become more engaged and motivated.

> **Quality assurance** is a system for ensuring the desired level of quality in the development, production and delivery of products or services.

Total quality management (TQM)

There are a number of different systems of quality assurance, of which **total quality management (TQM)** is probably the best known. TQM instils a culture of quality throughout the organisation. It places on all employees of a firm an individual and collective responsibility for maintaining high quality standards. By checking throughout the process, it aims for zero defects (see Figure 4.1).

> **Total quality management (TQM)** — where there is a culture of quality throughout the organisation.

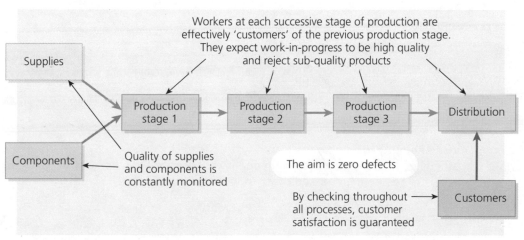

Figure 4.1 Total quality management

TQM has both an internal and an external dimension. Externally, the success of a firm depends on its ability to satisfy customers' demands. Product quality is likely to be a way in which a company can achieve a competitive advantage.

Internally, each department in a firm is viewed as a customer and/or a supplier. The firm has to meet consistently high standards in this 'internal' trading. Workers at each stage of the production process examine critically the work-in-progress they receive. Errors and faults are identified and rectified as soon as possible and customer satisfaction is assured.

Quality assurance systems are unlikely to succeed without the support of all employees. TQM seeks commitment to the highest quality standards in each of the internal stages of production. It minimises the time and money spent on quality by preventing quality problems.

Kaizen

Kaizen is the Japanese business philosophy of continuous improvement, where all employees are encouraged to identify and suggest possible improvements in the production process. Such a system requires a culture of participation and involvement.

The benefits and difficulties of improving quality

REVISED

The main **benefits** of improving quality are:
- an enhanced reputation and increased brand loyalty
- a competitive advantage in that quality may give a USP
- increased revenue due to higher sales and perhaps higher selling price
- greater flexibility in terms of price

The **difficulties** of improving quality might include:
- Bearing the cost of training of staff, the administration of the system and any equipment that might be needed.
- Employees can be resistant to change and convincing them that change is necessary might prove a stumbling block. Once convinced they might demand higher pay due to the increased responsibility.

The consequences of poor quality

REVISED

The consequences of poor quality revolve around the issue of increased costs including:
- the cost of scrapping or reworking products
- the additional costs if goods are returned for repair or replacement under warranty
- the costs resulting from the damage to the business's reputation

Exam tip

Implementing a system of TQM has enormous implications for the management of the workforce. It is likely to result in recruitment and training and can have a positive effect on motivation. Do seek to explore these links when responding to high-mark examination questions in this area.

Typical mistake

Only quality assurance is mentioned in the specification, and although some textbooks will cover quality control it is important the two are not confused.

Now test yourself

TESTED

12 Briefly explain the importance of quality to a business.
13 Explain one benefit to a business of introducing a system of quality assurance such as TQM.
14 Outline why poor quality is likely to result in increased costs for a business.

Answers on p. 206

Making operational decisions to improve performance: managing inventory and supply chains

Inventory is the term used to describe stock. A business might hold stock in the form of raw materials and components, work in progress (products in the process of being made) and finished goods.

The **supply chain** encompasses three areas: the supply of materials to the manufacturer, the manufacturing process and the distribution of the finished goods to the consumer. In other words, the supply chain is the whole process of getting a good (or service) to the consumer.

> **Inventory** is the stock a business holds in the form of raw materials, components and work in progress.

Ways and value of improving flexibility, speed of response and dependability

REVISED

Whether it is a consumer buying the finished product or service or a business purchasing supplies, the dependability, speed of response and flexibility of the supplier are important factors that will affect the decision to buy. As a result, businesses will set operational objectives in this area.

Flexibility

Flexibility refers to the ability of a business to meet a customer's requirements whether in terms of numbers ordered or of variations in specification. The former refers to the ability to vary production levels in order to cope with variations in the size of order. The latter is known as **mass customisation** which means tailoring goods to specific customer requirements, e.g. in the car industry where an individual customer can effectively build his/her own car. The customer decides on the colour, paint, trim, seating material, accessories etc., this information is then sent to the factory and the car is produced. Greater flexibility is likely to lead to greater customer satisfaction and act as a competitive advantage.

> **Mass customisation** is the production of custom-tailored goods or services to meet customers' diverse and changing needs.

Speed of response and dependability

Speed of response refers to how quickly a business fulfils an order, and **dependability** refers to its punctuality or whether it fulfils the order on time. Responding in this way can result in a competitive advantage as this will lead to greater customer satisfaction and therefore loyalty. Such a response, however, relies on there being good communication and relationships with suppliers.

> **Typical mistake**
>
> The term 'dependability' can be used in two ways: for punctuality as outlined above, and also in terms of reliability and durability. It is important to identify the correct context when responding to a question.

How to manage supply to match demand and the value of doing so

REVISED

It is important that a business is able to match supply with demand. This is a particular problem for those businesses that operate in a seasonal industry, but it can also affect other businesses. Problems will arise if there are insufficient supplies to match demand and also if there is too much supply. Too little and a business will not only miss out on lucrative orders but also future orders due to lack of dependability. Too much supply will incur costs of holding the excess, and a business may be faced with selling the good at a reduced price. In order to overcome these problems, a business might either try to manage demand or manage the supply more effectively.

Managing demand

The marketing mix might be used in order to try to influence demand. It may be possible to increase demand by additional marketing, price reductions or sales promotions and, if necessary, decrease demand by reducing promotion and increasing price. Hotels and airlines are good examples of businesses that try to match supply and demand in this way. Center Parcs does this too, charging significantly higher prices in the school holidays and having more promotions during term times. As a result, it has a capacity utilisation of over 90%.

Managing supply

Supply can be managed in a number of ways:
- **Flexible workforce.** This can be achieved through the use of a multi-skilled workforce, employing part-time workers or workers on zero hours contracts. This enables a business to increase or decrease the amount produced by simply varying the size of the workforce or number of hours worked.
- **Increase capacity.** If the market a business is operating in is growing and further increases in demand are likely, it makes sense to invest in further capacity in order to be able to satisfy the growing demand.
- **Produce to order.** Some businesses, such as restaurants, tailors and aircraft manufacturers produce to order, but for others this is more difficult. As we have seen, however, the introduction of mass customisation has enabled more businesses to adopt this approach and, as technology develops further, more businesses are likely to be able to produce to order.
- **Outsourcing**. This is when another business is contracted to produce the extra goods required in order to satisfy the demand.

> **Outsourcing** is the transfer of production that was previously done in house to a third party.

Influences on the amount of inventory held

REVISED

Inventory as outlined above may be in the form of materials for production, work in progress and finished goods. It is important that a business holds sufficient inventory to be able to satisfy demand reliably. If it cannot do this it will run the risk of losing sales and damaging its reputation. The level of inventory held will depend on the following:
- **Nature of the product.** It would be foolish to hold large stocks of perishable goods.
- **Nature of production.** A JIT method of production means that lower levels of stock are held.
- **Nature of demand.** Seasonal products may require a higher level of stock to be held than those that have regular demand.
- **Opportunity cost.** Any money tied up in stock represents an opportunity cost and could be better used elsewhere in the business.

In order to manage inventory effectively a business might use an inventory control chart as shown in Figure 4.2.

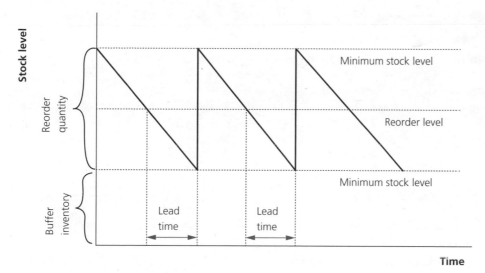

Figure 4.2 Inventory control chart

The key features of this chart are:
- **Buffer level of inventory:** the minimum amount of inventory held, designed to cover for emergencies such as late arrival of inventory.
- **Reorder level:** the level of inventory at which a new order is placed.
- **Lead time:** the time between an order being made and its arrival in the business.
- **Maximum stock level:** the highest amount of inventory a business is able to hold.
- **Reorder quantity:** the amount ordered.

Influences on the choice of suppliers

The choice of supplier may be influenced by a number of factors:
- **Dependability.** Is the supplier reliable and able to deliver on time?
- **Flexibility.** Is the supplier able to respond efficiently to changes in demand?
- **Quality.** Is the supplier able to produce at a consistent and reliable standard?
- **Price and payment terms.** Are the prices charged and payment terms (such as credit terms) competitive?
- **Ethics.** Does the supplier operate in a socially responsible manner? This might be of particular importance when dealing with overseas suppliers.

How to manage the supply chain effectively and efficiently and the value of this

A business will aim to have the right good in the right place at the right time. If it can achieve this effectively, it is likely to be able to gain customer loyalty and maximise revenues. This requires managers to make decisions about what to produce, when to produce and how much to produce. Getting this right requires not only good communication and relations with suppliers but also coordination with other functional areas — marketing, finance and human resources. It will also require an understanding of the external environment and how this might impact on both supply and demand.

Now test yourself questions

15 Briefly outline how the nature of the product and the nature of demand might affect the level of inventory held.
16 Identify four key features of an inventory control chart.
17 In what circumstances might payment terms be more important than flexibility when choosing a supplier?

Answers on pp. 206

The value of outsourcing

The value of outsourcing can be assessed by weighing up the benefits and drawbacks. One of the main benefits is that it enables a business to respond quicker to any increase in demand, thereby providing greater dependability for customers. It also means a business will save on costs as it will not have to invest in increasing capacity. This is particularly important if any increase in demand is only temporary.

Outsourcing does, however, have a number of drawbacks. One of the most important is the problem of quality: will the outsourced company be able to produce at the required level of quality? There is also the problem of cost: outsourcing is likely to be more costly than producing in house, and there may be other costs such as transport and distribution.

Outsourcing can work but it depends on the reliability and quality of work of the company undertaking the outsourced work and on the relationship established between the two companies.

Now test yourself

18 Briefly explain the benefits of mass customisation.
19 How might a company offering skiing holidays use the marketing mix to manage demand?
20 Draw up a table to show the advantages and disadvantages of outsourcing.

Answers on p. 206

Exam practice

Alpha and Beta

Alpha and Beta are two businesses operating in the same market but with different approaches to production. Alpha has a very labour-intensive approach, whereas Beta is much more capital intensive as shown in the figures in the table below.

	Alpha	Beta
Output	500,000	450,000
Number of people employed	750	150
Turnover	£7m	£7.5m
Labour costs	£2m	£3.75m

In the face of increasing competition, particularly from overseas, over the last 10 years Beta has invested heavily in technology and adopted a lean production approach. It is now considering a further measure, that of just-in-time production. This, however, is considered to be a move too far by some of the directors, who believe that reliability and dependability has been a USP for their customers. A JIT approach could threaten this, particularly as they have had problems with their suppliers in the past. On these occasions it has been their sizeable buffer inventory that has enabled them to continue to meet customer deadlines.

Questions

a Sketch a simple inventory control chart to illustrate buffer inventory.   [4]
b For both Alpha and Beta, calculate the labour productivity and labour costs as a percentage of
   turnover.   [6]
c Analyse the factors Beta may have considered before investing in technology.   [9]
d To what extent do you believe some of the directors at Beta are right to be concerned
   about a move to just-in-time production?   [16]

Answers and quick quiz 4 online

ONLINE

Summary

You should now have an understanding of all the points below.

Setting operational objectives

The value of setting and the internal and external influences on operational objectives

Analysing operational performance

- interpretation of operational data including calculation of labour productivity, unit costs, capacity and capacity utilisation
- the use of data in operational decision-making

Making operational decisions to improve performance: increasing efficiency and productivity

- capacity and its efficient utilisation
- the importance of labour productivity, how to increase it and difficulties involved
- choosing the optimal use of resources
- lean production including JIT
- using technology to improve operational efficiency

Making operational decisions to improve performance: improving quality

- the importance of quality and the consequences of poor quality
- methods of improving quality (including quality assurance) and benefits and difficulties of doing so

Making operational decisions to improve performance: managing inventory and supply chains

- ways and value of improving flexibility, speed of response and dependability
- the value of managing supply to match demand including outsourcing, producing to order and flexible workforce
- influences on the amount of inventory held including interpreting inventory control charts
- influences on the choice of suppliers

5 Decision-making to improve financial performance

Setting financial objectives

When judging the performance of a business, most analysts will first look at the financial information. It is therefore very important that a business sets objectives in terms of revenue, costs, profit, return on capital, cash flow and capital structure.

The value of setting financial objectives

REVISED

There are a number of benefits of setting financial objectives:
- They may act as a measure of performance.
- They provide targets which can be a focus for decision-making.
- Potential investors or creditors may be able to assess the viability of the business.

The distinction between cash flow and profit

REVISED

Cash flow and profit are very different. **Cash flow** is the difference between the actual amount of money a business receives (inflows) and the actual amount it pays out (outflows), whereas **profit** is the difference between all sales revenue (even if payment has not yet been received) and expenditure. It is possible for a profitable business to have cash-flow problems. In fact, many small businesses fail not because they are not profitable but because they have cash-flow problems. Such problems can occur for a number of reasons including:
- holding large amounts of inventory (stock)
- having sales on long credit periods
- using cash to purchase fixed assets

This distinction between cash flow and profit highlights the importance to a business of setting clear cash-flow objectives.

Now test yourself

TESTED

1 How is it possible that a seemingly profitable business can fail?

Answer on p. 206

The distinction between gross profit, operating profit and profit for the year

REVISED

When looking at profit it is important to distinguish between three aspects:
- **Gross profit.** This is the difference between a business's sales revenue and the direct costs of production such as materials and direct labour. It is calculated in the following way:

Sales revenue – direct costs of production = gross profit

- **Operating profit (profit of operations).** This is the difference between the gross profit and the indirect costs of production or expenses such as marketing and salaries. In other words, it is sales revenue minus both direct and indirect costs of production. It may be calculated in the following ways:

Sales revenue – all costs of production = operating profit

Gross profit – expenses = operating profit

- **Profit for the year.** The figure for operating profit does not include other expenditure such as interest payments or tax to be paid or other income such as interest received or money received from the sale of assets. It can be calculated in the following way:

Operating profit + other income – other expenditure = profit for the year

Now test yourself

TESTED

2 Distinguish between the following three measures of profit: gross profit; operating profit and profit for the year.

Answer on p. 206

Revenue, costs and profit objectives

REVISED

A business is likely to set targets in terms of **revenue**, **costs** and **profit**.

Revenue

A knowledge of the likely revenue of a business is essential and is the starting-point for creating a budget. Budgeted revenue might be based on the objective of increasing revenue by 5% per annum. The objective set might depend on the type of market a business is operating in and the state of the economy. In addition, any objective set would have to be coordinated with the other functional areas such as marketing and operations.

Cost

Businesses operate in a highly competitive environment and, as a result, face increasing pressure on costs. Cost minimisation, therefore, has become an important business objective. This involves trying to achieve the lowest possible unit costs of production. As an alternative to cost minimisation, a business might set an objective of reducing costs by a certain percentage or target a specific area of the business that is seen to be underperforming.

Profit

Making a profit is the aim of the majority of businesses in the private sector. A business might, however, set a specific objective for profit. This might be a particular figure, a percentage increase, or it might be set in terms of a profit margin. Profit maximisation is sometimes mentioned, but it is difficult to judge whether profit maximisation has actually been achieved, and a business making unreasonably high profit can be the subject of a great deal of criticism as in the case with some of the utility companies.

Cash-flow objectives

Cash flow is the flow of money into and out of the business and is vital to the health of any business. Although it is possible to survive as a business in the short to medium term whilst making a loss, it is impossible to survive for long without cash to make immediate payments. It is therefore vital that a business manages its cash flow carefully. This may involve setting cash-flow objectives such as:

- targets for monthly closing balances
- reduction of bank borrowings to a target level
- reduction of seasonality in sales
- targets for achieving payment from customers
- extension of the business's credit period to pay suppliers

These objectives are likely to vary according to the circumstances of the individual business.

> **Cash flow** is the money (cash) moving into and out of a business over a given period of time.

Objectives for investment (capital expenditure) levels

Capital expenditure is the money spent on fixed assets such as buildings and equipment and represents long-term investment into the business. Such investment will take place when a business first sets up, but it will also need to invest further as a business grows and develops. Objectives for investment will depend on the overall corporate objectives. For example, if there is an overall objective of growth, this is likely to require further capital expenditure. It will also depend on other factors such as the type of business and the state of the economy and market in which the business is operating. For example, with oil prices falling, many oil companies, such as BP and Shell, are cutting back investment in exploration.

> **Capital expenditure** is the money used to purchase, upgrade or improve the life of long-term assets.

Return on investment

A business might set itself an objective in terms of the return on an investment, e.g. 10%. This would be calculated using the following formula:

$$\frac{\text{return on investment (or profit)}}{\text{capital invested}} \times 100$$

This formula could also be used when a business is deciding between two different investments. With this type of decision, however, it is important to remember that any returns (profit) will only be forecasts, and any predictions made may be influenced by a manager's own bias towards a particular investment.

Capital structure objectives

The capital structure of the business refers to the long-term capital (finance) of a business. Long-term capital is made up of **equity** (share capital) and **borrowing** (loan capital). The proportion of borrowing to equity is an important consideration for a business. The higher the borrowing, the greater is the interest repayment. Having high interest payments could put a business at risk if profit should fall for any reason. In addition, any rise in interest rates could have a significant impact on

> **Equity** is the money a business raises through the issue of shares.
>
> **Borrowing** is the money a business raises through loan capital.

profit. A business may therefore set targets in terms of the proportion of long-term capital that is debt. This can be measured by the following gearing ratio:

$$\text{Gearing ratio} = \frac{\text{loan capital}}{\text{total capital}} \times 100$$

Total capital = loan capital + equity

Now test yourself

TESTED

3 What is the formula used for calculating return on investment?
4 Briefly explain how a highly geared business selling luxury items might be affected by a rise in interest rates.

Answers on p. 206

External and internal influences on financial objectives and decisions

REVISED

External influences

- **Competitor actions.** Businesses operate within a competitive environment and therefore financial objectives may be affected by the actions of competitors. This might be due to competitors launching a new marketing campaign, price cuts or the development of new products or services.
- **Market forces.** Markets and fashion change over time and, unless a business can lead or keep up with changes, financial targets may be missed. This can be illustrated by the changes in the music and film industry where HMV and Blockbuster failed to recognise the growth in downloading.
- **Economic factors.** Changes in the economy, such as the recession of 2008, are likely to result in financial targets being missed, whereas increasing growth may lead to better performance. Changes in interest rates can also impact on performance illustrating the need for all businesses to review targets in the light of any changes in the economy.
- **Political factors.** Change of government and legislation can also have an impact. For instance, an increase in the minimum wage or the introduction of new health and safety legislation will incur additional costs which, if not passed on to the consumer, will impact on financial targets.
- **Technology.** Changes in technology may impact in a number of ways such as facilitating quicker and easier monitoring of financial data. The introduction of new technology, which may, in the long term, lead to greater efficiency and improved performance, is likely to have a significant cost in the short term.

Internal influences

- **Corporate objectives.** Any financial targets need to be linked to the overall corporate objectives. For instance, an objective of growth might lead to improved financial performance in the long term, but in the short term to a decline in performance as more money is used to finance growth.

- **Resources available.** The ability to achieve financial targets may be limited by the resources available, such as the availability of skilled labour and the money available to finance the targets set.
- **Operational factors.** The ability to achieve financial targets will be limited in the short term by the physical capacity of a business.

Now test yourself

5 Why might a business not be able to achieve its financial targets even though market conditions are favourable?

Answer on p. 206

Analysing financial performance

How to construct and analyse budgets and cash-flow forecasts

A **budget** is a financial plan. Its purpose is to provide a target for entrepreneurs and managers as well as a basis for a later assessment of the performance of a business. A budget should have a specific purpose and must have a set of targets attached to it if it is to be of value. The detail of a budget should be the result of negotiation with all concerned. If it is to work as an effective motivator, those responsible for keeping to a budget should play a part in setting it.

> A **budget** is a financial plan.

Structure of income, expenditure and profit budgets

Income budgets

Income budgets are forecasted earnings from sales and are sometimes called 'sales budgets'. For a newly established business they will be based on the results of market research. Established businesses can also call upon past trading records to provide information for sales forecasts. Income budgets are normally drawn up for the next financial year, on a monthly basis, as shown in Table 5.1.

> An **income budget** is the forecasted earnings from sales, sometimes called a 'sales budget'.

Expenditure budgets

An **expenditure budget** sets out the expected spending of a business, broken down into a number of categories. The titles given to these categories will depend upon the type of business. A manufacturing business will have sections entitled 'Raw materials' or 'Components', whereas a service business may not. The categories in Table 5.1 may therefore vary according to the type of business.

> An **expenditure budget** is the expected spending of a business.

Profit (or loss) budgets

Profit and loss budgets are calculated by subtracting forecast expenditure (or costs) from forecast sales income. Depending on the balance between expenditure and income, a loss or a profit may be forecast. It is not unusual for a new business to forecast (and actually make) a loss during its first period of trading.

Table 5.1 shows forecast income, expenditure and profit/loss for a newly established manufacturer of surfboards for the first 3 months of trading.

Table 5.1 Viking Boards Ltd's budget (April to June)

	April (£)	May (£)	June (£)
Cash sales	10,215	15,960	17,500
Credit sales	0	0	4,125
Total sales	**10,215**	**15,960**	**21,625**
Purchases of raw materials and components	19,500	14,010	15,550
Interest payments	1,215	1,105	1,350
Wages and salaries	3,000	2,850	2,995
Marketing and administration	2,450	2,400	2,450
Other costs	975	1,100	1,075
Total costs	**27,140**	**21,465**	**23,420**
Profit/(loss)	**(16,925)**	**(5,505)**	**(1,795)**

Exam tip

In an examination, you should be able to complete budgets such as Table 5.1 by inserting any missing figures, or be able to recalculate it if, for example, there is a change in the forecast income from sales.

The process of setting budgets

As Table 5.1 shows, budgets have a common structure. The top of the budget shows income, and this is followed by expenditure and finally by profit or loss. This is also the sequence in which budgets are set. Figure 5.1 summarises this process.

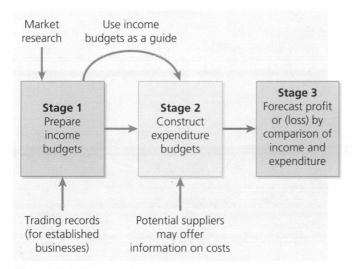

Figure 5.1 The process of setting budgets

Businesses set budgets because:
- They are an essential element of a business plan. A bank is unlikely to grant a loan without evidence of this particular form of financial planning.
- Budgets can help businesses to decide whether or not to go ahead with a business idea. If the budget shows a significant loss in its first year of trading, with little improvement evident, then the business idea may be abandoned.
- Budgets can help with pricing decisions. If a large loss is forecast, the business may decide to adjust the price to improve the business's financial prospects.

Difficulties of setting budgets

Those in charge of budgets can expect to face several difficulties when drawing up a first set of budgets:

- In some cases there may be no historical evidence available to a business, particularly for a new business or an existing business entering a new market. There will be no trading records to show the level of sales income, costs or how these figures fluctuated throughout the year.
- Forecasting costs can also be problematic. A business may lack the experience to estimate costs such as those for raw materials or wages.
- Competitors may respond to the actions of a business by cutting prices or promoting their products heavily. This can affect the sales income of a business and it may receive less income than it forecast. As a result, expenditure on promotion may have to increase, so increasing costs.

> **Exam tip**
>
> Remember financial information given in an examination paper is often a forecast. It may not be accurate. You should treat this with caution, especially if you think that the quality of market research was poor.

How to calculate and interpret variances

Variance analysis is the study by managers of the differences between planned activities in the form of budgets and the actual results that were achieved. Table 5.2 is an example of a monthly budget for a restaurant.

As the period covered by the budget unfolds, actual results can be compared with the budgeted figures and variances calculated and examined.

A **positive (or favourable) variance** occurs when costs are lower than forecast or profit or revenues higher, as in the case of sales revenue and profits in Table 5.2.

A **negative (or adverse) variance** arises when costs are higher than expected or revenues are less than anticipated. Examples are wages costs and food and drink in Table 5.2.

> **Variance analysis** is the study by managers of the differences between planned activities in the form of budgets and the actual results that were achieved.

Table 5.2 An example of calculating variances

Item	Budget figure (£)	Actual figure (£)	Variance (£)
Sales revenue	39,500	42,420	2,920 (favourable)
Fixed costs	9,500	9,500	0
Wages costs	10,450	11,005	555 (adverse)
Food and drink	8,475	9,826	1,351 (adverse)
Other costs	5,300	6,000	700 (adverse)
Total costs	33,725	36,331	2,606 (adverse)
Profit/loss	5,775	6,089	314 (favourable)

How to use variances to inform decision-making

Positive variances might occur because of good budgetary control or by accident, e.g. due to rising market prices. Possible responses to positive variances are:

- to increase production if prices are rising, giving increased profit margins
- to reduce prices if costs are below expectations and the business aims to increase its sales
- to reinvest into the business or pay shareholders higher dividends if profits exceed expectations

Exam practice answers and quick quizzes at **www.hoddereducation.co.uk/myrevisionnotes**

Negative variances might occur because of inadequate control or factors outside the firm's control, such as rising raw material costs. Possible responses to negative variances are:

- to reduce costs (e.g. by buying less expensive materials)
- to increase advertising in order to increase sales of the product and revenues
- to reduce prices to increase sales (relies on demand being price elastic)

The key issue about using the results of variance analysis to help decision-making is to take into account the causes of the adverse or favourable variances. Just because a result is favourable does not mean that everything is in order. Neither does an adverse variance mean that the area responsible has been inefficient. A favourable production material variance could be generated from using lower-quality raw materials, which in turn could manifest itself as a drop in sales. Similarly, an adverse cost variance may occur because sales are higher than forecast and the business has incurred extra costs in supplying customers' demands.

The value of budgeting

The value of budgeting can be assessed by weighing up the benefits and drawbacks of using budgets.

Benefits of budgets

- Targets can be set for each part of a business, allowing managers to identify the extent to which each part contributes to the business's performance.
- Inefficiency and waste can be identified, so that appropriate remedial action can be taken.
- Budgets make managers think about the financial implications of their actions and focus decision-making on the achievement of objectives.
- Budgeting should improve financial control by preventing overspending.
- Budgets can help improve internal communication.
- Delegated or devolved budgets can be used as a motivator by giving employees authority and the opportunity to fulfil some of their higher-level needs, as identified by Maslow (see pp. 106–107). At the same time, senior managers can retain control of the business by monitoring budgets.

> **Typical mistake**
>
> When answering questions on the value of budgets students often write only about the use of budgets in preventing overspending. Make sure that you can argue a wider range of points.

Drawbacks of budgets

- The operation of budgets can become inflexible. For example, sales may be lost if the marketing budget is followed when competitors implement major promotional campaigns.
- Budgets have to be accurate to have any meaning. Wide variances between budgeted and actual figures can demotivate staff and waste the resources used to prepare the budgets.

> **Exam tip**
>
> Look for the relationships between revenues, costs and profits when considering variances. For example, if sales revenue has recorded a negative variance, it would be reasonable to expect costs, especially variable costs, to show a positive variance. If they do not, profits are likely to have a negative variance.

Now test yourself

6 Draw up a table to show four possible causes of favourable variances and four possible causes of adverse variances. For each cause of variance that you have listed, identify an appropriate response.

7 Briefly outline three benefits of budgeting.

Answers on pp. 206–207

The structure of a cash-flow forecast

Cash-flow forecasts are a central part of a business plan for a new business. They comprise three sections:

- **Receipts** in which the expected total month-by-month receipts are recorded.
- **Payments** in which the expected monthly expenditure by item is recorded.
- **Running balance** in which a running total of the expected bank balance at the beginning and end of each month (see Figure 5.1) is recorded. These are termed 'opening' and 'closing balances'. The closing balance at the end of one month becomes the opening balance at the start of the next month.

Negative figures in cash-flow forecasts are usually shown in brackets.

Month	Jan	Feb	Mar	Apr	May	June
Receipts						
1 Sales cash	4,500					
2 Sales credit	3,650		.			
3 Total cash in (1 + 2)	8,150					
Payments						
4 Supplies	2,500					
5 Wages	1,900					
6 Fuel	900					
7 Electricity	200					
8 Heating	200					
9 Rates	400					
10 Mortgage payment	900					
11 Interest on loan	450					
12 Total cash out (4 + 5 + 6… + 11)	7,450					
13 Net cash flow (3 – 12)	700					
14 Opening bank balance	(250)	450				
15 Closing bank balance (14 + 13)	450					

Figure 5.2 An example of a cash-flow forecast completed for the month of January

---

Typical mistake

It is not unusual for a cash-flow calculation in an examination to include negative figures. Many students have difficulty carrying out calculations involving negative figures and make errors when adding and subtracting where one or more figure is negative.

How to construct and interpret breakeven charts

A breakeven chart is a graph used in breakeven analysis to illustrate the point at which total costs are equal to total revenue, in other words, the output at which it makes neither a profit nor a loss.

How to construct a breakeven chart

One way of representing the breakeven point is through the use of a breakeven chart, as shown in Figure 5.3. The step-by-step points below show how to draw a breakeven chart.

1 Give the chart a title.
2 Label axes (horizontal — output in units; vertical — costs/revenues in pounds).
3 Draw on the fixed cost line.
4 Draw on the variable cost line.
5 Draw on the total cost line.
6 Draw on the sales revenue line.
7 Label the breakeven point where sales revenue = total cost.
8 Mark on the selected operating point (SOP): that is, the actual or forecast level of the company's output.
9 Mark on the margin of safety (the difference between the SOP and the breakeven level of output).
10 Mark clearly the amount of profit and loss. Note that this is a vertical distance at any given level of production, and not an area.

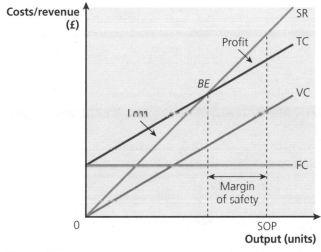

Figure 5.3 A breakeven chart for product X

> **Exam tip**
>
> It is unlikely that you will be asked to draw a complete breakeven chart in an examination as this would take too long. It is probable that you will be asked to add lines to an incomplete chart or to show the effects of changes in costs or prices. You should practise these types of activity.

Contribution and the calculation of breakeven output

The breakeven output can also be identified through calculation, and doing so enables the accuracy of charts to be checked. An understanding of the concept of **contribution** is necessary for this. Contribution is the difference between sales revenue and variable costs and can be calculated as follows:

> sales revenue – variable costs

Contribution is the amount of money left over after variable costs have been subtracted from sales revenue.

It can also be calculated per unit as follows:

> sales price per unit – variable cost per unit

From this second calculation you may have already spotted that total contribution could also be calculated by multiplying unit contribution with output:

> Total contribution = unit contribution × output

Contribution can be used to calculate two things:
- the breakeven point
- the level of profit

The calculation for breakeven is:

$$\frac{\text{fixed costs}}{\text{contribution per unit}}$$

This tells us the number of units that need to be sold to break even.

Profit can be calculated as follows:

> contribution total – fixed costs

Figure 5.4 illustrates how the profit calculation works.

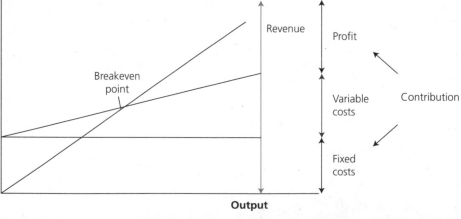

Figure 5.4 Profit calculation

From Figure 5.4 it can be seen that contribution is made up of profit and fixed costs. Therefore, by subtracting the fixed costs we are left with profit. Note also that at the breakeven point no profit is made, so the value of contribution must be equal to the value of fixed costs. This means that below the breakeven point any contribution sales goes towards covering the fixed cost, and above the breakeven point it goes towards profit.

8 What is the formula used to calculate breakeven?
9 A business sells 100,000 burgers per year for an average price of £2.50. The average variable cost for each burger is £1.50. Calculate the total contribution for the year.
10 A business produces 10,000 units. It has a sales price of £5 per unit, variable costs of £3 per unit and fixed costs of £15,000. Calculate (i) the breakeven output and (ii) the level of profit made.

Answers on p. 207

How to calculate and illustrate on a breakeven chart the effects of changes in price, output and cost

REVISED

Breakeven analysis can illustrate the effects of changes in price and costs, and assist entrepreneurs in making decisions by the use of 'what if?' scenarios:

● What level of output and sales will be needed to break even if we sell at a price of £x per unit?
● What would be the effect on the level of output and sales needed to break even of an x% rise (or fall) in fixed or variable costs?

Using breakeven analysis in this way, entrepreneurs can decide whether it is likely to be profitable to supply a product at a certain price or to start production. This aspect of breakeven analysis makes it a valuable technique. Few businesses trade in environments in which changes in prices and costs do not occur regularly.

Figure 5.5 illustrates the effects of changes in key variables on the breakeven chart. These are further illustrated in Table 5.3.

Typical mistake

When adding or amending lines on breakeven charts do not waste time by plotting figures at each level of output before drawing the new line. All lines on breakeven charts are straight, so it is only necessary to plot the new figures at zero and maximum output and to join up these two points using a ruler.

Note: Figure 5.5(b) only illustrates a rise in fixed costs to avoid the diagram becoming too complex. A fall in fixed costs would have the exact opposite effect. For the same reason, Figure 5.5(c) only illustrates a fall in variable costs. A rise in variable costs would have the exact opposite effect.

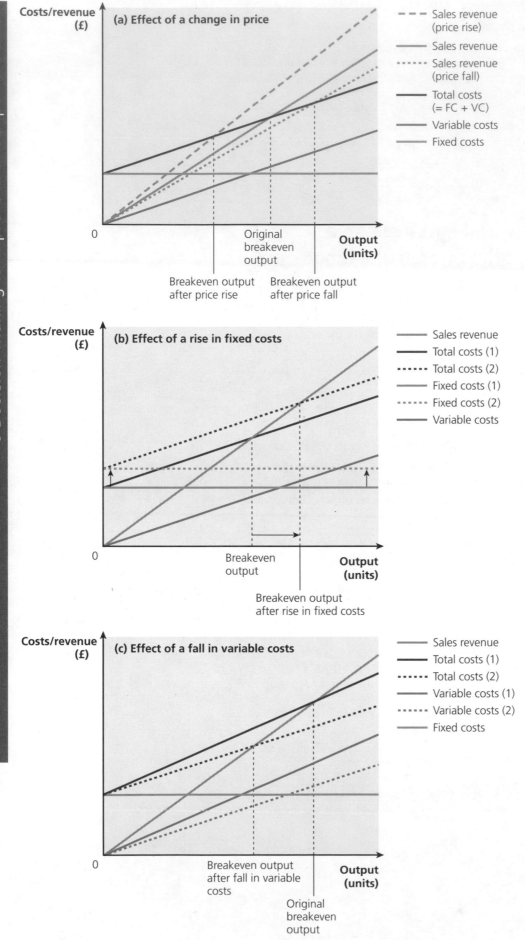

Figure 5.5 Effects of changes in key variables on the breakeven chart

Table 5.3 Effects of changes in key variables on the breakeven chart

Change in key variable	Impact on breakeven chart	Effect on breakeven output	Explanation of change	Illustrated in figure
Increase in selling price.	Revenue line pivots upwards.	Breakeven is reached at a lower level of output.	Fewer sales will be necessary to break even because each sale generates more revenue, while costs have not altered.	Figure 5.5(a)
Fall in selling price.	Revenue line pivots downwards.	A higher level of output is necessary to reach breakeven.	Each sale will earn less revenue for the business and, because costs have not altered, more sales will be required to break even.	Figure 5.5(a)
Rise in fixed costs.	Parallel upward shift in fixed and total cost lines.	Breakeven occurs at a higher level of output.	More sales will be required to break even because the business has to pay higher costs before even starting production.	Figure 5.5(b)
Fall in fixed costs.	Parallel downward shift in fixed and total cost lines.	Smaller output required to break even.	Because the business faces lower costs, fewer sales will be needed to ensure that revenue matches costs.	
Rise in variable costs.	Total cost line pivots upwards.	Higher output needed to break even.	Each unit of output costs more to produce, so a greater number of sales will be necessary if the firm is to break even.	
Fall in variable costs.	Total cost line pivots downwards.	Lower level of output needed to break even.	Every unit of production is produced more cheaply, so less output and fewer sales are necessary to break even.	Figure 5.5(c)

The value of breakeven analysis

The value of breakeven analysis can be assessed by weighing up the benefits and shortcomings.

Benefits include:
- **Starting a new business.** A business can estimate the level of sales required before it would start to make a profit. From this it can see whether or not the business proposal is viable. The results of market research are important here.
- **Supporting loan applications.** A business will be unlikely to succeed in negotiating a loan with a bank unless it has carried out a range of financial planning, including breakeven analysis.
- **Measuring profit and losses.** In diagrammatic form, breakeven analysis enables businesses to tell at a glance what their estimated level of profit or loss would be at any level of output and sales.
- **Modelling 'what if?' scenarios.** Breakeven analysis enables businesses to model what will happen to their level of profit if they change prices or are faced by changes in costs.

Although breakeven analysis is quick to perform, it is a simplification and as such it has several **drawbacks**:

● No costs are truly fixed. A stepped fixed cost line would be a better representation, as fixed costs are likely to increase in the long term and at higher levels of output if more production capacity is required.
● The total cost line should not be represented by a straight line because this takes no account of the discounts available for bulk buying.
● Sales revenue assumes that all output produced is sold and at a uniform price, which is unrealistic.
● The analysis is only as good as the information provided. Collecting accurate information is expensive, and in many cases the cost of collection would outweigh any benefit that breakeven analysis could provide.

Exam tip

It is common for examination questions to ask you to read data from breakeven charts. You may be required to read off profit or loss, revenue or variable costs. You should practise doing this.

Now test yourself

TESTED

11 What will be the effect on breakeven output of (i) a rise in fixed costs and (ii) an increase in price?
12 Explain two weaknesses of using breakeven analysis as a technique of financial planning.

Answers on p. 207

How to analyse profitability

REVISED

The figures for gross profit, operating profit and profit for the year can be used to analyse the performance of a business in terms of its profitability. On their own, however, they show very little and, in order to be useful, they need to be compared either with previous years or other companies. The most useful way of doing this is to convert them into ratios and calculate the percentage profit margins. This can be done as follows:

$$\text{Gross profit margin} = \frac{\text{gross profit}}{\text{sales revenue}} \times 100$$

$$\text{Operating profit margin} = \frac{\text{operating profit}}{\text{sales revenue}} \times 100$$

$$\text{Profit for the year margin} = \frac{\text{profit for the year}}{\text{sales revenue}} \times 100$$

Once calculated, these figures make comparisons both with previous years and other firms simpler and easier to understand. For example, when comparing different supermarket chains, their levels of turnover and profit will be different. By calculating operating profit margins it will be possible to see at a glance what percentage of every pound of turnover is profit — the higher the figure the better. In addition, the gross and operating profit margins give an indication of a business's ability to control both its direct and indirect costs. A falling gross profit margin could indicate either rising direct costs of production or a more competitive environment and falling prices. A falling operating profit margin could indicate rising indirect costs (expenses).

Exam tip

When assessing the performance of a business try to make comparisons either with previous years' figures or the performance of other similar businesses.

Now test yourself

13 Briefly explain how it might be possible for a business to have an improving gross profit margin but a falling operating profit margin.

Answer on p. 207

How to analyse the timings of cash inflows and outflows

Money leaving a business is known as **payables**, and money coming into the business is known as **receivables**. The analysis of this relationship is important as it will enable a business to:

- Forecast periods of time when cash outflows might exceed cash inflows and take action (e.g. arrange a loan) in order to avoid the business being unable to pay bills on time.
- Plan when and how to finance major items of expenditure (e.g. vehicles or machinery), which may lead to large outflows of cash.
- Highlight any periods when cash surpluses, that could be used elsewhere, may exist.
- Assess whether an idea will generate enough cash to be worthwhile putting into action.
- Give evidence to lenders (e.g. banks) that any loans given can and will be repaid.

> **Payables** (sometimes called 'trade creditors') — money owed for goods and services that have been purchased on credit.
>
> **Receivables** (sometimes called 'trade debtors') — money owed by a business's customers for goods or services purchased on credit.

Now test yourself

14 Distinguish between payables and receivables.
15 Why is it important that a business draws up a cash-flow forecast? Identify three reasons.

Answers on p. 207

The use of data for financial decision-making and planning

A business today has enormous amounts of data at its disposal, which can be manipulated in a variety of ways. This involves employing a scientific decision-making approach using budgets, cash flows, breakeven and profit ratios, which will hopefully reduce risk. Any data used, however, will either be historical or forecast and should be treated with a certain amount of caution.

Making financial decisions: sources of finance

Internal and external sources of finance

Figure 5.6 summarises the various sources of finance available to a business.

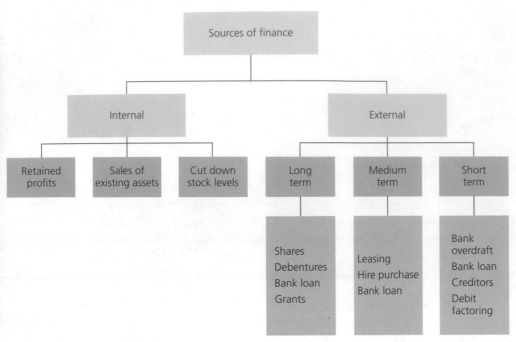

Figure 5.6 Sources of finance

External

The two main external sources of long-term capital, **equity** and **loans**, were outlined when discussing the capital structure of a business above (see p. 74).

- **Equity** is the money provided by the owners or shareholders. Its key characteristics are that it will not have to be paid back and there is no interest to pay on it. If a shareholder wishes to regain his/her money, he/she will simply sell his/her shares to someone else through the Stock Exchange. Although the owners of the shares receive no interest payment, they will be hopeful of receiving a share of the profit made through a dividend payment.
- **Loans** is money raised from a creditor, but unlike equity loans have to be paid back and there will also be interest payments to be made.

Other sources of long-term external finance include:

- **Venture capital.** This applies to mainly small and medium-sized businesses that may struggle to raise money from traditional sources. A venture capitalist may provide funds as a loan or in return for a share of the business.
- **Mortgages.** A loan granted for the purpose of buying land or buildings.
- **Crowdfunding.** This is a method of raising finance from a large number of people who each contribute a small amount of money. This has been made possible through the internet, an example being Lunar Missions Ltd, a private moon drilling mission that has raised over $1m by this method.

Internal

There are two major sources of internal finance: **retained profit** and **sale of assets**.

- **Retained profit.** This is profit that is not paid to shareholders and is kept within the business for future investment. A business will only have access to this source if it is profit-making, but the great benefit is that it does not have to be paid back and has no interest or dividend payment attached to it.

- **Sale of assets.** This is when a business sells assets it no longer requires, such as machinery, warehouse and factory space or land. Although this can sometimes raise large amounts, a business has to be sure that these assets will not be required in the future.

Short-term sources of finance

Short-term sources of finance include the following:

- **Overdraft.** This is when a bank allows a business to overspend on its bank account up to an agreed limit. Overdrafts are easy to arrange and are a very flexible form of finance. They can be expensive, but interest will only be charged on the amount overdrawn.
- **Debt factoring.** This is when a business sells its bills (invoices) that have not been paid to a bank or financial institution in order to access this money up front. The business receives 80% of the sum owed immediately and the remainder less any charges once the bank or finance institution has collected the money.
- **Trade credit.** This is when a business receives materials but pays for them at a later date. Trade credit periods can vary from a week to several months.

Advantages and disadvantages of different sources of finance for short- and long-term uses

REVISED

Table 5.5

Source	Advantages	Disadvantages
Retained profit	• No interest to pay. • Does not have to be paid back. • No dilution of shares.	• Shareholders may have reduced dividends.
Sale of assets	• No interest to pay. • Does not have to be paid back. • No dilution of shares.	• Once sold gone forever.
Equity	• No interest to pay. • Does not have to be paid back.	• Might upset existing shareholders.
Loans	• No dilution of shares.	• Interest payments. • Set maturity date.
Overdraft	• Quick and easy to set up and very flexible. • Interest paid only on amount overdrawn.	• Interest payments higher than for a loan.
Debt factoring	• Immediate cash. • Improves cash flow. • Protection from bad debts. Reduced administration costs.	• Expensive. • Customer relations may be affected.
Trade credit	• Eases cash flow.	• If late paying, can damage credit history.

Now test yourself

TESTED

16 How does an overdraft differ from a bank loan?
17 Explain why retained profit and equity might be viewed as preferable sources of finance to borrowing.

Answers on p. 207

Making financial decisions: improving cash flow and profits

Cash-flow problems

REVISED

Cash-flow problems may occur for a number of reasons:

- **Poor management.** If managers do not forecast and monitor the business's cash flow, problems are more likely to arise and lead to a serious financial situation. Similarly, the failure to chase up customers who have not paid can lead to lower inflows and cash shortages.
- **Giving too much trade credit.** When a firm offers trade credit, it gives its customers time to settle their accounts — possibly 30, 60 or 90 days. This is an interest-free loan, and while it may attract customers it slows the business's cash inflows, reducing its cash balance.
- **Overtrading.** This occurs when a business expands rapidly without planning how to finance the expansion. A growing business must pay for materials and labour before receiving the cash inflow from sales. If it does this on an increasing scale it may struggle to fund its expenditure.
- **Unexpected expenditure.** A business may incur unexpected costs, resulting in a cash outflow. The breakdown of a machine can lead to significant outflows of cash, weakening the enterprise's cash position.

Methods of improving cash flow

REVISED

There are a number of methods of improving cash flow.

Factoring

Factoring enables a business to sell its outstanding debtors to a specialist debt collector, called a factor. The business receives about 80% of the value of the debt immediately. The factor then receives payment from the customer and passes on the balance to the firm, holding back about 5% to cover expenses. This improves the business's cash-flow position as it does not have to wait for payment. Factoring, however, reduces profit margins, as approximately 5% of revenue is 'lost'.

Sale and leaseback

Here the owner of an asset (such as property) sells it and then leases it back. This provides a short-term boost to the business's finances, as the sale of the asset generates revenue. However, the business commits itself to paying rent to use the asset for the foreseeable future.

Improved working capital control

Working capital is the cash available to a business for its day-to-day operations. This can help cash-flow management and be improved by:
- selling stocks of finished goods quickly, prompting cash inflows
- making customers pay on time and offering less trade credit (although this may damage sales)
- persuading suppliers to offer longer periods of trade credit, slowing cash outflows

Other possibilities are:
- stimulating sales, by offering discounts for cash and prompt payment
- selling off excess material stocks

> **Working capital** is the cash available to a business for its day-to-day operations.

18 Draw up a two-column table to show four possible causes of cash-flow problems and an appropriate solution for each cause.

Answer on p. 207

Answer on p. 207

Exam tip

Try to match the solution for cash-flow problems to their cause. This makes it much easier for you to justify your solution.

Methods of improving profits and profitability

REVISED ☐

Profitability measures profits against some yardstick, such as the sales revenue achieved by the business. Firms can increase their profits and/or profitability by taking a variety of actions:

- **Increasing prices.** An increase in price may increase revenue without raising total costs. However, this is a risk because an increase in price may cause a fall in sales, leading to a reduction in profits if the fall in sales more than offsets the increase in price. The extent to which this happens depends upon price elasticity of demand (see pp. 38–39).
- **Cutting costs.** Lower costs of production can increase profit margins but possibly at the expense of quality. Reduced quality could reduce the volume of sales and the firm's reputation.
- **Using its capacity as fully as possible.** If a business has productive capacity that is not being utilised, its profits will be lower than they could be. If train companies run services that are only 50% occupied, their revenue is much lower. Offering incentives to customers to use the trains could increase profits, as it costs little more to run a full train than a half-full one.
- **Increasing efficiency.** Avoiding waste in the form of poor quality and unsaleable products, using staff fully and using minimal resources to make products are all ways of improving the efficiency of a business. Improving efficiency is likely to result in increased profits.

> **Profitability** measures profits against some yardstick, such as the sales revenue achieved by the business.

Difficulties of improving cash flow and profit

REVISED ☐

It is relatively easy in theory to identify ways of improving cash flow and profit but much more difficult in practice. This is due to the difficulties associated with each method. The relative difficulties are summarised below.

Cash flow

- **Factoring.** The profit margin is reduced due to cost of factoring. In addition, customers might become concerned that their supplier has cash-flow difficulties.
- **Sale and lease back.** The asset is removed forever and rent now has to be paid.
- **Working capital control.** Customers may be put off by reduced credit periods and suppliers may be unwilling to extend credit periods.

Profit

- **Increasing prices.** This may reduce sales and revenue and attract criticism from customers.
- **Cutting costs.** This is likely to result in a reduction in quality if inferior raw materials are used. It could also mean job losses and upset labour relations.
- **Use capacity fully.** This may cause problems in matching supply with demand. It could result in price reductions and lower revenues.
- **Increasing efficiency.** This may result in redundancies if technology is introduced.

Now test yourself

19 Identify two ways in which a business could increase its profit.
20 For each of the methods of increasing profit, outline the difficulties that might be encountered.

Answers on p. 207

Exam practice

Opportunity knocks for ABC plc

ABC currently operates on two separate sites, which although workable does mean higher costs than necessary. The opportunity has arisen to purchase land adjacent to one of the sites and consolidate production into one area. This would have a significant impact on costs, especially fixed costs, and as a result lower the breakeven output.

Financially, ABC has been struggling over the last 5 years, making only a very small profit in 2 of those years. Cash flow has also been an issue, with an increasing dependence upon its overdraft and the likelihood of having to extend its limit in the near future.

Being able to consolidate into one site would eventually improve ABC's position and make consistent profit a realistic possibility. In the short term, however, there is the problem of financing the purchase of the land. The situation is even more pressing due to the fact that it needs to act quickly. The best option appears to be a loan, but will the bank be willing to advance the money, especially considering the company's current cash-flow problems?

Questions

a Sketch a simple breakeven chart to illustrate how a fall in fixed costs would reduce the breakeven output. [4]
b Explain the possible benefits to ABC of using an overdraft. [6]
c Analyse the potential problems for ABC of raising the finance needed through loan capital. [9]
d To what extent do you believe achieving a positive cash flow is more important to ABC than achieving consistent profit? [16]

Answers and quick quiz 5 online

ONLINE

Summary

You should now have an understanding of all the points below.

Setting financial objectives

- financial objectives including those for cash flow, capital expenditure, revenue costs and profit
- the value of setting financial objectives and internal and external influences on them
- the distinction between profit and cash flow as well as between gross, operating and profit for the year

Analysing financial performance

- construction of budgets and their value including variance analysis
- construction and analysis of cash flows
- construction of, interpretation and value of breakeven charts

- illustration of changes in price, output and cost on breakeven charts
- analysis of profitability including gross, operating and profit for the year ratios
- the use of data for financial decision-making

Making financial decisions: sources of finance

- advantages and disadvantages of different sources of internal and external finance for short- and long-term purposes

Making financial decisions: improving cash flow and profits

- methods and difficulties of improving cash flow, profit and profitability

6 Decision-making to improve human resource performance

Human resources is the function of an organisation that is focused on activities related to employees. This includes manpower planning, recruitment and selection, training and development, retention and employee motivation, welfare and benefits and finally dismissal and redundancy.

Setting human resource objectives

The value of setting human resource objectives

The AQA specification outlines the following human resource objectives:
- **Employee engagement and involvement.** If employees are fully engaged and involved in the business they are more likely to be motivated, leading to higher productivity and quality of output.
- **Talent development.** This relates to the development and guidance of the future stars of a business so that they can contribute to the business success and growth. It involves not just developing their talents but also the retention of these employees.
- **Training.** The development of employee skills in order to improve performance.
- **Diversity.** This concept encompasses acceptance and respect in terms of race, gender, age sexual orientation, physical abilities, religion etc. It means understanding that each individual is unique and recognises individual differences.
- **Alignment of values.** This means bringing together employee and business values.
- **Number, skills and location of employees.** This involves manpower planning in order to ensure a business always has the right employees in the right numbers, in the right place and with the correct skills.

A business that is able to fulfil these objectives is likely to benefit from:
- a lower labour turnover
- higher labour retention rates
- higher productivity
- full compliance with any UK and EU labour legislation

Internal and external influences on human resource objectives

Human resources is no different from the other functional areas in that decision-making will be affected by a variety of external and internal factors.

External

Economy

If the economy is growing, there may be a greater requirement for human resources. Linked to this is the aspect of demographics and the availability of labour with the skills required.

Political

The UK government and the EU have passed a variety of measures that affect human resource planning, e.g. equality measures and the minimum wage.

Technology

The introduction of technology into manufacturing has resulted in not only a reduced requirement for labour but also for new skills. The decline of manufacturing and development of the service sector in terms of employment also emphasises the changing nature of work and the importance from a business perspective of developing the skills required.

Competitive environment

Changes in the market and competitor actions are likely to affect demand for a product or service, which in turn will impact on a business's human resource requirement.

Internal

Corporate objectives

Human resource objectives must be aligned with corporate objectives. If there is an overall objective of growth, human resources need to prepare for this by ensuring the availability of sufficiently skilled workers.

Type of product or service

A business must make sure the skills of the workforce are appropriate for that particular product or service as well as the image of the business.

Style of management

Whether a business has a **hard** or **soft approach** to human resource management is likely to influence decision-making. With a hard approach, managers see employees as just another resource that has to be used as efficiently as possible, whereas with a soft approach, employees are seen as a valuable asset that needs to be developed.

A **hard human resource approach** treats employees as just another asset that must be used as efficiently as possible.

A **soft human resource approach** treats employees as a valuable asset that needs to be developed.

Table 6.1 Hard and soft HR strategies

	Hard HR approach	Soft HR approach
Philosophy	Employees are no different from any other resource used by the business.	Employees are the most valuable resource available to the business and a vital competitive weapon.
Timescale	HR management operates in the short term only: employees are hired and fired as necessary.	Employees are developed over a long period of time to help the firm fulfil its corporate objectives.
Key features	• Pay is kept to a minimum. • Little or no empowerment. • Communication is mainly downwards. • Leaders have a Theory X view of the workforce. • Emphasis is on the short term in recruiting and training employees.	• Employees are empowered and encouraged to take decisions. • Leaders have a Theory Y view of the workforce. • Employees are encouraged to extend and update skills. • Employees are consulted regularly by managers. • A long-term relationship is developed with employees through use of internal recruitment and ongoing training programmes.
Associated leadership style	This approach is more likely to be adopted by leaders using an autocratic style of leadership.	This approach is more likely to be adopted by leaders using a democratic style of leadership.
Motivational techniques used	Principally financial techniques with minimal use of techniques such as delegation.	Techniques intended to give employees more control over their working lives, e.g. delegation and empowered teams.

Now test yourself

TESTED

1 Define the term 'human resource objectives' and give two examples.
2 Identify three potential benefits of having a fully engaged workforce.
3 State two internal and two external influences on human resource objectives.
4 Distinguish between a hard and a soft human resource strategy.

Answers on pp. 207–208

Analysing human resource performance

Calculating and interpreting human resource data

REVISED

Labour turnover and retention rates

Labour turnover refers to the proportion of a business's staff leaving employment over a period of time. It is calculated as follows:

$$\frac{\text{number leaving during year}}{\text{average number of staff}} \times 100$$

> **Labour turnover** is the proportion of a business's staff leaving their employment over a period of time.

Labour retention is the number of employees with more than one year of service. It is calculated as follows:

$$\frac{\text{number of employees with one or more years of service}}{\text{overall workforce numbers}} \times 100$$

Employees may leave a business for a number of reasons:
- Low/inadequate wages levels leading employees to defect to competitors.
- Poor morale and motivation.
- A buoyant local labour market offering more attractive opportunities.

From a business point of view, lower rates of labour turnover and higher rates of labour retention are preferable, as costs of recruitment will be lower, as is the likelihood of low morale and productivity.

> **Labour retention** is the proportion of employees with one or more years of service.

Labour productivity

Labour productivity is a key measure of business efficiency and measures the output per employee over a specified time period. It is calculated using the following formula:

$$\frac{\text{total output per time period}}{\text{number of employees}}$$

Higher rates of productivity are preferable, but it is important that this is not achieved at the expense of poorer quality. In addition, when comparing to other similar businesses, it is important to take into account other factors such as wage rates, technology and the way the workforce is organised.

> **Labour productivity** measures the output per worker over a given time period.

> **Typical mistake**
>
> It is important to express answers to calculations in the correct format. When calculating productivity, for example, many students express their answers as percentages and not as a number of units of output per time period.

Employee costs as a percentage of turnover

For a number of businesses, such as premiership football clubs and independent schools, labour represents their biggest cost and it is important that this is monitored and kept to a sustainable level. It is calculated as follows:

$$\frac{\text{labour costs}}{\text{turnover}} \times 100$$

Monitoring employee performance is very important to a business as it may help in identifying a business's needs in terms of recruitment, training and redundancy or redeployment.

Labour cost per unit

This measures how much it costs to produce one unit of output and is calculated as follows:

$$\frac{\text{labour costs}}{\text{output}}$$

Unit labour cost is directly related to productivity because unit labour cost will fall as each employee produces more (becomes more productive), and will rise as each worker produces less (becomes less productive).

> **Unit labour cost** is a measure of the average labour cost of producing one unit of output.

Exam tip

It is important to look behind any labour force data that are provided. For example, two sets of productivity data may suggest that firm A has a clear advantage. This may become less clear cut when the following factors relating to firm B are taken into account:
- Wage rates are significantly lower.
- Morale is excellent.
- A training programme is being implemented, causing short-term disruption.
- There is a low incidence of industrial relations problems.
- A reputation for craftsmanship and quality products has been established.

Now test yourself

TESTED

5 Distinguish between labour turnover and labour retention.
6 A business employing 300 employees makes 25m units of output producing a £15m turnover per year. Its total labour costs are £7.5m. Calculate (i) unit labour costs and (ii) labour costs as a percentage of turnover.

Answers on p. 208

The use of data for human resource decision-making and planning

REVISED

Human resource planning is a key area of business decision-making, and in order to make effective decisions, managers will require relevant information and data. Such data may be derived both internally and externally. The main aspects are summarised in Table 6.2.

Table 6.2 Summary of internal and external data

Internal	External
Productivity	Wage rates
Unit labour costs	Sales forecasts
Retention rates	Market trends
Labour turnover	Competitor actions
Skills	Unemployment rates
Age profile of workers	Skills available
Corporate objectives	Operational capacity

Once managers have analysed relevant data, key decisions can be made regarding numbers, training, skills and development of the labour force.

Exam tip

It is important to recognise that much of the data used by HR will come from other functional areas such as operations and marketing.

Now test yourself

TESTED

7 Briefly outline how a knowledge of labour turnover and market trends may affect human resource planning.

Answer on p. 208

Making human resource decisions: improving organisational design and managing the human resource flow

Influences on job design

The influences on job design are summed up in Table 6.3.

Table 6.3 Factors affecting job design

Organisational factors	Environmental factors	Behavioural factors
Task characteristics	Employee availability and ability	Feedback
Process or flow of works in organisation	Social and cultural expectations	Autonomy
Ergonomics		Variety
Work practices		

- **Organisational factors** such as the nature of the work and the culture of the business will determine the extent to which a business is able and willing to design jobs in such a way that enrichment and empowerment exist.
- **Environmental factors** that will influence job design include the availability of employees and their abilities as well as their social and cultural expectations.
- **Behavioural factors** and the extent to which a job or task/s offer autonomy, diversity and the use of skills will determine the level of enrichment and empowerment possible and impact on job design.

Job design

This is the process of deciding on the contents of a job in terms of its duties and responsibilities, on the methods used to carry out the job and on the relationships that should exist between job holder and superiors, subordinates and colleagues. Through job design or redesign, an organisation aims to make jobs interesting, challenging and rewarding with the aim of creating a fully engaged and motivated workforce. Some of the methods used include:

- **Job rotation.** This is the regular switching of employees between tasks of a similar degree of complexity. Rotating jobs provides variety and may relieve the monotony of just doing one task.
- **Job enlargement.** This extends the employees' range of duties. Instead of rotating round different tasks, the job itself is extended to include more tasks of a similar nature. This is called 'horizontal loading' and can help lessen the monotony and repetition on production lines.
- **Job enrichment.** Unlike enlargement, which is horizontally loaded, enrichment is vertically loaded with the job designed in such a way as to include more challenging tasks. Enrichment attempts to give employees greater responsibility by increasing the range and complexity of tasks they undertake with the aim of improving motivation and engagement.

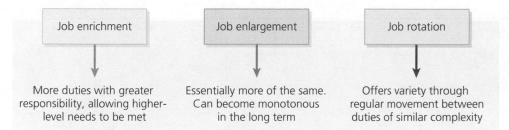

Figure 6.1 Job enrichment, enlargement and rotation

- **Empowerment.** This involves giving employees control over their working lives and can be achieved by organising employees into teams, setting them targets and allowing them to plan their own work, take their own decisions and solve their own problems.

The ideas of enrichment and empowerment have been taken further in the Hackman and Oldham job characteristics model (see Figure 6.2).

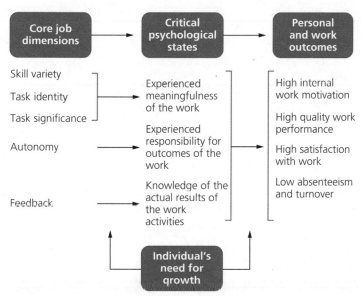

Figure 6.2 Hackman and Oldham job characteristics model

The model identifies five core characteristics (skill variety, task identity, task significance, autonomy and feedback) which impact on three critical psychological states (experienced meaningfulness, experienced responsibility for outcomes and knowledge of actual results) in turn influencing work outcomes (motivation, quality of work, job satisfaction, reduced absenteeism).

The core characteristics and psychological state operate in a continuous feedback loop, which allow employees to continue to be motivated through owning and understanding the work they are involved in. Skill variety, task identity and task significance will directly impact on the meaningfulness of the work, autonomy on responsibility and task significance on knowledge of results.

According to this model, the goal should be to design jobs in such a way that the core characteristics complement the psychological states of the worker and lead to positive outcomes. As a result, employees should achieve greater job satisfaction and motivation.

Now test yourself

8 Briefly outline why job enrichment might be a better way to redesign a job than job rotation.
9 Briefly outline the Hackman and Oldham job characteristics model.

Answers on p. 208

Influences on organisational design

REVISED

Organisational design is the process of shaping the organisational structure so that it can achieve its objectives effectively. Key factors in organisational design are likely to be related to the span of control possible, the amount of delegation given and the level of centralisation or decentralisation. Other influences include:

● **The size of business.** The larger the business, the more complex it becomes and the greater the need for a formal organisational structure.
● **Life cycle of the organisation.** A business will evolve and change over time and, as a result, the organisational design and structure is likely to evolve with it.
● **Corporate objectives.** The organisational structure will need to fit with the corporate objectives. A business whose main objective is growth and innovation may require a different structure to one whose aim is to maintain its position in current markets.
● **Technology.** Developments in technology have changed the nature of production, impacting on organisational design and structure.

> **Organisational design** is the process of shaping an organisation's structure in order to meet its objectives effectively.

Organisational structure

An organisation is a group of people who work together to achieve a common goal. To work together effectively, a clear structure is required that defines how tasks are divided, grouped and coordinated. The structure clarifies the roles organisational members perform so that everyone understands their responsibilities to the group.

The organisational structure will often be depicted in an organisational chart. Such charts will illustrate the **hierarchy** within the business and the **chain of command** that provides a line of **authority** from the top of the business to the bottom showing who reports to whom.

The organisational chart may also show the **span of control**. This is the number of subordinates that may be controlled effectively by one manager. The span of control may depend on a number of factors such as the ability of the manager, the type of work being done and the skills of the employees. It may also be determined by whether the organisation structure is tall or flat. Organisations with wider spans of control require fewer managers and have a flatter structure, as shown in Figure 6.3a, whereas those with narrower spans are likely to have more managers and taller structures (Figure 6.3b). Flatter structures with wider spans tend to become more predominant as this gives greater scope for worker empowerment lower down the hierarchy.

Flatter structures result in cost saving due to fewer middle management and can lead to greater engagement of the workforce due to more empowerment.

> **Hierarchy** — how different levels of authority are ranked in an organisational structure.
>
> **Chain of command** is the order in which authority and power in an organisation is exercised and delegated from top management down.
>
> **Authority** is the power or right to give orders or make decisions.

> **Span of control** is the number of subordinates who can be controlled effectively by one manager.

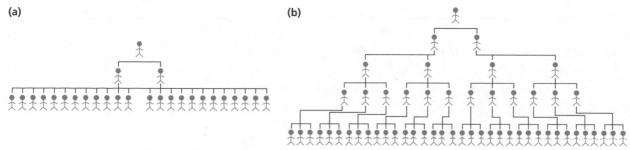

(a)

(b)

Figure 6.3 (a) A flat hierarchy/wider span of control; (b) A tall hierarchy/narrower span of control

Influences on delegation, centralisation and decentralisation

REVISED

Delegation

Delegation is the passing of authority to a subordinate within an organisation. It is the power to undertake a task that is delegated and not the responsibility for it — this remains with the manager. A manager must therefore choose delegates carefully — they must have the skills and ability to perform the task, and there has to be complete trust in the delegate. Successful delegation relieves managers of routine decisions, enabling them to concentrate on the more important decisions.

Centralisation and decentralisation

Whether an organisation is **centralised** or **decentralised** will determine where authority and decision-making lie in the organisation. A centralised structure is one where decision-making lies with management at the top with little input from lower down. A decentralised structure is one where those lower down the hierarchy play a greater part in the decision-making process.

Influences

Decentralisation will involve a greater degree of delegation, and there are a number of influences on the level of centralisation or decentralisation:

- **Uniformity of decisions.** Where decisions are uniform there is little room for delegation and decentralisation. As a result, individual outlet managers in a business such as Pizza Hut have little or no input into decision-making.
- **Management style.** An autocratic style is more likely to lead to a centralised organisation, whereas a more democratic or laissez-faire style gives greater scope for decentralisation.
- **Skills and ability of workforce.** A decentralised approach is only possible where the workforce has the necessary skills to make decisions. A business employing mainly professional skilled people is more likely to delegate and adapt a decentralised approach than one employing mainly unskilled workers.
- **Economic influences.** Changing economic circumstances can lead to different approaches. In difficult times a more centralised approach may be adopted, whereas if the economy is growing strongly there may be greater freedom for delegation and decentralisation.

> **Delegation** is the granting of authority by one person to another for agreed purposes.

> **Typical mistake**
>
> Students often suggest responsibility can be passed down the organisation structure. This is not the case, It is authority that is passed down.

> **Centralisation** is the process of concentrating management and decision-making power at the top of an organisation hierarchy.
>
> **Decentralisation** is the process of redistributing decision-making power away from a central location or authority.

- **Technology.** Developments in technology have resulted in a great deal of information being readily available to a business. This may provide greater scope for delegation and decentralisation, e.g. to individual branch or store managers.

Now test yourself

10 Briefly outline the reasons for a business introducing a flatter organisation structure.
11 What is delegation, and why is it important to business success?
12 Distinguish between centralisation and decentralisation.
13 Identify four possible influences on organisational design.
14 Briefly explain how Tesco can operate with a certain amount of decentralisation but McDonald's cannot.

Answers on p. 208

The value of changing job and organisational design

REVISED

The aim and value of changing organisational and job design is to be better able to meet human resource objectives. By making jobs more interesting, employees are likely to become more engaged and motivated, resulting in higher productivity, quality and less wastage, all of which may lead to a competitive advantage and the potential for higher revenue and profit. Changing organisational design may also lead to lower costs, particularly if it involves creating a flatter structure with fewer managerial levels.

> **Exam tip**
>
> Answers in this area frequently reveal a lack of understanding about the relationship between organisational structure and business performance. It can be a complex topic and is one you should spend time on.

Now test yourself

TESTED

15 In what ways may changing organisational and job design help in achieving human resource objectives?

Answer on p. 208

How managing the human resource flow helps meet human resource objectives

REVISED

The aim of human resources is to have the right number of people employed, with the right skills in the right place at the right time. This can be achieved creating a **human resource plan** and managing the **human resource flow**, i.e. the recruitment, selection, placement, appraisal, promotion of employees plus termination of employment.

> **Human resource planning** is the process that identifies the current and future human resource needs of an organisation in order to achieve its objectives.
>
> **Human resource flow** is the movement of employees through an organisation including recruitment, promotion and employment termination.

Recruitment and selection

The recruitment and selection process is summed up in Figure 6.4.

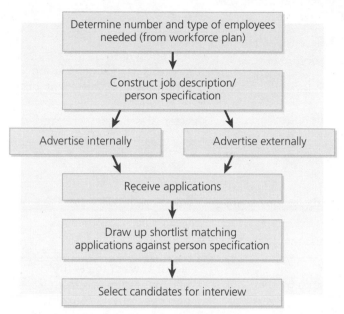

Figure 6.4 The process of recruitment

Once the number and type of employees has been determined, **job descriptions** and **specifications** can be drawn up. The job can then be advertised both internally and externally. Internal recruitment is likely to be cheaper, but new ideas are more likely to come from external candidates. From the applications, a shortlist can be drawn up for interview, and, once interviewed and selected, the ideal candidate can be appointed.

Training

Training is the provision of job-related skills and knowledge. Almost all employees receive some training when they first start a job, known as 'induction training'. This is designed to familiarise the employee with the business procedures and policies. Training to improve the skills of the worker may be undertaken either on the job, learning from an experienced worker, or off the job at college or some other training agency.

Appraisal and promotion

Performance appraisal is the process by which a manager examines and evaluates an employee's work by comparing it to set standards, documenting the results and using these to provide feedback to employees to show where improvements need to be made. Performance appraisal can be used to determine training needs and likely candidates for promotion. Promoting from within the business is an example of internal recruitment.

Redundancy, redeployment and termination

The final stage of human resource flow is that of termination of employment or dismissal. When a job no longer exists due to the introduction of technology, moving location or closure, those employees no longer required are made redundant. The process of **redundancy**

A **job description** sets out the duties and tasks associated with particular posts.

A **job specification** sets out the qualifications and qualities required of an employee.

Training is the provision of job-related skills and knowledge.

Performance appraisal is a systematic and periodic process that assesses an employee's job performance in relation to established criteria.

Redundancy is when an employee is dismissed due to their job no longer existing.

may take place on a voluntary basis, and an organisation must consult with individual employees as well as worker representatives if 20 or more employees are made redundant. Those who have been employed for over two years are entitled to redundancy pay.

As an alternative to redundancy, an employee may be offered **redeployment** within the business. This, however, may not be popular as it may involve a change of location and or changes in the conditions of work.

> **Redeployment** is the process of moving existing employees to a different job or location.

Besides redundancy, an employee may be dismissed in the following circumstances:
- **Gross misconduct**, such as violence towards a customer or colleague, or theft.
- **Persistent minor misconduct**, such as regularly turning up late for work, but only after set procedures have been adhered to in terms of verbal and written warnings.
- **A substantial reason**, such as not agreeing to new reasonable terms of employment.

It should also be noted that employment may be terminated by the employee. This might be due to family reasons or retirement. Every business expects a number of its employees to leave in this way and this is known as **natural wastage**.

> **Natural wastage** is the loss of employees from a business due to retirement, resignation or death.

Efficient management of the human resource flow providing a business with the right employees, in the right place, with the right skills should enable a business to meet its objectives more effectively.

Now test yourself

TESTED

16 Briefly explain the importance of workforce planning.

Answer on p. 208

Making human resource decisions: improving motivation and engagement

The benefits of motivated and engaged employees

REVISED

Employee engagement is a workplace approach designed to ensure that employees are committed to their organisation's goals and values and are motivated to contribute to organisational success. There are a number of potential benefits of a motivated and engaged workforce:
- **Productivity.** A fully engaged and motivated workforce is not only likely to work harder so producing more, but will probably put in the extra work to make sure deadlines are met etc.
- **Recruitment and retention.** An organisation that has a fully engaged workforce is more likely to be seen as the employer of choice, and is more likely to be able to retain its workers.
- **Absenteeism.** This is likely to be lower.

- **Innovation.** A close link has been shown to exist between innovation and engagement.
- **Profitability.** This is likely to be higher.

What is motivation?

Analysts disagree on the precise meaning of the term '**motivation**'. Some believe it is the will to work due to enjoyment of the work itself. This suggests that motivation comes from within an employee. An alternative view is that it is the will or desire to achieve a given target or goal due to some external stimulus. Many of the differences in the theories of motivation can be explained in terms of this fundamental difference of definition. Figure 6.5 shows the various schools of thought relating to motivation.

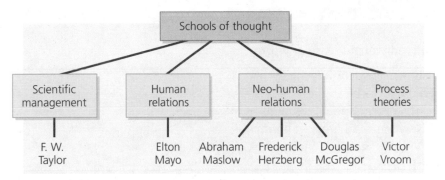

Figure 6.5 Schools of thought relating to motivation

The school of scientific management

A 'school of thought' is simply a group of people who hold broadly similar views. The school of scientific management argues that business decisions should be taken on the basis of data that are researched and tested quantitatively. Members of the school believe that it is vital to identify ways in which costs can be assessed and reduced, thus increasing efficiency. This school of thought supports the use of techniques such as work-study.

A member of the school of scientific management was **F. W. Taylor** (1856–1915). Taylor was a highly successful engineer who began to advise and lecture on management practices and was a consultant to Henry Ford. His theories were based on a simple interpretation of human behaviour.

Taylor's ideas were formulated during his time at the Bethlehem Steel Company in the USA. He believed in firm management based on scientific principles. He used a stopwatch to measure how long various activities took and sought the most efficient methods. He then detailed 'normal' times in which duties should be completed, and assessed individual performance against these. Efficiency, he argued, would improve productivity, competitiveness and profits. This required employees to be organised, closely supervised and paid according to how much they produced.

Taylor believed that people were solely motivated by money. Workers should have no control over their work, and the social aspect of employment was considered irrelevant and ignored.

Taylor's views were unpopular with shop-floor employees. As workers and managers became more highly educated, they sought other ways of motivating and organising employees.

The human relations school of management

A weakness of the scientific school was that its work ignored the social needs of employees. This, and the obvious unpopularity of the ideas, led to the development of the human relations school. This school of thought concentrated on the sociological aspects of work.

A key writer was **Elton Mayo**. He is best remembered for his Hawthorne Studies at the Western Electric Company in Chicago between 1927 and 1932. He conducted experiments to discover whether employee performance was affected by factors such as breaks and the level of lighting. The results surprised Mayo. The productivity of one group of female employees increased both when the lighting was lessened and when it was increased. It became apparent that they were responding to the level of attention they were receiving. From this experiment, Mayo concluded that motivation depends on:

- the type of job being carried out and the type of supervision given to the employee
- group relationships, group morale and individuals' sense of worth

Mayo's work took forward the debate on management in general and motivation in particular. He moved the focus on to the needs of employees, rather than just the needs of the organisation. Although Mayo's research is nearly 80 years old, it still has relevance to modern businesses.

The neo-human relations school

Abraham Maslow and **Frederick Herzberg** are recognised as key members of this school of thought. While the human relations school associated with Elton Mayo highlighted the *sociological* aspects of work, the neo–human relations school considered the *psychological* aspects of employment.

Abraham Maslow

Abraham Maslow was an American psychologist who formulated a famous hierarchy of needs (Figure 6.6). According to Maslow, human needs consist of five types that form a hierarchy:

1 **Physiological:** the need for food, shelter, water and sex.
2 **Security:** the need to be free from threats and danger.
3 **Social:** the need to love and be loved, and to be part of a group.
4 **Esteem:** the need to have self-respect and the respect of colleagues.
5 **Self-actualisation:** the need to develop personal skills and fulfil one's potential.

Maslow argued that all individuals have a hierarchy of needs and that once one level of needs is satisfied, people can be motivated by tasks that offer the opportunity to satisfy the next level of needs.

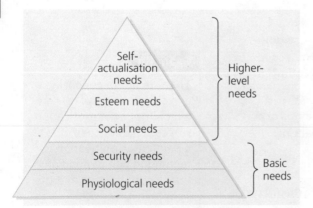

Figure 6.6 Maslow's hierarchy of needs

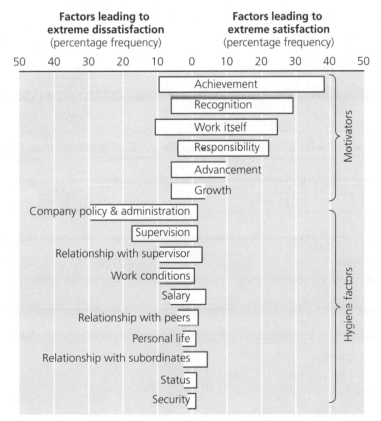

Some writers doubt the existence of a hierarchy of needs. They argue that social needs and esteem needs may coexist and that people do not move smoothly up a hierarchy, as Maslow's model suggests. However, his work brings psychology into motivational theory and highlights the range of individual needs that may be met through employment.

Frederick Herzberg

The research carried out by Frederick Herzberg offered some support for Maslow's views and focused on the psychological aspects of motivation. Herzberg asked 203 accountants and engineers to identify those factors about their employment that pleased and displeased them. Figure 6.7 summarises Herzberg's findings.

This research was the basis of Herzberg's two-factor theory, published in 1968. Herzberg divided the factors motivating people at work into two groups:

- **Motivators.** These are positive factors that give people job satisfaction (e.g. receiving recognition for effort) and therefore increase productivity as motivation rises.
- **Hygiene (or maintenance) factors.** These are factors that may cause dissatisfaction among employees. Herzberg argued that motivators should be built into the hygiene factors. Improving hygiene factors will not positively motivate but will reduce employee dissatisfaction. Examples of hygiene factors are pay, fair treatment and reasonable working conditions.

Herzberg did not argue that hygiene factors are unimportant. On the contrary, he contended that only when such factors are properly met can motivators begin to operate positively.

Factors leading to extreme dissatisfaction (percentage frequency)

Factors leading to extreme satisfaction (percentage frequency)

50 40 30 20 10 0 10 20 30 40 50

Motivators:
- Achievement
- Recognition
- Work itself
- Responsibility
- Advancement
- Growth

Hygiene factors:
- Company policy & administration
- Supervision
- Relationship with supervisor
- Work conditions
- Salary
- Relationship with peers
- Personal life
- Relationship with subordinates
- Status
- Security

Figure 6.7 Herzberg's factors causing satisfaction and dissatisfaction

Process theories of motivation

The foremost writer on process theory is **Victor Vroom**, who published *Work and Motivation* in 1964. Vroom's theory expressed the view that motivation depends on people's expectations of the outcome. If working life offers opportunities for workers' expectations to be met, motivation is likely to be high. If the outcome of their actions is expected to be desirable, they will be motivated. The stronger the desire for the outcome, the greater is the level of motivation.

The value of theories of motivation REVISED

The motivation theories do not set out a blueprint of how to motivate a workforce but rather their value lies in the insight they give to management and employee attitudes. Although it is easy to dismiss Taylor and the scientific school today, he did establish management as a subject worthy of study, and ideas such as time and motion study and work study are still used today by management consultants. The human relations school recognised that employees did not just work for money, and factors such as involvement in decision-making, recognition for work done well and responsibility were all important in achieving an engaged and motivated workforce. These factors are perhaps key to the non-financial methods of motivation.

Now test yourself TESTED

17 How does the scientific school of management differ from the human relations school of management?

Answer on p. 208

How to improve employee engagement and motivation REVISED

The benefits of a fully engaged workforce make improving engagement and motivation of the workforce an essential element of the work of the human resources function. The methods used include both financial and non-financial.

The use of financial methods of motivation REVISED

Some writers, such as Herzberg, believe that money is not a positive motivator, although the lack of it can demotivate. Nevertheless, pay systems are designed to motivate employees financially.

Wages and salaries

Employees are normally paid a wage or salary. Wages are usually paid weekly at an hourly rate for a set working week with any extra hours (overtime) being paid at a higher rate. Salaries are expressed in annual terms but are usually paid monthly. Salaried staff do not normally have a set number of hours to work per week, although there may be a minimum number.

Piece-rate pay

Piece-rate pay gives a payment for each item produced. This system encourages effort, but often at the expense of quality. Piece rate is common in agriculture and the textile industry.

Commission

Commission is a payment made to employees based on the value of sales achieved. It can form all or part of a salary package.

Profit-related pay

Profit-related pay gives employees a share of the profits earned by the business. It encourages all employees to work hard to generate the maximum profits for the business. It also offers some flexibility: in a recession, wages can fall with profits, reducing the need for redundancies.

Performance-related pay

Performance-related pay is used in many industries, from banking to education. It needs to be tied into some assessment or appraisal of employee performance. Whatever criteria are used to decide who should receive higher pay, the effect can be divisive and damaging to employee morale.

Share ownership

Employees are sometimes offered shares in the company in which they work. Shares can be purchased through savings schemes. However, share ownership may cause discontentment if this perk is available only to the senior staff.

> **Exam tip**
>
> Do consider the financial position of the business (in terms of profits and cash flow) when developing arguments in support of and against financial methods of motivation. There is likely to be numerical evidence in a case study if such a question has been asked.

The use of non-financial methods of motivating employees

REVISED

The Hackmann and Oldham job characteristics model (see p. 99) and the work of the motivation theorists give us some clues as to the non-financial methods of motivating employees. Hackmann and Oldham suggested that motivation is linked to the three psychological states: meaningful work, responsibility and knowledge of outcomes. In Herzberg's theory responsibility, involvement and recognition are key motivators, and Maslow suggested these same three factors are key in achieving self-actualisation. Key characteristics of non-financial methods of motivation can therefore be summarised as follows:

- **Meaningful work**, providing jobs that are both interesting and challenging.
- **Involvement** with the decision-making process.
- **Responsibility and recognition** for the job.

For this to be achieved it is necessary for the following to be in place:
- The **leadership and management style** is more likely to be soft and democratic.
- **Opportunity** needs to be provided for involvement and responsibility.
- The **culture** of the business needs to be one of involvement and communication.

Influences on the choice and assessment of the effectiveness of financial and non-financial reward systems

REVISED

The factors that might influence the choice and effectiveness of reward systems include:
- **Finance.** In some ways this relates to the success of an organisation as a business must operate within its means. It will also want to keep a careful check on both unit labour costs and labour costs as a percentage of turnover.
- **Nature of the work.** It is not just the type of work that will have an influence but also the skills of the workforce involved. Reward and conditions of work need to be appropriate to attract and retain employees. If a business gets this right, it may well be able to establish a reputation as a good employer to work for.
- **Culture.** The culture of the business and the management style adopted — a hard approach may favour financial incentives, whereas a soft approach may favour non-financial ones.
- **External factors.** This might include the economic cycle, e.g. it may be difficult to have performance related pay systems in times of economic recession.

Now test yourself

TESTED

18 Briefly outline the links between the non-financial methods of motivation and the motivation theories of Maslow and Herzberg.

Answer on p. 208

Making human resource decisions: improving employer–employee relations

Influences on the extent and methods of employee involvement in decision-making

REVISED

Having a fully engaged and motivated workforce requires good employer–employee relations. Employees need to feel involved and appreciated and the extent may be influenced by the following:
- **Management style.** A soft management style is more likely to lead to involvement in decision-making than a hard management style.

- **Nature of the work.** Those working in highly skilled and technical industries are more likely to have an input into decision-making than those doing unskilled repetitive tasks.
- **Legislation.** The UK government and EU legislation in terms of trade unions and works councils can have an influence on employee involvement in decision-making.

Methods of employee representation

Trade unions

A **trade union** is an organised group of employees that aims to protect and enhance the economic position of its members. They offer a number of benefits to members:
- They negotiate on pay and conditions of work.
- They discuss major changes in the workplace, such as redundancy, and help protect job security.
- They provide a range of services including financial and legal advice.

When a trade union negotiates with an employer on behalf of its members on matters such as pay and conditions, it is called 'collective bargaining'. A trade union is in a much better position to negotiate than an individual worker. This not only benefits workers but also can be easier and less time-consuming for the employer.

> A **trade union** is an organised group of employees that aims to protect and enhance the economic position of its members.

The changing role of trade unions in the UK

Union membership has fallen steadily since its peak in 1979. This decline has been due to:
- **Legislation:** the Conservative governments of the 1980s and 1990s passed a series of measures to control the activities of trade unions.
- **Decline of traditional industries:** e.g. coal mining, steel and ship building.
- **Increasing number of small businesses:** such businesses are not strongly unionised.

There has also been a move towards union derecognition and single union agreements in workplaces.

> **Typical mistake**
>
> Trade unions are often depicted by students as being a disruptive influence in business. This approach ignores much of the good work they do in terms of conditions of work, employee protection and health and safety.

Work councils

Workers might also be represented by **work councils**. Work councils are bodies composed of both employee and employer representatives elected to negotiate with management about working conditions, wages etc. Since they are normally elected and have both employer and employee representatives, they may provide for better communication and increased involvement of employees and result in more conciliatory relationships than those with a trade union.

> A **work council** is a body composed of both employer and employees convened to discuss and negotiate on matters of common interest including pay and conditions.

Now test yourself

TESTED

19 Briefly explain why trade union membership has declined since 1979.

Answer on p. 208

How to manage and improve employer–employee communications and relations

Good relations between employer and employees do not just happen but need to be worked upon. Key to good relations is communication. If communication is effective and employees feel a part of the decision-making process, they are more likely to be engaged and motivated. This is perhaps more likely to occur where there is a soft approach to human relations.

Advisory, Conciliation and Arbitration Service (ACAS)

Disputes, however, can and do happen and when they do, the help of ACAS can be sought. ACAS was set up by the government in 1975 as an independent body with the responsibility of preventing and resolving industrial disputes. It provides the following services:

- **Advice:** to employers, trade unions and employee associations on topics such as payment systems, absenteeism and sickness.
- **Conciliation:** it encourages continuation of negotiation rather than industrial action.
- **Arbitration:** it can act to resolve a dispute by making recommendations that may be either binding or non-binding.

ACAS can also investigate individual cases of discrimination, and overall has the aim of improving business practices to reduce the possibility of industrial disputes.

> **Typical mistake**
>
> Many students ignore the importance of communication in fostering good relations between employers and employees. Good communication can prevent disputes and remove the need for resolution.

The value of good employer–employee relations

The value of good employer–employee relations can be seen in the following areas:

- **Productivity.** Where relations are good, employees are more likely to be committed and motivated, leading to higher productivity, less wastage and better quality.
- **Employee loyalty.** Labour turnover rates are likely to be lower and retention rates higher.
- **Decision-making.** Decisions are likely to be taken faster, and the introduction of change is likely to be easier.

Now test yourself

20 Briefly outline ACAS's main responsibility.

Answer on p. 209

Exam practice

Labour problems at XYZ plc

XYZ has been struggling to meet its human resource targets for a number of years.

	XYZ	Industry average
Labour turnover	20%	10%
Labour productivity	80	100
Unit labour costs	£10	£8

Managing director Harvey Jones has decided on a radical change of approach. He wants to move from the current hard management approach to a soft approach. This will involve flattening the present tall hierarchical structure and a significant amount of job redesign. He was partly influenced in this decision by an article he read on the Hackman and Oldham job characteristics model and the importance of designing jobs with motivational properties. Further reading related to the motivational theories and particularly to Herzberg suggested that if jobs are redesigned appropriately, key motivational influences can lead to significant improvements in workforce performance.

Labour relations have not been good at XYZ and the key to the success of Harvey's plan will be in persuading the workforce to accept the ideas. For this to happen, effective communication will be necessary.

Questions

a Distinguish between a hard and soft approach to management. [4]
b Explain the possible implications for XYZ of missing its human relations targets. [6]
c Analyse the potential benefits for XYZ of job redesign. [9]
d To what extent do you believe motivational theories are useful in practice? [16]

Answers and quick quiz 6 online

ONLINE

Summary

You should now have an understanding of all the points below.

Setting human resource objectives

- the value of setting and the internal and external influences on human resource objectives

Analysing human resource performance

- the use of data in human resource planning including the calculation of labour turnover and retention, labour productivity, employee costs as a percentage of turnover and unit labour cost

Making human resource decisions: improving organisational design and managing human resource flow

- influences on job design — Hackman and Oldham model
- influences on organisational design including authority, span, hierarchy, delegation, centralisation and decentralisation
- the value of changing organisational design
- how managing human resource flow helps meet human resource objectives

Making human resource decisions: improving motivation and engagement

- the benefits of a motivated and engaged workforce and how to improve it
- the value of theories of motivation — Taylor, Maslow and Herzberg
- financial and non-financial methods of motivation and influences on their choice and effectiveness

Making human resource decisions: improving employer–employee relations

- the value of good employer–employee relations
- influences on and methods of employee involvement including trade unions and works councils
- how to manage and improve employer–employee relations

7 Analysing the strategic position of a business

Mission, corporate objectives and strategy

Influences on the mission of a business

REVISED

The **mission** of a business defines what an organisation is, why it exists and its reason for being. It is a declaration of its core purpose and focus. Two examples of mission statements are given on p. 7. A number of factors will influence the mission statement of a firm.

> The **mission** is normally encompassed in the mission statement, which is a written declaration of a company's core purpose and focus and defines the reason for its existence.

Philosophy and values

The philosophy is the set of beliefs and principles that a business works toward and explains its overall goals and purpose. It is also likely to outline the values of the business, which are often a reflection of the leaders' values. A good example of this is the philosophy of online shoe retailer Zappos, which was created by Tony Hsieh. Other examples are the philosophies of Apple and Google. This is important as it gives employees a true sense of direction and purpose. The philosophy itself may also be influenced by the size of the business, its ownership and the activities undertaken.

The environment in which it operates

This is related to the external environment in which the business operates and includes such factors as the state of the economy, the level of competition and government regulation.

> **Exam tip**
>
> This section builds on the work covered in Chapter 1. It might be useful to review the section on understanding the nature and purpose of business.

Internal and external influences on corporate objectives and decisions

REVISED

Corporate objectives are those that relate to the business as a whole. They will be well defined, quantifiable, measurable, realistic goals that are likely to be set in a specified time frame (SMART). The corporate objectives set will be the means by which a business achieves its mission. They will lead to the development of the corporate strategy which, as shown in Figure 7.1, leads to the development of strategies in each of the functional areas as well as, in some cases, social strategies.

> **Corporate objectives** are the goals set for the business as a whole that will lead to the achievement of the mission.

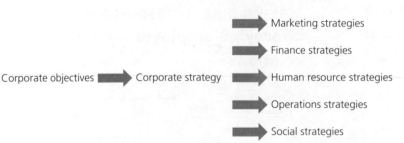

Figure 7.1 Corporate objectives

The corporate objectives are influenced by a number of factors that may be either internal or external.

Internal factors

Business ownership

The different forms of business ownership were discussed in Chapter 1 and the type of ownership is likely to have an impact on objectives and decisions. For example, sole traders and private limited companies will not be subject to the pressures of short termism and can focus more on the long-term value creation of the business. Also, whether the business is profit or non-profit making will have an impact on objectives and decisions.

Business culture

Business culture refers to the collective beliefs, values and attitudes within a business. Put simply, it is 'the way we do things around here'. For decisions to be implemented successfully, they must align fully with the organisational culture. This is discussed in more detail on in Chapter 10.

> The **business culture** (or corporate culture) refers to the beliefs and behaviours that determine how a company's employees and management interact.

Business performance

The performance of a business has an impact on decision-making as this has an effect on the resources available. Typically this is associated with finance available and the access to finance, but it can also be related to other resources such as human resources. A poorly performing business might struggle to employ and keep its employees whereas a strongly performing business is more likely to be able to attract and keep the best employees.

External factors

Pressures for short termism

Short termism refers to the excessive focus of decision-makers on short-term goals at the expense of longer-term objectives. The focus tends to be on short-term profit and return to shareholders with insufficient attention being paid to strategy, fundamentals and the long-term value creation of an organisation. The causes of short termism might include pressure from investors for short-term outcomes, the fact directors positions are dependent on shareholders and the frequency of financial reporting and scrutiny of the media. All of these causes may deter directors from undertaking the investment expenditure necessary for long-term value creation because of its short-term potential negative impact on finances and share price.

> **Short termism** refers to an excessive focus on short-term results (profit) at the expense of the long-term interests.

> **Exam tip**
>
> Short termism is about results. A good analogy to help remember its meaning is one of football club managers. If results are bad, they quickly find themselves out of a job. This is the fear of CEOs; if they do not produce results (profit), they too can find themselves out of a job.

> **Typical mistake**
>
> Do not view short termism, concentrating on short-term goals, as always being a problem. It is only a problem when long-term goals are neglected.

Other external factors might include the following:
- changes in the economy
- government policy
- environmental factors
- demographic trends
- competitors' actions
- technology

The distinction between strategy and tactics

REVISED

The terms **strategy** and **tactics** are often used interchangeably and can be confused. However, it is important to recognise the distinction between the two terms, as shown in Table 7.1. Strategy is about choosing the best plan for achieving long-term goals whereas tactics are the short-term actions or means of achieving those goals: in other words, strategy is *what* needs to be achieved and tactics are *how* it will be achieved.

Strategy is a plan of action to achieve a long-term goal. It relates to what needs to be achieved.

Tactics relate to the short-term actions necessary to achieve the plan or strategy.

Table 7.1 The distinction between strategy and tactics

Strategy	Tactics
What are we trying to accomplish?	*How* will we accomplish it?
Strategy is planning	Tactics involve carrying out the plan
Medium to long term	Short term
Plans are formulated at the top level of management	Actions are formulated at the middle level of management
Strategies are made for the future	Tactics are made to cope with the present

The links between mission, corporate objectives and strategy

REVISED

Figure 7.2 illustrates the links between the mission statement, corporate objectives and corporate strategies.

Mission statement ➡ Corporate objectives ➡ Corporate strategies

Figure 7.2 The links between the mission statement, corporate objectives and corporate strategies

Once a business has set its overall mission or purpose, it is in a position to set long-term targets that will enable it to achieve or fulfil its mission. Once targets have been set, strategies or plans can then be devised aimed at meeting those targets and therefore fulfilling the mission.

Typical mistake

Do not get confused with terminology as a lot of terms are used interchangeably. For example, corporate plan, strategic plan and corporate strategy all mean essentially the same thing.

The impact of strategic decision-making on functional decision-making

REVISED

Strategic decisions are likely to be related to the business as a whole, to be taken by senior management and medium to long term in nature. However, **functional decision-making** refers to decisions made within the functional areas of a business: marketing, finance, operations and human resources. Such decisions are made by the functional managers themselves and represent the action necessary on behalf of that function to implement and achieve strategic decisions and targets.

Functional decision-making relates to the decision-making within the functional areas of business: marketing, finance, operations and human resources.

For example, in order to provide a better service for their customers, supermarkets took the strategic decision to introduce an online facility with delivery. This decision impacted on each of the functional areas of the business. Finance had to be found, an online facility needed to be established as well as delivery vehicles sourced, employees needed to be recruited and trained, and consumers needed to be made aware of the facility. The strategic decision has to fit with the overall mission of the business; it is *what* the business wants to achieve — a medium- to long-term objective. However, the functional decisions are *how* the strategy or plan will be achieved — the tactics implemented to achieve the overall goal.

The value of SWOT analysis

REVISED

SWOT analysis is a tool that analyses the internal **S**trengths and **W**eaknesses as well as the external **O**pportunities and **T**hreats of an organisation, as shown in Figure 7.3.

> **SWOT analysis** is an analytical tool used in decision-making that examines the internal strengths and weaknesses of a business as well as the external opportunities and threats.

Internal

External

Strengths	Weaknesses
- Your specialist marketing expertise - A new, innovative product or service - The location of your business - Quality processes and procedures - Any other aspect of your business that adds value to your product or service	- A lack of marketing expertise - Undifferentiated products or services (i.e. in relation to your competitors) - The location of your business - Poor quality goods or services - A damaged reputation
Opportunities	**Threats**
- A developing market such as the internet - Mergers, joint ventures or strategic alliances - Moving into new market segments that offer improved profits - A new international market - A market vacated by an ineffective competitor	- A new competitor in your home market - Price wars with competitors - A competitor that has a new, innovative product or service - Competitors that have superior access to channels of distribution - Taxation is introduced on your product or service

Figure 7.3 SWOT analysis

Once a SWOT analysis has been undertaken, an organisation should have a reasonable idea of what it is good at and the opportunities that might exist, as well as an idea of its weaknesses and potential threats. From this analysis, managers can develop strategies that build on the positives while trying to alleviate the negatives. The value of SWOT analysis can be summed up as follows:

- It helps a firm to identify its core competencies, enabling it to build on its strengths.
- It helps a firm to focus on the future, given its past and present condition.

> **Typical mistake**
>
> In a SWOT analysis, when looking at the strengths of a business do not automatically assume a particular characteristic is a strength. For example, a loyal workforce is only a strength if it consistently performs better than a competitor's workforce.

● It may identify opportunities that a firm can focus on to achieve maximum gains.
● It is a source of strategic planning as well as marketing.
● It helps the firm to redefine and set its overall objectives.

Now test yourself

TESTED ☐

1 What is meant by the philosophy and values of a business?
2 What is the link between the mission of a business, its corporate objectives and the corporate strategy?
3 Why may short termism be a problem for business?
4 Distinguish between strategy and tactics.
5 How might a SWOT analysis help in the development of business strategies?

Answers on p. 209

Analysing the existing internal position of a business to assess strengths and weaknesses: financial ratio analysis

How to assess the financial performance of a business using balance sheets, income statements and financial ratios

REVISED ☐

An organisation always needs to assess its performance in order to determine how well it is doing in terms of achieving its mission. From the results achieved, the management can then decide what strategic changes, if any, need to be made. The financial performance is a key element in this and assessment in this area is normally achieved through ratio analysis. However, before this can be undertaken it is necessary to have an understanding of two key financial documents: the balance sheet and the income statement.

Balance sheets

The **balance sheet** represents a snapshot of a business's financial position at a given time. It shows what a business owns (its assets) and what it owes (its liabilities, including shareholders' equity). The report gets its name from the fact that the two sides of the equation must balance, as illustrated in Figure 7.4.

> The **balance sheet** is a report that summarises all of an organisation's assets, liabilities and equity at a given point in time.

Figure 7.4 A balance sheet

In other words, the value of the assets in a business will always be equal to the value of the money put into a business. The structure of a balance sheet is outlined in Figure 7.5.

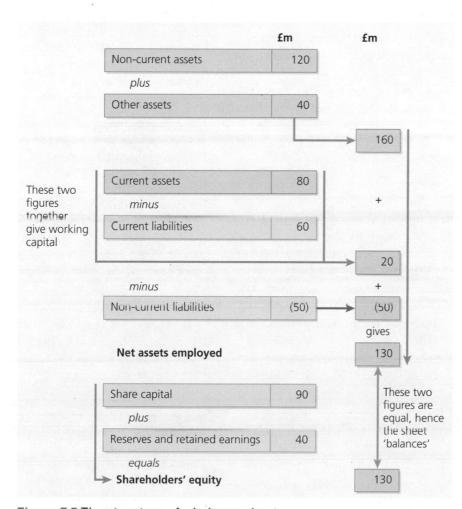

Figure 7.5 The structure of a balance sheet

Assets

Assets are listed from top to bottom in order of their liquidity, with the least liquid at the top and the most liquid at the bottom, as follows:

- **Non-current (or fixed) assets.** Examples include land, buildings, vehicles, machinery and equipment. These are assets that remain in a business for longer than 1 year.
- **Tangible v intangible assets.** The examples of non-current assets above can be described as tangible assets as they can be physically touched. However, a business might have other intangible assets that have real value to the business but do not have a physical presence, such as patents, trademarks, copyright, brand names and goodwill. On account of the difficulty of valuing such assets, they are not normally included in a balance sheet unless they have been specifically paid for, such as in a takeover.
- **Current assets.** These are assets owned for less than 1 year and include inventories, receivables and cash. Inventories include any stock, work in progress and finished products not yet sold. Receivables represent money owed to the business for goods sold which have yet to be paid for.

Liabilities

Liabilities on the balance sheet start with the most liquid and finish with the least liquid, as follows:

- **Current liabilities.** Debts of a business that will be repaid within 1 year and include payables (creditors), overdrafts and any corporation tax or dividends due for payment.
- **Non-current liabilities.** Debts of a business that will be repaid in more than 1 year and include bank loans, mortgages and debentures.
- **Shareholders' equity.** The money attributable to the business owners (shareholders), including the money invested by shareholders together with any reserves and retained earnings.

Usefulness of balance sheets

When drawing up the balance sheet, a number of important figures are identified:

- **Working capital of the business.** This may be shown in the balance sheet as net current assets and is the difference between current assets and current liabilities. It is the amount of money a business has available for day-to-day operations such as the payment of wages and the purchase of inventories. If a business has too little working capital, it may struggle to make payments and run into cash-flow problems. However, it is also important not to have too much working capital as this is an inefficient use of resources. For example, cash sitting in a bank account is not usually earning anything for a business.
- **Net assets (or net worth) of a business.** This shows the overall worth of a business to its shareholders and is the difference between non-current assets and working capital less non-current liabilities.

The balance sheet can also be used to work out the following:

- **Capital employed.** This is the value of total equity plus non-current liabilities and is the total amount of money invested into the business.
- **Assets employed.** This is the value of non-current assets plus current assets. Essentially, the assets employed represent what the money invested into the business (capital employed) has been spent on and therefore its value is equal to the capital employed.

> **Assets** are anything that a business owns, benefits from or has the use of in generating income.
>
> **Tangible assets** are physical assets such as land, buildings and machinery.
>
> **Intangible assets** are non-physical assets such as patents, copyrights and goodwill.

> **Liabilities** are what a business owes, the legal debts or obligations that arise during the course of business operations.

> **Typical mistake**
>
> Reserves in the balance sheet are not held in cash but are an entry indicating past profit that has been retained in the business and spent on further non-current or fixed assets.

> **Working capital** is a measure of an organisation's short-term financial health, calculated as current assets less current liabilities.

> **Exam tip**
>
> Although you will not be asked to construct a balance sheet or income statement, it is important that you fully understand their layout in order that you can assess a business's performance.

Income statements

The **income statement** measures a company's financial performance over a specific accounting period. It shows the income and expenditure over this accounting period and the resultant profit (or loss) made. The structure of the income statement is outlined in Figure 7.6.

The main elements of the income statement are as follows:
- **Revenue (or turnover):** the amount of money received from the sale of goods and services during the trading period.
- **Cost of goods sold:** the direct costs of producing the goods sold, such as materials and direct labour.
- **Gross profit:** the difference between the revenue received and the cost of goods sold.
- **Expenses:** the costs that are not directly related to production, such as marketing or general administrative costs.
- **Operating profit:** a measure of the profit or loss resulting from the day-to-day operations of the business. It is also known as earnings before interest and tax (EBIT).
- **Finance income and expenses:** this relates to interest received on accounts that are held and interest paid out on loans.
- **Profit before tax:** arrived at after adjusting operating profit for finance income and expenses.
- **Taxation:** corporation tax paid to the government.
- **Profit after tax:** the final profit (or loss) figure, often referred to as the bottom line.

Profit utilisation

Profits can be used in one of two ways and it is the responsibility of the board of directors to decide how they are split:
- **Retained profit:** profit kept within the business to fund expansion plans or capital investment. Any retained profit is added to the balance sheet in the reserve section of the liabilities and the cash section of the assets.
- **Distributed to shareholders:** paid in the form of dividends.

> **Exam tip**
>
> Earnings per share (EPS) is calculated by dividing the profit after tax figure by the number of shares. The dividend per share is calculated by dividing the profit for distribution by the number of shares.

Profit quality

Profit quality is the degree to which profit is likely to continue into the future, i.e. the sustainability of the profit. For example, it is important to check that profit has not resulted from one-off items such as the sale of an asset, something that will not be repeated in the future.

Financial ratios

Although both the balance sheet and the income statement provide useful information regarding the performance of a business, this information can be analysed further through the use of **ratio analysis**. Four areas for ratio analysis are outlined in the specification.

The **income statement** is a financial statement that measures an organisation's financial performance over a specific accounting period.

	£m
Revenue (turnover)	250
less	
Cost of sales	190
gives	
Gross profit	60
less	
Expenses	40
gives	
Operating profit	20
plus	
Finance income	5
less	
Finance expenses	3
gives	
Profit before taxation	22
less	
Taxation	4
gives	
Profit after taxation	18

Figure 7.6 The structure of an income statement

Profit quality is the degree to which profit is likely to continue in the future — the sustainability of profit.

Ratio analysis is a tool used in financial analysis to express relationships between an organisation's accounting numbers in order to establish trends and comparisons.

Profitability (return on capital employed)

Profitability refers to the capacity of a business to make profit, and profitability ratios assess its ability to generate profit. Profit margins have been looked at in Chapter 5. These show the percentage of profit generated from each £ of revenue. There is one further ratio to investigate in the specification: the return on capital employed (ROCE). This ratio measures how efficiently a business generates profit from the capital employed (equity plus non-current liabilities).

$$\text{Return on capital employed (ROCE)} = \frac{\text{net operating profit}}{\text{capital employed}} \times 100$$

The figure for ROCE is expressed as a percentage. We would expect a figure above the rate at which the business borrows money – typically above 20%. The actual figure achieved, however, will vary from industry to industry and business to business according to circumstances.

Liquidity (current ratio)

Liquidity measures the extent to which a business is able to pay its short-term debts. Many business failures result from a lack of cash and an inability to pay short-term debts. An investigation into a business's liquidity position through ratios can therefore provide a valuable insight into this issue. The specification only requires that the current ratio is known and understood. This is calculated as follows:

$$\text{Current ratio} = \frac{\text{current assets}}{\text{current liabilities}}$$

The current ratio demonstrates a business's ability to pay its short-term debts from its short-term assets. A result of 2:1 indicates the business can pay its debts twice over. In the past a figure of 2:1 was recommended, but this is now not the case as firms can operate comfortably on a figure around 1.5:1, although this varies from business to business and industry to industry. What is clear from the current ratio is that a figure less than 1:1 could present problems and a figure greater than 2:1 could indicate an inefficient management of resources.

Gearing

The capital structure of a business can be analysed further through the **gearing ratio**. It is calculated as follows:

$$\text{Gearing ratio} = \frac{\text{non-current liabilities}}{\text{total equity + non-current liabilities}} \times 100$$

Gearing investigates whether or not a business is at risk from increases in interest rates and falling profit. A figure above 50% is considered high gearing and could cause problems with servicing debt should profit fall or interest rates rise. A figure below 50% is low gearing and allows a business greater flexibility should profit levels fall or interest rates rise. The gearing ratio helps analyse the longer-term liquidity position of a business.

Efficiency ratios

Efficiency ratios are used to analyse how well a business uses its assets and liabilities internally. The specification details three ratios in this area: payables days, receivables days and inventory turnover.

Liquidity is a measure of the extent to which an organisation can meet its immediate short-term financial obligations.

Typical mistake

Just because a business has a current ratio of less than 1.5:1, do not automatically assume it is bad. The figure needs to be compared to the industry average and previous years' figures in order to make a useful judgement.

The **gearing ratio** is a measure of an organisation's leverage and shows the extent to which its operations are funded by loans rather than by equity.

Exam tip

Do not always assume a highly geared business is risky. If a business has high levels of profitability that are sustainable, it may be little affected by high gearing, just as a low-geared business with unsustainable profits could face problems.

Payables days

This ratio calculates the average number of days a business takes to pay its bills. It is calculated as follows:

$$\text{Payables days} = \frac{\text{payables}}{\text{cost of sales}} \times 365$$

A business might look to achieve a figure that is higher than its receivable days: in other words, money comes in before it has to be paid out, although this is not always possible. A business might also look to improve its own liquidity position by increasing the payable days figure, but this could damage its relationship with suppliers and lead to higher payments.

Receivables days

This ratio shows the number of days it takes to convert receivables into cash and is calculated as follows:

$$\text{Receivables days} = \frac{\text{receivables}}{\text{revenue}} \times 365$$

This shows the number of days it takes to collect payments; the lower the figure, the better. This is important as allowing customers lengthy credit periods can lead to cash-flow problems.

Inventory turnover

This efficiency ratio calculates the number of times per period a business sells and replaces its entire stock of **inventories**. It is calculated as follows:

$$\text{Inventory turnover} = \frac{\text{cost of goods sold}}{\text{average inventories}}$$

A high inventory turnover in general indicates efficient operations but in analysing the figure it needs to be compared to the industry average.

The value of financial ratios when assessing performance

REVISED

Analysing a business's financial performance through ratio analysis can be a useful tool, but analysts need to be aware of its limitations.

Comparisons

On their own, ratios tell analysts little; to be useful, the figures need to be compared against previous years' results to see if there is an improving or declining trend. Only by undertaking such a comparison can analysts judge if a business is doing better, worse or about the same as in previous years. A further comparison that can be made is with other businesses in the same industry. This is important; although a business may be showing improving trends, others in the same industry may be improving at a faster rate and the reasons for this may need to be investigated. On the other hand, although figures may be declining, it may be at a slower rate than others in the industry, which may indicate that the business is coping better with worsening economic conditions.

Historical

It should also be remembered that any ratios calculated are based on past results and are not necessarily an indicator of future performance. Changes in the economy, the actions of competitors, advancements in technology etc. can all have an impact on future performance.

Typical mistake

Students have a habit of not showing their workings when making calculations. Do not fall into this trap as marks can be earned for the correct identification of figures and the workings undertaken, even if the final answer is incorrect.

Exam tip

Having a high figure for receivables days may act as a USP for a business and any attempt to reduce it could result in dissatisfied customers.

Inventories relate to a business's holdings of raw materials, work in progress and finished goods.

'Window dressing'

Sometimes, financial statements can be 'dressed up' to make them appear better than they are. For example, 'window dressing' can improve the impact of one-off events such as the sale of an asset on the profit figure. We have already looked at the problem of valuing intangibles such as a brand name and goodwill, which could be used to create an inflated value for the business. It is also possible to artificially improve the liquidity position of a business, such as by short-term borrowing to improve the cash position or by bringing sales forward to improve revenue.

> **'Window dressing'** relates to the actions taken by organisations to improve the appearance of their financial statements.

Limited focus

Ratio analysis focuses on just the financial performance of a business, which makes it limited in scope. It ignores other areas, such as the market and the position of the business and its competitors in that market, technological advancement and the economic environment, all of which can have an impact on a business.

However, if the limitations outlined above are taken into account, there is no doubt that ratio analysis can provide an excellent indicator of business performance.

> **Typical mistake**
>
> When undertaking ratio analysis, do not jump to conclusions: just because a particular ratio looks bad, this does not necessarily mean it is. There may be an explanation for it, which underlines the importance of reading any case study material carefully.

Now test yourself

TESTED ☐

6 What do you understand by the term 'profit quality' and why is it important?
7 Distinguish between gross profit, operating profit and profit for the year.
8 Using examples, distinguish between liabilities and assets.
9 Explain why a business should not have too much or too little working capital.
10 In assessing a business's financial position, name two ratios you might use and suggest on what basis you could make a judgement as to whether the business has improved its position.
11 Why is an understanding of gearing useful when making a major capital investment?
12 Suggest three limitations of ratio analysis.

Answers on p. 209

> **Exam tip**
>
> When analysing a business's financial position through ratio analysis, look for trends or make comparisons with the industry average in order to reach justified conclusions.

Analysing the existing internal position of a business to assess strengths and weaknesses: overall performance

The overall success of a business is not determined by its financial performance alone. In order to complete the analysis of the strengths and weaknesses of a business's internal position, it is necessary to investigate data from the other functional areas, such as marketing, operations and human resources.

How to analyse data other than financial statements to assess the strengths and weaknesses of a business

REVISED

Marketing data

In Chapter 3 possible marketing objectives such as sales volume and value, market share and sales growth were investigated and these can provide numerical evidence of a business's performance. However, there is a wealth of additional data on areas such as consumer behaviour, the market itself and competition which a business's performance can be judged against.

Operations data

The operational objectives investigated in Chapter 4 included measures such as productivity, unit costs and capacity utilisation, as well as measures of quality. Again, these can be used to assess a business's performance.

Human resource data

In terms of human resource data, Chapter 6 investigated such measures as labour productivity, absenteeism, labour turnover and labour cost per unit. A well-motivated, loyal and engaged workforce is likely to be considered a strength for a business and therefore human resource data can be a good indicator of a business's performance.

As with financial ratios, any performance measures from other functional areas need to be compared to make them useful. This might be with previous years' figures, other businesses in the same industry or the industry as a whole. It is also important to recognise that the relative importance of any one piece of data is likely to vary from business to business, depending on the nature of production, the market, technological advancement and the external environment. Remember that any measures used are also a reflection of the past rather than what might happen in the future.

The importance of core competencies

REVISED

Another way of looking at the relative strengths of a particular business is that of **core competencies.** This is a relatively new concept originating from a *Harvard Business Review* article in 1990. Core competencies give a company one or more competitive advantages in creating and delivering value to its customers in its chosen market: they are the main strengths or strategic advantages of a business. Theoretically, core competencies should be difficult for competitors to replicate and they provide opportunities for a business to expand into new markets, as well as providing significant benefits to customers. Examples of core competencies include Apple's design capabilities and Netflix's content-delivery platform.

> **Core competencies** are the combination of pooled knowledge and technical capacities that allow a business to be competitive in the market place.

Competencies need to be nurtured and protected, and unlike physical assets that deteriorate over time they can be enhanced as they are applied. As a result, once a core competency has been identified, a strategy needs to be developed in order to maximise its potential.

However, there have been some criticisms of core competencies, such as the problems associated with **outsourcing**. In order to focus on core competencies, a business may lose some control of other areas, which may affect its overall performance. It must also be recognised that things change over time and a business must be prepared to move with the times. Kodak is a good example of a business that focused on its core competency of film products and as a result missed the rise of the digital age.

> **Outsourcing** is the sub-contracting of non-core activities of an organisation in order to free up cash, time, personnel and facilities, thereby concentrating on other areas in which it has a competitive advantage.

Assessing short- and long-term performance

REVISED

The problem of short termism was covered on p. 115 and refers to the excessive focus on short-term results at the expense of long-term interests. The measures of financial performance do perhaps focus too heavily on the short term and the need to satisfy ever-more demanding shareholders. In fast-changing industries such as social media and technology, this may not necessarily be a problem as it is essential to keep up to date and move with the times. In these fast-changing industries, a business cannot simply pass off a fall in profit or return on capital employed: it has to tackle any underlying problems head on.

> **Exam tip**
>
> In a fast-changing industry, short termism may not be a problem as profit generation is essential for future development.

However, there is an argument that businesses should be acting in the interests of all **stakeholders**, not just shareholders. They should be looking for long-term, sustainable shareholder value and not just short-term profit. This might be achieved through investment in research and development of new products and processes, together with a focus on achieving customer satisfaction and loyalty as well as employee engagement and loyalty. Attention paid to these areas in the short term may have a high financial cost initially but could lead to more sustainable profit in the future.

> **Stakeholders** are people, groups, organisations or members of society that have an interest in a business such as customers, employees and the local community.

The value of different measures of assessing business performance

REVISED

Assessing organisational performance to see how well a business is doing in terms of its mission and goals is a vital aspect of strategic management in order to determine what strategic changes need to be made. The performance measures looked at so far focus heavily on financial performance based on past performance and are often short term in nature. As a result, a number of alternative methods of assessing organisational performance have been put forward in recent years, two of which are included in the specification.

Kaplan and Norton's Balanced Scorecard model

Proposed by Kaplan and Norton in 1992, the **Balanced Scorecard model** attempts to achieve a balance between financial and other measures of performance that can lead to sustained, long-term performance. The model recommends that managers track a small number of key measures that collectively measure four dimensions: financial, customer, internal business process, and learning/growth. This is shown in Figure 7.7.

> The **Balanced Scorecard model** is a strategic planning and management system that is used in organisations to align their activities to their mission and strategy.

Figure 7.7 Kaplan and Norton's Balanced Scorecard model

The four dimensions need to be measured, analysed and improved together, ignoring any one dimension could result in a business losing balance and failing to thrive. Although initially popular with organisations, the model is less so today. It is complex, some areas can be difficult to quantify, and achieving the right balance between each dimension can be difficult and dependent on the compiler's perspective. However, there is no doubt that it provides a broader view that may detect weaknesses early, as well as allowing employees to see their importance within an organisation and thereby acting as a motivator.

Elkington's Triple Bottom Line

First used in 1994, the **Triple Bottom Line** concept emphasises the three Ps: **P**rofit (economic concerns), **P**eople (social concerns) and **P**lanet (environmental concerns), which are also known as the 'three pillars'. The model (Figure 7.8) was mainly intended to advance the idea of sustainability in business practice.

- In terms of profit, it means the economic value of the business in relation to the benefit to the surrounding community and society.
- In terms of people, it means fair practices in labour employment and in the community in which it operates.
- In terms of planet, it means the use of sustainable environmental practices and the reduction of environmental impacts.

> **Triple Bottom Line** assesses an organisations performance through three dimensions of performance, social, environmental and financial.

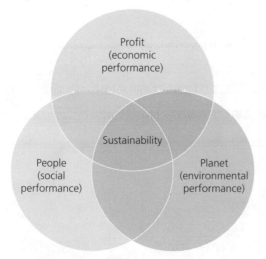

Figure 7.8 Elkington's Triple Bottom Line

As a way of looking at a business's social responsibility, this approach perhaps has some merit, but in measuring business performance it has some problems. The biggest issue is that of comparing profit, which is measured in cash terms, with people and planet, which are difficult to quantify in the same way. As a result, the Triple Bottom Line concept has become less popular.

Now test yourself

TESTED

13 For each of the following functional areas — marketing, operations and human resources — draw a table to show two performance measures and their formulae.
14 What do you understand by the term 'core competencies'?
15 Outline one benefit and one drawback of Kaplan and Norton's Balanced Scorecard model.
16 Briefly outline:
   (a) the four elements of the Balanced Scorecard model
   (b) the three aspects of the Triple Bottom Line.

Answers on p. 209

> **Exam tip**
>
> Triple Bottom Line may help a company become more socially and environmentally conscious, particularly now that corporate social responsibility (CSR) has become much more important. For example, Nike has changed its employment practices in overseas countries whereas Starbucks perhaps goes a stage further with a sustainability strategy of supporting growers and using environmentally friendly napkins and cups, as well as taking care of its employees.

Exam practice

Pizza Dreams plc

Paul Sagebrush established Pizza Dreams plc in 1999. It now operates 502 takeaway stores across the UK and Ireland, selling pizza and other simple fast food. It offers a home delivery service that has received praise for its speed and efficiency. Paul and the other company directors hold large numbers of shares in the business. The company's early growth was spectacular, although it has slowed in recent years. It has recently faced tough competition from rivals such as Domino's and prices in the pizza market have been drifting downwards for the last 2 years.

Over the last year, the market for pizzas has grown by 7.1%. Demand for pizzas is price elastic: the latest estimate was –1.7. A major competitor cut its prices by 5% last year and was still able to achieve a ROCE of 18.9%. After its initial opening promotions, Pizza Dreams has relied almost exclusively on word-of-mouth advertising. Other than its chefs, it relies on part-time employees, mainly students, which results in a high labour turnover figure. At times, this has affected the efficiency of its delivery service.

The following is an extract from the company's accounts.

Financial item	This financial year (£000)	Last financial year (£000)
Sales turnover	50,457	49,899
Operating profit	3,699	3,457
Current assets	4,071	4,002
Current liabilities	3,120	4,325
Non-current liabilities	20,568	19,045
Total equity	16,535	14,201
Total dividends	1,202	990

Although Paul believes his business is financially successful, the share price has fallen over the last 12 months from 128p to 120p.

Questions

a Explain why the Balanced Scorecard model might be a better way of assessing Pizza Dreams's performance rather than just looking at its financial performance. [9]
b Paul says his business is financially successful. To what extent do you agree with his view? (You should use relevant calculations to support your answer.) [16]

Answers and quick quiz 7A online

ONLINE

Analysing the external environment to assess opportunities and threats: political and legal change

Continuing the SWOT analysis approach (see p. 117), we now turn to the external opportunities and threats faced by a business. In terms of the political and legal environment, the specification requires 'a broad understanding of the scope and effects of UK and EU law related to competition, the labour market and environmental legislation'. It also requires an understanding of 'the impact of UK and EU government policy related to enterprise, the role of regulators, infrastructure, the environment and international trade'.

The impact of changes in the political and legal environment on strategic and functional decision-making

REVISED

The scope and effects of UK and EU law

In order to avoid incrimination, strategic and functional decisions must be formed and undertaken within the UK and EU legal framework. This covers the following areas.

Competition

The objective of competition law is to promote economic efficiency through the sound development of the market economy and to protect the consumer from excessive market power. This has resulted in a number of important laws designed to promote healthy competition and prevent anti-competitive practices. These are designed to prevent businesses taking advantage of a dominant market position (greater than 40% market share) or forming **cartels** or other trade agreements such as price fixing, which could be used to exploit consumers and trading partners. There are two key pieces of legislation:

- **The Competition Act 1998.** This act prevents anti-competitive agreements between businesses such as price fixing, where competitors collude to sell a good or commodity at the same price, limiting production and sharing out markets. It also addresses the potential abuse of a dominant position in a market. This act is supported by similar EU legislation.
- **The Enterprise Act 2002.** This act further strengthens the Competition Act 1998, particularly in the area of cartels.

These two acts are supported and overseen by the **Competition and Markets Authority (CMA)**, which was formed in 2014 with the merger of the Office of Fair Trading and the Competition Commission. It is responsible for the enforcement of competition and consumer law. Part of its role is also to investigate mergers and takeovers when either the business being taken over has a turnover of at least £70m or the merged business gains control of 25% or more of the market.

> A **cartel** is where businesses or countries act together as a single producer in order to influence prices, production and marketing of certain goods or services.
>
> The **Competition and Markets Authority (CMA)** is a non-ministerial government department responsible for strengthening business competition and preventing and reducing anti-competitive activities.

Within the financial services sector, responsibility for overseeing competitive practices lies with the Financial Conduct Authority (FCA).

The labour market

UK labour legislation is designed to prevent the exploitation of employees by businesses by regulating the relations between workers, employees and trade unions. It seeks to ensure reasonable working conditions and prevent exploitation and **discrimination**. The relevant legislation falls into two main areas: that which applies to individual workers and that which applies to workers collectively, such as those in trade unions. In terms of individual workers, one of the most important pieces of legislation has been the **Equality Act 2010**. This brought together all previous acts related to discrimination in the workplace into one act. This includes discrimination on the grounds of age, race, sex, disability, religion and sexual orientation.

In 1998 the **Minimum Wage Act** was introduced with rates reviewed annually by the Low Pay Commission. In October 2015 the rate stood at £6.70 for workers over the age of 21. The Conservative Government has introduced a national living wage of £7.20 for all workers over 25 as of 1 April 2016.

The **Employment Rights Act** sets out employees' statutory rights in relation to pay and conditions of work. However, in order to receive redundancy pay an employee needs to have worked for at least 2 years. The **Health and Safety at Work Act** is the primary piece of legislation covering health and safety at work.

In terms of EU legislation, the **Working Time Regulations 1998** are important as they limit the hours an employee can be legally required to work to a maximum of 48.

Legislation has also been introduced in the UK in terms of industrial relations. This was designed to control a number of aspects of trade union behaviour that were considered unfair, such as:
- closed shops, which meant that in order to work for a business an employee had to belong to a trade union
- open ballots on strike action — ballots are now secret
- picketing, where the number of striking workers able to congregate outside a workplace is limited, and secondary picketing, where picketing of a business not directly related to a dispate (e.g. a supplier or customer business) is banned

The main pieces of legislation in this area are the **Employment Act 1980** and the **Trade Union Act 1984**. There have been further refinements to this legislation and the whole area of employment law has been the subject of a government review, with one of the main aims to make employment practices in the UK more flexible and family friendly.

Environmental legislation

Environmental legislation is designed to minimise the negative impact of business on the environment. The legislation in this area falls into two main categories: pollution and climate change.

Pollution is related to air, water and land and the two main acts here are the **Environmental Protection Act 1991**, which prevents pollution from emissions, and the **Environment Act 1995**, which set up the **Environment Agency** to oversee environmental protection.

> **Discrimination** is bias or prejudice resulting in the denial of opportunity or unfair treatment regarding the selection, promotion or transfer of employees.

> The **Environment Agency** is a public body established in 1996 to protect and improve the environment and promote sustainable development.

Two key pieces of legislation related to climate change are the **Climate Change Act 2008**, which aims to make the UK a low-carbon economy, and the **Energy Act 2013**, which focuses on setting decarbonisation targets for the UK and reforming the energy market.

Much of this legislation has been shaped by the EU, which has some of the highest environmental standards in the world.

Legislation inevitably has an impact on business. Not only does it increase the amount of bureaucracy and red tape, it is also likely to add to its costs. The introduction of the living wage is an example of how costs can rise and the requirement to provide more flexible working environments is likely to impact on both the costs and the administrative burden of a business. Addressing tighter environmental controls could also increase costs. Although the burden of legislation from both the UK and EU poses challenges for business, it is not all bad news. All businesses are treated the same and measures such as those against anti-competitive behaviour may make it easier for firms to compete.

The impact of UK and EU government policy

As well as the legal framework, the UK government and the EU also have an impact in the following areas.

Enterprise

It is in the government's best interest to encourage **enterprise** — to encourage people and businesses to take initiative and to be innovative in building businesses — as this will lead to a stronger, more vibrant economy. One way it can do this is by reducing the amount of red tape faced by businesses, particularly new and small businesses. Another way is by reducing the tax burden. The UK has one of the lowest rates of corporation tax in the EU and schemes such as the **Patent Box** allow further relief to be gained. Direct financial help can also be gained through such schemes as Enterprise Allowance and the Enterprise Finance Guarantee.

The role of regulators

Regulatory bodies exercise a regulatory function within a wide variety of industries and professions. Their primary activity is to protect the public through imposing requirements, restrictions and conditions; setting standards in relation to any activity; and ensuring compliance and enforcement. Examples include the regulators of privatised industries such as Ofwat (water and sewage) and Ofcom (communications such as television, radio and fixed-line telecoms), as well as bodies such as the Civil Aviation Authority, the Legal Services Board and the Financial Conduct Authority.

Infrastructure

Infrastructure refers to the basic physical systems of a country that allow the economy to run smoothly, such as transportation, communication and utilities (electricity, gas, water, etc.) Infrastructure represents a high-cost investment and yet is vital to the economy. The importance of infrastructure is often taken for granted and yet it is one of the biggest issues facing governments across the world. Investment in schools, roads, hospitals and communication is essential for both economic development and quality of life. As a result, the quality and reliability of a country's infrastructure is a key determinant of inward investment. It is therefore in a government's best interest to maintain and

> **Exam tip**
>
> Remember that legislation, although burdensome at times, creates a level playing field where all businesses are treated in the same way. This leads to the effective operation of the market economy and can sometimes lead to cost savings.

> **Typical mistake**
>
> It is often assumed that legislation just leads to higher costs, but this may not always be the case; sometimes it can lead to cost savings. For example, the introduction of filters in cement factories required by environmental legislation resulted in cost savings because of the reduction in wastage created.

> **Enterprise** in this context refers to the willingness to take initiative in setting up or taking on a project or business venture.
>
> **Patent Box** is a special tax regime for intellectual property revenues that businesses have been able to elect to enter.
>
> **Infrastructure** is the basic physical and organisational structures (transport, communications, utilities etc.) needed for the operation of society or enterprise.

improve the UK's infrastructure with projects such as the high-speed train line HS2, Heathrow's third runway and investment in the next generation of nuclear power reactors.

The environment

Governments like to show a commitment to the protection of the environment and this is evidenced by such schemes as the establishment of green belt areas around cities, the granting of subsidies for those installing renewable energy systems (e.g. solar) and the introduction of environmental legislation. However, commitment to the environment faces many conflicts and challenges, such as those surrounding building new roads, runways and nuclear power stations and the increased demand for housing.

International trade

International trade is the exchange of goods and services between countries and is essential to maintaining the standard of living in the UK. Some goods and materials cannot be produced in the UK and therefore have to be imported. Therefore, those countries that sell them have a competitive advantage in this respect. In other areas the UK may have an advantage, such as in banking and finance, the UK's location within Europe and in terms of innovation (e.g. Dyson). The government recognises the importance of trading internationally to the success of the economy and therefore takes steps to support it. This might be in the form of trade fairs or financial support for exporters.

> **International trade** is the exchange of goods and services between countries.

Until the referendum in June 2016 one of the key aspects of international trade had been the UK's membership of the EU, which gave it free access to over 500 million consumers. EU membership also brought significant direct foreign investment from firms such as Nissan, as membership gave foreign companies producing in the UK direct access to the EU. The 'Leave' vote, however, means that trade deals will now have to be negotiated with the EU, a process that is likely to be both time-consuming and complicated. The period of uncertainty until new deals are thrashed out will make future strategic planning difficult for many UK businesses. It also remains to be seen how leaving the EU will affect both future foreign direct investment into the UK and what impact it will have on the future strategic thinking of companies such as Nissan.

Changes in the law and policy can have a significant impact on business, not only in terms of cost but also in terms of the demand for individual businesses. Construction firms benefit from infrastructure investment, renewable energy firms from subsidies offered, and start-up businesses and innovative firms from grants and tax incentives.

Now test yourself

TESTED

17 With examples, explain what is meant by the term 'anti-competitive practices'.
18 Outline the role of the Competition and Markets Authority.
19 What do you understand by the term 'discrimination in the workplace'?
20 Identify three aspects of trade union behaviour that have been targeted by trade union legislation.
21 List three pieces of legislation related to the environment.
22 By what means has the government encouraged enterprise?
23 List three regulatory bodies.
24 Briefly explain why it is important to maintain investment in infrastructure.

Answers on p. 210

Analysing the external environment to assess opportunities and threats: economic change

This section covers the macro-economic environment, for which the specification requires students to have an understanding of economic factors such as GDP, taxation, exchange rates, inflation, fiscal and monetary policy and more open trade v protectionism. As a result, it should be possible to interpret changes in these data from a UK, EU and global perspective and the implications of such changes for businesses. Ideally, the government wishes to achieve a growing domestic economy and to be operating in a growing world economy, as this provides opportunities for businesses to flourish and the standard of living of consumers to improve. However, this is not always possible.

The impact of changes in the UK and the global economic environment on strategic and functional decision-making

REVISED

GDP

GDP is a measure of a nation's overall economic activity and represents the value of all finished goods and services produced within a country. It is an indicator of a nation's economic health and a gauge of its standard of living. It can also be used to compare one country with another, such as comparing how different countries are coping with the aftermath of global financial crisis.

Although governments would like to achieve steady and sustained growth in GDP, this rarely happens. The rate of economic growth varies and sometimes even becomes negative (recession). These regular fluctuations in the level of GDP are known as the **business cycle**. As shown in Figure 7.9, business cycle is generally seen to have four stages: upswing/expansion, boom, recession and trough/slump. The implications and responses of businesses to these stages are summarised in Table 7.2.

It is important to recognise that the business cycle within the UK is likely to follow a different pattern to other countries and therefore businesses within the UK will be affected differently according to how much they are exposed to the UK and world markets.

> **GDP** is a measure of the value of all goods and services produced within a country over a specific time period and as such provides a primary indicator of a country's economic health.
>
> A **business cycle** or trade cycle shows the fluctuations in economic activity, as measured by GDP, that an economy experiences over time.

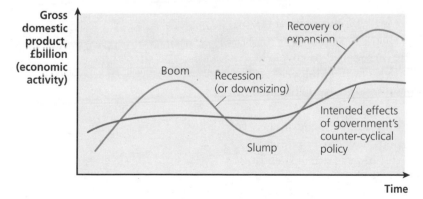

Figure 7.9 The stages of the business cycle

Table 7.2 Businesses and the business cycle

Stage of the business cycle	Possible implications for business	Possible responses of businesses to changing trading conditions
Upswing or expansion	• Rising incomes and expenditures • Possible labour shortages, pushing up wages • Possible rise in output, encouraging expansion	• Opportunity to charge higher prices • Adoption of more technology to replace expensive labour • Decide to invest in fixed assets • Operate nearer to full capacity
Boom	• Possible rise in inflation • Bottlenecks in supply of materials and components • Unable to satisfy levels of demand as consumption rises • Profits likely to be high	• Face increasing pressure to raise prices regularly • Seek methods to increase output (maybe producing at overseas plants) • Offer wage rises to avoid threat of industrial action • Managers plan for falling levels of demand
Recession	• Consumers' disposable incomes start to fall • Demand for many products begins to fall • Some businesses experience financial problems • Excess stocks	• Begin to emphasise price competitiveness in advertising • Seek new markets for existing products • Lay off some workers or ask them to work short time • Possible reduction in trade credit provided
Slump	• Government may initiate counter-cyclical policies, e.g. lower interest rates • Rise in number of bankruptcies • Increased frequency of bad debts • High levels of unemployment	• Offer basic products at bargain prices • Review credit control policies • Continue to target new markets • Seek to diversify product range and sell income-inelastic products • Reduce wage levels

Taxation

In order to fund government expenditure, it is necessary to impose taxes on individuals and businesses. These may be **direct taxes** or **indirect taxes** and the main ones used by the UK government and their impact on businesses are outlined below.

- **Income tax.** Paid on all income earned over the personal allowance (currently £11,000), this includes income from employment, investments and pensions. Changes in the level of personal allowance and rates of income tax can affect consumer disposable income and, as a result, the level of spending within the economy.
- **Corporation tax.** This is a tax levied on business profit and the rate at which it is charged can affect the attractiveness of the UK as a business location. It currently stands at 20%, which is one of the lowest in the EU. The UK also offers incentives for innovation through the Patent Box system (see p. 131), leading to a lower level of corporation tax on the resulting profit from innovations.
- **National insurance payments.** Initially introduced to cover the cost of the welfare state, this is a tax paid jointly by both employees and employers. Changes in the rates paid can affect the disposable income of both businesses and consumers.
- **Value added tax (VAT).** This is a consumption or spending tax. In the UK the rate is 20%, although some goods have lower rates and most food items are zero-rated. Changes in rates can affect spending as VAT has a direct impact on the price of goods.
- **Excise duty.** This is a tax on the sale of specific goods such as alcohol, tobacco and fuel.

> **Direct taxes** are taken directly from individuals' or organisations' income.
>
> **Indirect taxes** are taxes on expenditure.

- **Green taxes.** These are paid by consumers for products or services that are not considered environmentally friendly, such as air transport tax. They also cover measures such as levies on consumer energy bills, which have been used to encourage the expansion of low-carbon power such as solar.

Exchange rates

The **exchange rate** is the price at which the currency of a country can be exchanged for another country's currency. As with changes in interest rates, changes in exchange rates can cause uncertainty for business and affect competitiveness.

Rising exchange rates make goods exported from the UK more expensive and goods imported less expensive. This may have the impact of reducing the competitiveness of UK-producing businesses. If a business is importing materials for production, however, these will be cheaper, which could possibly offset an increase in the export price.

Falling exchange rates have the effect of making exports cheaper but imports more expensive, although again, in terms of exports, if materials are imported this could offset any reduction in export price.

Businesses can take measures to limit the uncertainty presented by the fluctuating £ exchange rate. For example, a number of businesses producing in the UK and selling to the EU deal in euros and use the forward foreign currency market to reduce their exposure to fluctuations.

Inflation

Inflation is the rate at which the general level of prices for goods and services is rising and consequently the purchasing power of a currency is falling. Since 2003 the main measure of inflation has been the consumer price index (CPI). Each month it measures the change in price of a basket of goods and services purchased by households.

The objective of the Bank of England's **Monetary Policy Committee (MPC)** is to deliver price stability and low inflation, and it has a target rate of 2%. Interest rates can be increased if there is a danger of inflation rising above 2%. In this way, the Bank of England is trying to avoid the uncertainty associated with volatile inflation and increase business confidence. High inflation poses a number of problems for business:

- **Cost pressures.** These might be in terms of higher borrowing costs on account of interest rate rises, higher material costs as well as pressure on wage rates from employees due to their wages declining in value as a result of inflation.
- **Reduced sales.** This might be because of lower demand as a result of lower consumer disposable income because of the fall in value of money or because of a tendency for consumers to save more in periods of inflation. Lower sales might also be a result of lower competiveness if overseas competitors are not experiencing the same levels of inflation and therefore cost pressures.

However, inflation is not all bad news for business. If a business can cope with interest payments, the value of any borrowings declines. Some inflation allows revenues to grow and, if costs can be kept the same, profits can grow.

Fiscal and monetary policy

The way in which the government adjusts its own spending levels and tax rates to monitor and influence the economy is known as **fiscal policy**.

> The **exchange rate** is the price for which the currency of one country can be exchanged for another country's currency.

> **Typical mistake**
>
> Students often assume that all businesses are affected in the same way by changes in interest rates or exchange rates, but this is not the case. It depends on the individual circumstances of the business concerned.

> **Inflation** is the general increase in prices and the fall in the purchasing power of money.

> The **Monetary Policy Committee (MPC)** is a committee of the Bank of England that regulates interest rates in an attempt to maintain economic stability.

> **Fiscal policy** is the means by which the government adjusts its spending levels and tax rates to monitor and influence the country's economy.

Changes in taxation can affect the level of spending within the economy and could be used to stimulate growth in the economy or to curtail it, as shown in Table 7.3. The government can also affect the level of spending within the economy by its own spending and investment, such as that on infrastructure projects (Table 7.4).

Table 7.3 The effects of increases and reductions in taxation

The effects of increases in taxation	The effects of decreases in taxation
● Increases in indirect taxes such as VAT result in higher prices, cutting consumer demand. ● Producers may pay the increase in indirect taxes to avoid raising prices. This will cut profits and may reduce investment levels by businesses. ● Increases in income tax leave consumers with less disposable income, again reducing demand.	● Cutting indirect taxes reduces prices, which may boost spending, especially for price-elastic products. ● Reductions in income tax result in consumers having higher incomes. This increases demand, particularly for luxury products. ● Falling corporate taxation promotes investment and output for business, increasing economic activity. ● Reductions in corporate taxation may attract investment by foreign individuals and businesses.

Table 7.4 Fiscal policy and levels of economic activity

	Falling level of economic activity	Rising level of economic activity
Caused by	Reduced government spending or increased taxation.	Increased government spending or lower rates of taxation.
Likely effects	Increased unemployment, declining spending and production.	Inflation may appear while unemployment falls as imports increase.
Impact on business	● Falling sales and downward pressure on prices. ● Rising numbers of bankruptcies, especially among small firms. ● Increased levels of inventories.	● Rising wages and possible skill shortages. ● Sales rise and possibility of increasing prices. ● Increasing costs of raw materials and components.

The level of consumer spending in the economy is also affected by **monetary policy**. This involves using interest rates and other monetary tools such as credit controls to control consumer spending. It is the role of the Bank of England and the Monetary Policy Committee (MPC) to determine interest rates. During a period of expansion in the business cycle where inflationary pressures are growing, interest rates are likely to be increased to reduce consumer spending and ease inflationary pressures. When growth in the economy is falling and inflationary pressures easing, the MPC may need to lower interest rates to stimulate demand. The UK is currently experiencing one of the longest periods of low interest rates as a result of global economic problems and the need to stimulate spending.

Monetary policy is the process by which the monetary authority controls the money supply and interest rates in order to achieve healthy economic growth.

More open trade v protectionism

Free trade is the unrestricted purchase and sale of goods and services between countries without the imposition of constraints. The EU provides one of the biggest free trade areas in the world. **Protectionism** is where constraints are used to restrict the purchase and sale of goods and services between countries. Examples of constraints include:

● **tariffs:** taxes on imported goods that increase the price, thereby making the import less competitive
● **quotas:** physical restrictions on the number of goods imported into a country

Free trade is the unrestricted purchase and sale of goods and services between countries.

Protectionism refers to the policies and actions by governments to restrict or restrain international trade, such as import tariffs, quotas or subsidies to local businesses.

Exam practice answers and quick quizzes at **www.hoddereducation.co.uk/myrevisionnotes**

- **non-tariff barriers:** these might include excessive rules and regulations that make importing difficult, and exacting standards or specifications designed to make the cost for the exporting nation excessive.

The arguments for the introduction of protectionist measures include the protection of domestic industries and employment as well as the prevention of 'dumping'. This is when a country exports or sells products in a foreign country for less than either the price in the domestic country or the cost of making the products.

With the growth of **globalisation** there are greater demands for more open trade or trade liberalisation. This aims to free up world trade by breaking down the barriers to trade. Although this exposes businesses to greater competition, it should lead to the more efficient use of resources.

> **Globalisation** is the increased interdependence of economies, industries and markets around the world.

Reasons for greater globalisation of business

REVISED

The Organisation for Economic Co-operation and Development (OECD) defines globalisation as 'the process of deeper economic integration between countries and regions of the world'. It refers to the breakdown of barriers that prevent the exchange and integration of finances, trade and ideas across the world. Reasons for greater globalisation include:

- **Improved transport.** The use of containers to transport goods and the introduction of bigger ships has made transport cheaper and more efficient. The rapid growth of air transport has also made the movement of both people and some goods across the globe easier.
- **Technology.** Improvements in technology have made it easier and quicker to communicate, share information and trade across the world. Some services such as website creation can be sourced anywhere in the world.
- **More open trade.** The World Trade Organization (WTO) encourages reduced tariff barriers and more open trade. There has also been a reduction in national barriers through the development of the EU and other trading blocs such as NAFTA and ASEAN.
- **Multinational companies.** Many firms now have a global presence, seeking to benefit from the increased opportunities for economies of scale.
- **Other reasons.** These include the increasing by global nature of the financial system, leading to a reduction in capital barriers and making it easier for capital to flow between countries.

The importance of globalisation for business

REVISED

Globalisation is important for business for a number of reasons that affect strategic and functional decision-making.

Positive reasons

- **Freer trade.** This is likely to lead to increased sales and profit. It also means countries and businesses can specialise in producing goods and services where they have a comparative advantage, leading to economies of scale and lower costs.

- **Free movement of labour.** Although this is a controversial topic, this has allowed UK business to fill job vacancies (both skilled and unskilled) with migrants such as nurses and doctors working in the NHS.
- **Increased investment.** The UK has benefited from direct inward investment from multinational companies such as Nissan and Toyota.

Negative reasons

- **Greater competition.** Globalisation leads to greater competition, which results in lower costs and prices and might put pressure on domestic firms if they cannot compete.
- **Takeovers.** The growth of large multinationals has led to a number of high-profile takeovers such as Kraft taking over Cadbury and Tata Steel taking over Jaguar Land Rover. Although not necessarily bad, this can pose a threat to 'British' businesses.
- **Global economy.** Business is likely to be influenced by not only the UK economy but also the global economy. Lower growth and demand in China or the USA has consequences for UK businesses.

One final issue that is very much in the news is taxation and how the growth of large multinationals has enabled tax avoidance. Companies such as Google, Amazon and Starbucks have been able to significantly reduce their tax bills as a result. This is good for the individual business but not so good for governments of host countries.

> **Exam tip**
>
> Tax avoidance is a complex issue as the UK government does not want to deter direct inward investment. Companies such as Amazon and Starbucks have provided a large number of jobs and their associated income tax and national insurance contributions.

The importance of emerging economies for business

REVISED

Emerging markets are countries in the process of rapid growth and industrialisation, the most notable of which are Brazil, Russia, India and China (the BRICs). Others include South Africa, Vietnam and Turkey, as well as a number of Latin American and Eastern European countries. They are important for a number reasons:

> An **emerging market** describes a national economy that is progressing towards becoming more advanced through rapid growth and industrialisation.

- **Large and growing markets.** The BRIC nations as well as other emerging markets have large populations that provide a growing middle class as their economies develop.
- **Growth of middle classes.** As economies grow, a wealthy middle class develops with aspirations for more up-market, high-quality goods, providing further opportunities for business.
- **Low-cost locations.** Emerging markets can also provide low-cost locations for producing products.

Strategies for businesses entering emerging markets include:

- **Knowledge.** An understanding of the market and its consumers, suppliers and competitors is crucial and an essential first step when entering an emerging market. Note the failure of companies such as Tesco when first entering the Chinese market.
- **Local partners.** Having a local partner and not just knowledge eases entry to a market and aids success.
- **Well-made and locally tailored products.** The aspiring middle classes in emerging economies want known brands and quality, but having something that is tailored specifically to them also aids success.

Now test yourself

25 What do you understand by the term 'GDP'?
26 Briefly outline how a downturn in the business cycle might affect a UK car manufacturer.
27 Using examples, distinguish between direct and indirect taxation.
28 How does fiscal policy differ from monetary policy?
29 What would be the impact of a rise in interest rates on the following:
   (a) Consumers.
   (b) A high-geared consumer-durable manufacturer.
   (c) Supermarkets.
30 What difficulties might a UK manufacturer face from a stronger pound?
31 With the use of examples, illustrate what is meant by the term 'protectionism'.
32 Briefly outline two reasons for the growth of globalisation.
33 What do you understand by the term 'emerging market'?

Answers on p. 210

Analysing the external environment to assess opportunities and threats: social and technological

Changes in the social and technological environment provide both opportunities and threats for a business. This might include changes in the age and structure of a population, as well as changes in tastes, habits and environmental awareness. Technological change influences not only what we produce and the way it is produced but also the way in which consumers go about their everyday lives.

The impact of the social and technological environment on strategic and functional decision-making

Social changes

Urbanisation and migration

Demographic change most commonly refers to shifts in a population structure, its size, composition and make-up. Two important aspects of the UK population are longer life expectancy and increasing immigration. Such changes affect the types of goods and services demanded and the overall structure of the workforce. Businesses need to respond to these changes in terms of the goods and services offered, as well as the structure and training needs of their workforces.

Migration is the movement of people between countries. UK net migration is the difference between the numbers leaving and the numbers arriving in the UK. The 5-year period between 2009 and 2014 saw UK net migration boost the population by around 1 million. One positive of this is an increase in the labour force, which adds to the skills available particularly in the health sector. It also boosts demand in the economy and can have a positive impact on some sectors such higher education, where foreign students contribute to the financing for domestic students.

> **Migration** is the movement of people between countries.

Urbanisation is the movement of people from the countryside to the cities. This happened in the UK as a result of the Industrial Revolution and is now happening on a large scale in emerging nations such as China. Urbanisation can cause problems such as traffic congestion, over-crowding, a lack of suitable housing and inequalities. Advancements in technology and more flexible working have meant that the UK's cities are perhaps less attractive than they used to be.

> **Urbanisation** is the movement of people from the countryside to towns and cities.

Changes in consumer lifestyle and buying behaviour

Over time, consumer tastes change and evolve because of changing fashion and increased awareness of alternative lifestyles. Rising incomes afford more opportunities, more leisure time allows for a wider variety of opportunities and advances in technology make communication and life altogether much easier. Consumers now have a vast amount of information at their fingertips on a whole range of issues including health, the environment, holiday destinations and shopping in general. Some of the resulting changes in lifestyle include:

- **Organic and fair-trade produce.** Although this has been affected by the recession, this sector represents a large market with organic food commanding £1.86 billion worth of sales.
- **Health.** There is a growing awareness of issues surround health, ranging from the dangers of smoking, alcohol, salt and sugar consumption to the benefits of a healthy diet and exercise.
- **Holidays.** With more leisure time and greater affluence, people take more holidays, expect to travel overseas and go further afield with long-haul flights and cruises.
- **Ready meals and eating out.** The growth in the number and variety of restaurants and fast-food outlets in our towns and cities illustrates the greater demand for eating out. The variety of ready meals on supermarket shelves indicates that when consumers do eat in, it is often the easy option they take.

Some of these changes have come about on account of demographics such as an ageing population and the demand for cruises and a greater variety in holidays and destinations. Others are the result of improvements in communication and the expectancy of 24/7 shopping that has come with **online shopping**.

> **Online shopping** is the act of purchasing goods and services over the internet.

The growth of online businesses

There was a time when online shopping was mistrusted with worries over using credit cards and giving personal information, but that has all changed. It is now possible to buy just about anything online from anywhere in the world, and businesses today ignore this medium at their peril. In the 20 years between 1995 and 2015, the number of internet users and the percentage of world population using the internet have grown from 16 million to 3,366 million and from 0.4% to 46.4% respectively. The internet has been a big driver of economic growth.

This growth has had a big impact on supermarkets, which at one time were competing for prime out-of-town retail space and adopting longer opening hours and bigger stores. With the advent of online business including home delivery and 'click and collect', the size of stores and opening hours are less important. With more consumers turning to online shopping, Tesco has even closed some of its bigger stores and in January 2016 announced that 70 of its stores would no longer offer 24/7 opening. The necessity for actual retail floor space has therefore declined and, as illustrated by Amazon and ASOS, it is possible operate through a website and distribution centres.

This has not only helped large, well-known businesses and brands, it has also helped smaller and start-up businesses. For a business to achieve its full potential in this internet age, it not only needs a good product or service but also a highly respected internet presence. This is likely to involve:

- the creation of a high-quality, user-friendly website
- a carefully targeted audience
- content that is increasingly personalised
- mobile capabilities for modern consumers
- integrated sales channels

These changes in consumer tastes and the growth of online business are in many respects the result of technological change.

Technological changes

There is no doubt that **technological changes** have had a big impact on the goods and services produced and the processes used to produce them. It has also revolutionised the way in which organisations conduct their business. Computer-aided design (CAD) has shortened lead times and computer-aided manufacture (CAM) has made production more efficient. As a result, new products are brought to the market more quickly and cheaply. Technology has also provided access to greater information about consumers and their buying habits, as well as access to wider markets. The benefits of technological change can be summed up as follows:

> **Technological changes**
> relate to innovation in services provided, products manufactured or processes of production.

- **Lower costs.** These are a result not only of improved efficiency and reduced waste in production, but also of reduced administration expenditure and distribution costs.
- **Improved communication.** This is now quicker and easier, allowing a flexible business to be more responsive to customer needs.
- **Increased sales.** Access to wider markets is possible, particularly for small- and medium-sized business.
- **Working environment.** This has generally become cleaner, quieter and safer, especially in manufacturing.
- **Quality.** CAD and CAM (often known as CADCAM) have generally brought improvements in the quality and reliability of products.

Technological changes are not without their problems, including:

- **Pace of change.** Businesses must keep moving forward in order to stay ahead of competition, which can sometimes prove costly.
- **Competition.** Technology has resulted in a more competitive market, not only because of globalisation but also as a result of the fact that smaller businesses have found it easier to access markets.
- **Security.** This is an increasing problem with hackers able to access confidential material and customer information. This results in the need for higher-security systems, adding further to costs.

The advancement in technology has implications for each functional area:

- operations in the way products are designed and made
- marketing in the way products are sold to consumers
- human resources in terms of the skills required and the working environment
- finance in terms of the costs and potential savings to be made

The social environment including corporate social responsibility

Corporate social responsibility (CSR) is the continuing commitment by business to behave ethically and contribute to economic development, while improving the quality of life of the workforce and their families as well as the local community and society at large. This is a significant area where greater consumer environmental awareness has led to increased pressure for CSR reporting, but there are a number of reasons both for and against corporate social responsibility.

> **Corporate social responsibility (CSR)** is a business approach that contributes to sustainable development by delivering economic, social and environmental benefits to all stakeholders.

Reasons for and against CSR

Reasons for include:

- **Cost savings.** These might arise from using less packaging or less energy. For example, the installation of energy-monitoring metres can help save energy.
- **Brand differentiation.** Although more difficult now, CSR reporting could lead to a competitive advantage for a company that took it seriously.
- **Customer and employee engagement.** Customers and potential employees are aware of an organisation's position on social reporting.
- **The 'right thing to do'.** Business is responsible for some of society's problems such as pollution and working conditions and therefore it should take responsibility for them.
- **Resources.** Some would argue that business has the resources to be able to take action.
- **Prevent government intervention.** By taking action, business can offset the need for government intervention and regulation.

Reasons against include:

- **Profit.** Socially responsible policies have a cost and some would argue that business should focus on profit and let governments deal with social and environmental issues.
- **Customer perception.** Although some consumers may be willing to pay more for products that are produced by environmentally aware businesses, others may not be. The success of Primark illustrates this point.
- **State of the economy.** In periods of high growth and profit, it may be possible to take a more socially aware approach, but during periods of low growth/recession and lower profit this may be difficult.
- **The market.** Milton Friedman argued that the market should decide what is best rather than businesses. In some ways, we can see this happening, in that CSR is just an extension of a business's market orientation. For example, the move to hybrid and electric cars has been undertaken because of the potential profit available.
- **Stakeholders' views.** Different stakeholders have different views, making it difficult to achieve agreement on socially responsible behaviour.

The difference between stakeholder and shareholder concepts

A stakeholder is anyone who has an interest in business, such as employees, consumers and suppliers. Shareholders are also stakeholders, but they own part of the business and are primarily interested in its financial performance.

The shareholder concept was proposed by Milton Freedman and it states that it is the responsibility of business to increase profit within the basic rules of society. After all, the management is hired by the shareholders to run the business for their benefit.

The awareness of CSR, however, has encouraged businesses to take the interests of all stakeholders into consideration during the decision-making process, rather than just those of shareholders. This is the stakeholder concept: that a business owes a responsibility to a wider group of stakeholders than just shareholders. Some would argue that in the long term this can result in increased shareholder value because:

● by treating employees properly, they are likely to be more engaged
● by providing higher-quality products, consumers are more likely to buy
● by having a socially responsible image, consumers may again be more likely to buy

However, this may not work in practice — consider why consumers continue to shop at certain clothes shops despite their record on the use of sweatshops, for example. In an economic downturn, CSR is low on the list of priorities. As a result, a happy medium of enlightened shareholder value (ESV) may be a more acceptable concept. This states that businesses should seek shareholder wealth that promotes sustainable growth and profits based on a responsible attention to a full range of stakeholder interests: in other words, gaining shareholder value while having full regard for the long-term external impacts of wealth creation.

Carroll's corporate social responsibility pyramid

In 1991 A. B. Carroll proposed the **pyramid of corporate social responsibility**, which shows four main areas that a business's duties to its stakeholders fall under. This is illustrated in Figure 7.10.

> The **pyramid of corporate social responsibility** is the pyramid proposed by Carroll to illustrate the four layers of corporate responsibility: economic, legal, ethical and philanthropic.

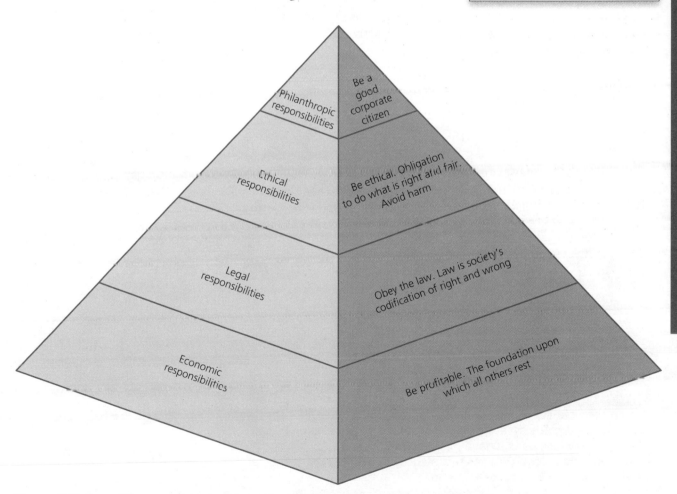

Figure 7.10 Carroll's corporate social responsibility pyramid

It is sometimes claimed that the basis of what we consider to be CSR is rooted in the four types of responsibility depicted. The four areas are outlined below:

- **Economic.** This is the responsibility to be profitable, to provide a return to shareholders, to create jobs and to contribute useful products and services to society.
- **Legal.** This is the responsibility to ensure that business practices are legal. This involves obeying laws and regulations relating to employees, consumers and the environment.
- **Ethical.** This responsibility extends beyond the letter of the law to do what is 'right' in terms of, for example, waste, recycling and the working environment: in other words, looking after its stakeholders.
- **Philanthropic.** This is the responsibility to be good corporate citizens and to improve the lives of others in society.

The relevance of this pyramid perhaps lies in the framework it provides for a business to understand the necessary principles of social responsibility, enabling practices and strategies to be developed to achieve it.

The pressures for socially responsible behaviour

REVISED

Concerns for CSR have grown significantly over the last two decades, adding to the pressures on business to act in a responsible manner. Other pressures include:

- **Pressure groups.** The actions of pressure groups such as Greenpeace can draw unwanted attention to a business's activities and in extreme cases influence consumer purchasing choices.
- **Regulation.** Strong and well-enforced state regulation makes socially responsible behaviour more likely.
- **Self-regulation.** Businesses are more likely to act in a socially responsible way if there is a well-organised and effective system of industrial self-regulation in place.
- **The media.** These can have a big impact on business, making CSR more likely as businesses aim to avoid negative publicity.
- **Consumer perception.** Consumers are more aware and through social media could have a big impact on a business that is not acting responsibly.

> A **pressure group** is a group of people who work together in order to influence business and government decision-making.

Now test yourself

TESTED

34 List three benefits of increased immigration to the UK.
35 Briefly outline two ways in which consumer lifestyles have changed over recent years.
36 What benefits does online shopping bring for UK producers?
37 How does the stakeholder concept differ from the shareholder concept?
38 What do you understand by corporate social responsibility (CSR) and for what reasons should businesses undertake CSR reporting?
39 What is Carroll's pyramid of corporate social responsibility and what relevance does it have for business?
40 Briefly explain two reasons for the growth in pressure for social responsibility in decision-making.

Answers on p. 210

Analysing the external environment to assess opportunities and threats: the competitive environment

The competitive environment refers to the market structure and the dynamic system in which a business competes. The state of the system is likely to impact on the flexibility of the businesses that operate within it. An individual business's power within the competitive environment can be analysed through the framework provided by Porter's five forces model.

Porter's five forces

The five forces

Michael E. Porter first put forward the **five forces** model in his book *Competitive Strategy: Techniques for Analysing Industries and Competitors* in 1980. It provides a simple but powerful tool for understanding where power lies in an industry, enabling a business to understand more clearly its own competitive strengths. Figure 7.11 illustrates the model.

> Porter's **five forces** model is an analytical tool that provides a framework for analysing the nature of competition within an industry.

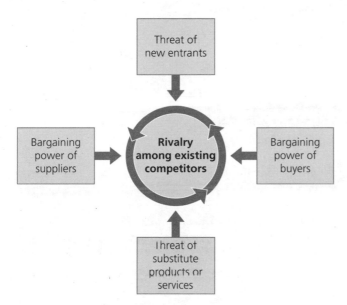

Figure 7.11 Porter's five forces model

Entry threat (barriers to entry)

It is not just existing firms in an industry that may pose a threat; this may also come from new entrants to the industry. Although it should be possible for a firm to enter any market, in practice there may be significant barriers to entry:

- **Cost of entry.** Some industries may involve a high cost to enter, e.g. aircraft manufacture.
- **Government barriers.** Government legislation can sometimes inhibit a new entrant.
- **Patents.** These give the holder a competitive advantage, which may make it more difficult for a new entrant to access a market.

● **Economies of scale.** Whether a new entrant or how quickly a new entrant would benefit from economies would act as a barrier to entry.
● **Access to suppliers.** Whether or not a new entrant has access to suppliers is a potential barrier.

To sum up, a market is likely to be easier to enter where brand loyalty is weak, there is easy access to suppliers, there is common technology available and there is a low threshold to economies of scale.

Buyer power

This relates to the impact the customers have on a business. In general, the fewer the customers and the more the suppliers, the stronger the buyer will be. The relative strength of buyers is summarised in Table 7.5.

Table 7.5 Buyer power

More likely to be powerful	More likely to be weak
● Few buyers and/or buys a significant proportion of output ● Buyers have a credible backward integration threat	● Many buyers ● Producers have a credible forward threat ● There are significant switching costs

Supplier power

Any producing business requires supplies, which necessitates relationships with suppliers. If suppliers are powerful, they are more likely to be able to exert influence on the producing business. The relative strength of suppliers is summarised in Table 7.6.

Table 7.6 Supplier power

More likely to be powerful	More likely to be weak
● A business uses a single supplier ● Credible forward integration threat by suppliers ● Customers are powerful ● High cost to switch suppliers	● There are many competitive suppliers ● Credible backward integration threat by purchasers ● Customers are weak ● Low cost to switch

Rivalry

This refers to the rivalry between firms in the same industry. Rivalry is likely to be high in the following situations:

● **Many firms of similar size.** Rivalry is more likely to be intense where there are a large number of firms all targeting the same customers, as well as if competitors are of a similar size.
● **Low levels of product differentiation.** Customers are more likely to switch between products in this situation, whereas if there is strong brand identification and loyalty rivalry will be less intense.
● **Slow market growth.** This results in increased rivalry as firms fight for market share.
● **High exit costs.** This means firms are more likely to stay and compete as the assets may not be sold easily or transferred to other uses.

The intensity of rivalry is described in various ways, such as cut-throat, aggressive or weak. To gain a competitive advantage, a firm may try to improve differentiation or change its pricing policy.

Substitute threat

A business's ability to achieve profitability is affected by the threat of substitutes, giving consumers the ability to choose an alternative product. A substitute product is one from another industry that offers similar benefits to the one produced by a particular business. For example, bottles provide an alternative to cans, airlines provide an alternative to train companies for domestic travel, e-readers are a substitute for books.

How the five forces shape competitive strategy

As a result of analysis of the five forces, Porter identified three generic strategies that could be implemented by a business to create a competitive advantage:

- **Cost leadership strategy.** This strategy may result from economies of scale, proprietary technology, preferential access to raw materials or other factors. The low-cost producer needs to sustain cost leadership in order retain customers and maintain an above average performance.
- **Differentiation strategy.** With this strategy, the producer seeks to be unique within the industry, giving consumers a reason to buy its product over others. As a result, a higher price can be charged.
- **Focus strategy.** This strategy entails a narrow competitive scope where a particular segment or segments in the market are targeted. The focus on that segment may then be on the basis of either cost leadership or differentiation.

Cost leadership strategy aims to gain a competitive advantage by having the lowest costs in the industry.

Differentiation strategy calls for the development of a product or service which offers unique attributes that are valued and perceived to be different from competitors by customers.

Now test yourself
TESTED

41 List the forces in Porter's five forces model.
42 How does a differentiation strategy differ from a cost leadership strategy?

Answers on p. 210

Analysing strategic options: investment appraisal

An essential element of a successful business is investment, which may be to renew capital equipment and machinery or an investment in new capital stock that will lead to the long-run expansion of the business. Not only will an investment involve risk, but there are always choices to be made because of the size and the limit of the capital investment budget. **Investment appraisal** can help in both reducing risk and enabling the correct choice to be made.

Investment appraisal is an analytical tool used to evaluate the attractiveness (or unattractiveness) of an investment proposal.

Financial methods of assessing an investment
REVISED

It is important that a business estimates the benefits of an investment in financial terms in order to identify the best option and thereby reduce risk. The different appraisal techniques allow an organisation to assess the effects an investment will have on its cash flow. This is achieved by evaluating the costs and benefits of the investment over its useful or expected life span. As a result, the expected net cash flow can be estimated for each year of the investment's life by taking the expected costs from the estimated returns. There are three methods of financial investment appraisal, as shown in this example.

Example

XYZ plc is considering the capital investment of £60,000 in technology, which it estimates will produce the following net cash flows over the next 5 years:

Year	Net cash flow (£)
0	(60,000)
1	24,000
2	21,000
3	20,000
4	18,000
5	18,000

Payback

The **payback** method measures the length of time needed to recover the initial investment (£60,000). In this example it is 2.75 years, which is 2 years and 9 months. This is found by using the following formula:

$$\text{Payback} = \text{number of full years} + \left(\frac{\text{the amount of cost left}}{\text{the revenue generated in the next year}} \right)$$

> The **payback** method calculates the length of time taken to recover the initial outlay of an investment from net income.

After 2 years £45,000 has been generated, leaving a further £15,000 to cover the full £60,000 cost. The net cash flow in year 3 is £20,000. Therefore:

$$\text{Payback} = 2 + \left(\frac{15,000}{20,000} \right)$$

$$= 2.75 \text{ years}$$

This technique is quick and simple but it ignores the timings of cash flows. £1 received today compared to a pound received in 3 or 4 years' time not only carries lower risk but can also be reinvested at a positive rate of return.

Average rate of return

The **average rate of return** calculates the average annual return as a percentage of the initial outlay. There are a number of steps to this calculation.

> The **average rate of return** calculates the average return of an investment and expresses this as a percentage of the initial outlay.

1. The **net return** is calculated by taking the initial outlay (the cost of the investment) from the total net cash flows:

   Net return = total net cash flows – initial outlay

   = 101,000 – 60,000

   = 41,000

2 The **average annual return** is calculated by dividing the net return by the life expectancy:

$$\text{Average annual return} = \frac{\text{net return}}{\text{life expectancy}}$$

$$= \frac{41{,}000}{5}$$

$$= 8{,}200$$

3 The **average rate of return** is found using the following formula:

$$\text{Average annual return} = \frac{\text{average annual return}}{\text{initial outlay}} \times 100$$

$$= \frac{8{,}200}{60{,}000} \times 100$$

$$= 13.66\%$$

This method is useful as it enables percentages to be compared for different investments but, like payback, it ignores the timing of cash flows.

Net present value

Net present value takes into account the timings of cash flows by using a technique called discounting. It converts future cash flows into their present values: in other words, it is showing what cash flows received in future years would be worth today. £100 in your pocket today is much better than the promise of £100 in, say, 3 years' time. This is because, due to inflation, it will be worth less in 3 years' time. Discounting cash flows tells you what that £100 in 3 years' time would be worth to you today. The **discount factor** used depends on a number of things such as current interest rates or the percentage return on an investment expected by shareholders, but this need not concern us here.

Using the example above and a discount factor of 10%, we can work out the net present value for XYZ plc. For each year, this is calculated by multiplying the net cash flow by the discount factor. The net present value for each year is then added together and the cost of the initial investment is deducted to arrive at the overall net present value of £17,609. This is shown in the Table 7.7.

Table 7.7 **Calculating net present value**

Year	Net cash flow (£)	Discount factor	Net present value (£)
0	(60,000)	1.000	(60,000)
1	24,000	0.909	21,816
2	21,000	0.826	17,346
3	20,000	0.751	15,020
4	18,000	0.683	12,249
5	18,000	0.621	11,178
			17,609

> **Net present value** is the current value of future income from an investment.
>
> The **discount factor** is the percentage rate used to calculate the present value of a future cash flow.

> **Exam tip**
>
> If you are asked to calculate net present value in the exam, you will be supplied with the relevant discount factor to use.

> **Typical mistake**
>
> In order to avoid errors in calculating net present value, it is sensible to set out your workings in a table such as the one shown here. Not only will this help with your accuracy, it will also enable the examiner to see clearly what you are doing and identify any mistakes.

If the resulting net present value figure is positive, the investment can be considered worthwhile, and the higher the figure, the better. Although it is more complex to calculate it than payback or average rate of return, it overcomes the problem of the timings of cash flows.

Financial investment appraisal does not eliminate risk completely because it is based on two key assumptions:
- Costs and revenues can be forecast accurately for future years.
- Key variables such as interest rates will not change.

Factors influencing investment decisions

REVISED

When making investment decisions, a business needs to consider a range of factors besides the quantitative analysis undertaken through investment appraisal. These further qualitative factors include:
- **The economy.** Investment might be postponed if economic conditions appear to be deteriorating or fast-tracked if there is a sudden improvement.
- **Competitive environment.** An organisation may need to undertake capital investment in order to keep up with competitors, such as the move by supermarkets into online retailing.
- **Industrial relations.** A business may need to consider the impact on its workforce and the strength of any trade unions when, for example, the introduction of new technology may lead to a reduction in employees.
- **Corporate image and objectives.** Is an investment aligned with the business's corporate objectives and its attitude to corporate social responsibility?
- **Logistics.** This relates to the availability of the machinery or equipment purchased, particularly if there is a choice to be made between different options. A least favourable option from a quantitative standpoint may be taken as if it can be delivered at short notice.

All investment decisions are undertaken in conditions of risk and uncertainty. There is a risk associated with estimating the potential costs and payoffs of an investment, so accuracy is not guaranteed. Estimates are based on past experience, relevant information available and the decision-maker's judgement; the outcome could be vastly different. The difference is because of the uncertainty involved if the decision-maker is unable to foresee the overall consequences of a decision. This may be on account of competitors' actions, unexpected changes in the economy or consumers' tastes and fashions.

The value of sensitivity analysis

REVISED

Sensitivity analysis is a 'what if' tool that can be used to address the problem of uncertainty in a number of situations in business, including investment appraisal. This is achieved by examining the impact of a change in a variable using the payback, average rate of return or net present value method. For example, what if the revenues achieved from an investment were lower than expected? This would result in a reduced net cash flow and a longer payback period, lower average rate of return and lower net present value. The impact of other variables can also be examined, such as using a higher or lower discount factor in a net present value calculation. The benefits of using sensitivity analysis are its simplicity and ease of use, enabling better and more informed decisions to be made.

> **Sensitivity analysis** is an analytical tool (a 'what if' tool) that enables the impact of a change in a variable on a given project or investment to be examined.

Now test yourself

TESTED

43 List three methods of investment appraisal.
44 Calculate the payback for capital equipment that costs £100,000 and generates a positive net cash flow of £12,500 each year.
45 What is the average rate of return for capital equipment that generates a total cumulative net cash flow over a period of 4 years of £1m and costs £2m to purchase?
46 What do you understand by the term 'discount factor'?
47 Why might net present value be considered a better method of investment appraisal than payback or average rate of return?
48 Explain two qualitative factors that could influence an investment decision.
49 Why does sensitivity analysis allow a more informed decision to be made?

Answers on p. 211

Exam practice

XYZ plc

Due to increasing demand in all markets, XYZ plc needs to expand its production facilities. Its luxury products are extremely popular within its main European market and there is a small but fast-growing market in the Far East, especially China. As a result, it is looking at two propositions: expand its current factory or build a new plant in China in order to be well placed to take advantage of that fast-growing market. Lower production costs mean that the Chinese plant could also be used to satisfy demand in its other markets. The cost and net annual cash flows for the two options are outlined in the following table.

Year	Expand existing factory (£)	Build new factory in China (£)
0	2,500,000	4,000,000
1	500,000	1,000,000
2	1,000,000	1,500,000
3	1,000,000	1,500,000
4	1,000,000	2,000,000
5	1,000,000	2,500,000

However, the directors are undecided over which option to choose. XYZ plc is very much a 'British' business that prides itself on the quality of its products. It also has an experienced, skilled and loyal workforce and a reputation for looking after that workforce.

Discount factor at 10%:

Year 1: 0.909
Year 2: 0.826
Year 3: 0.751
Year 4: 0.683
Year 5: 0.621

Questions

c Calculate payback, average rate of return and net present value for the two options and state which is the best option from a financial perspective. [9]
d To what extent do you believe financial factors should be the most important consideration in XYZ plc's decision? [16]

Essay

US multinational companies Apple and Amazon have responded to technological change by producing new products that incorporate the latest technology. Do you think this is the best way for businesses to respond to changes in technology? Justify your answer with reference to Apple/Amazon or any other business with which you are familiar. [25]

Answers and quick quiz 7B online

ONLINE

Summary

You should now have an understanding of all the points below.

Mission, corporate objectives and strategy

- influences on the mission of a business
- internal and external influences on corporate objectives and decisions including pressure for short termism, business ownership, the external and internal environment
- the links between mission, corporate objectives and strategy, and the distinction between strategy and tactics
- the impact of strategic decision-making on functional decision-making
- the value of SWOT analysis

Internal strengths and weaknesses: financial ratio analysis

- how to assess the financial performance of a business using balance sheets, income statements and the following financial ratios: profitability (return on capital employed), liquidity (current ratio), gearing and efficiency ratios (payables days, receivables days and inventory turnover)
- the value of financial ratios when assessing performance including the importance of analysis over time and comparison with other businesses

Internal strengths and weaknesses: overall performance

- how to analyse data other than financial statements to assess the strengths and weaknesses of a business including operations, human resource and marketing data; this should be done over time and in comparison with other businesses

- the importance of core competencies
- assessing short- and long-term performance
- the value of different measures of assessing business performance including Kaplan and Norton's Balanced Scorecard model and Elkington's Triple Bottom Line (Profit, People and Planet)

External opportunities and threats: political and legal change

- the impact of changes in the political and legal environment on strategic and functional decision-making
- the political and legal environment including a broad understanding of the scope and effects of UK and EU law related to competition, the labour market and environmental legislation
- the impact of UK and EU government policy related to enterprise, the role of regulators, infrastructure, the environment and international trade

External opportunities and threats: economic change

- the impact of changes in the UK and the global economic environment on strategic and functional decision-making
- relevant economic factors including GDP, taxation, exchange rates, inflation, fiscal and monetary policy and more open trade v protectionism
- relevant economic data including an ability to interpret any changes for the UK, EU and globally and to consider the implications of such changes for business
- reasons for and the importance of greater globalisation of business
- the importance of emerging economies for business

External opportunities and threats: social and technological

- the impact of the social and technological environment on strategic and functional decision-making
- social changes including demographic and population movements, urbanisation and migration, changes in consumer lifestyle and buying behaviour, and the growth of online business
- the social environment including corporate social responsibility (CSR) and the reasons for and against it, the difference between the stakeholder and shareholder concepts, and Carroll's corporate social responsibility pyramid
- technological change including the impact of such change on the functional areas and strategy
- the pressures for socially responsible behaviour

External opportunities and threats: the competitive environment

- Porter's five forces (entry threat/barriers to entry, buyer power, supplier power, rivalry and substitute threat), how and why these might change and the implications of these forces for strategic and functional decision-making and profit
- consideration should be given to how these five forces shape competitive strategy

Analysing strategic options: investment appraisal

- financial methods of assessing investment including the calculation and interpretation of payback, average rate of return and net present value
- factors influencing investment decisions including investment criteria, non-financial factors, risk and uncertainty
- the value of sensitivity analysis

8 Choosing strategic direction

Strategic direction: choosing which markets to compete in and what products to offer

Strategic direction relates to a course of action that it is hoped will lead to the achievement of the goals and mission of an organisation. This involves decisions about which markets to operate in and what products to offer.

> **Strategic direction** refers to a course of action or plan that it is hoped will lead to the achievement of long-term goals.

Factors influencing which markets to compete in and which products to offer

When an organisation undertakes a SWOT analysis, it examines the internal strengths and weaknesses and external opportunities and threats. This analysis can be used in choosing the organisation's strategic direction, seeking to build on its strengths or develop any opportunities identified. Alternatively, it may wish to address any weaknesses or threats. The choice of strategic direction can be further analysed using the **Ansoff matrix**.

> **Ansoff's matrix** is a strategic or marketing planning tool that links a business's marketing strategy with its general strategic direction.

The Ansoff matrix

Created by Igor Ansoff and first published in 1957, this matrix (Figure 8.1) was designed to help managers consider how to grow their business through existing or new markets and existing or new products. The matrix identifies four strategies:

- **Market penetration:** increased market share in existing markets achieved by selling more products to either existing customers or new customers.
- **Market development:** involves finding new markets for existing products using market research and segmentation to identify new groups of customers.
- **New product development:** involves producing new products for existing markets.
- **Diversification:** the most risky strategy, involving new products in new areas.

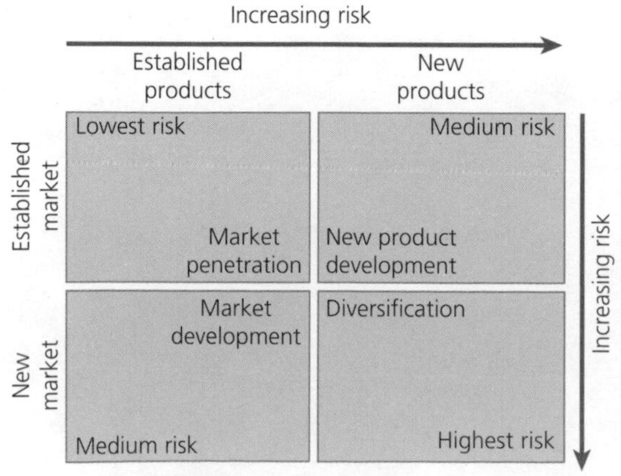

Figure 8.1 The Ansoff matrix

The following factors are likely to have an impact on the choice of strategic direction:

- **Objectives and attitude to risk.** Some organisations may be risk averse and therefore pursue strategies that are more conservative, focusing on what they know and steady growth rather than adopting a more risky strategy that offers fast growth.
- **Cost.** The budget available is likely to have an impact on strategic direction, which will be analysed in relation to the expected returns in a **cost–benefit analysis**.
- **Barriers to entry.** Some markets may have high barriers to entry, making entry very difficult. This might be in the form of tariffs, quotas and regulations. Access to these markets might be enabled by strategies involving setting up production facilities in the market, collaboration with existing businesses or takeover of existing businesses within the market.
- **Competitors' actions.** Organisations will seek proactive strategies to enable them to stay ahead of competitors, although sometimes they will need to be reactive, responding to competitors.
- **Ethics involved.** With greater attention attached to corporate social responsibility, the ethics involved may be an important consideration.

> A **cost–benefit analysis** is a process by which business decisions can be analysed, where the benefits and costs are quantified and then the costs subtracted from the benefits.

Strategic decisions are medium- to long-term decisions that require detailed analysis in order to guide an organisation on the right strategic direction. Failure to achieve this can be costly, as demonstrated by Kodak. It invented the first digital camera in 1975, but instead of marketing the technology it held back for fear of damaging its film business.

The reasons for choosing and the value of different options for strategic direction

REVISED

The reasons for and value of choosing the four strategies suggested by Ansoff are as follows.

Market penetration (existing products in existing markets)

This strategy can be implemented quickly with limited risk. It avoids the commitment in terms of the expense and time involved in developing new products or investigating and analysing unfamiliar markets. However, it does require there to be the potential for growth within the market, otherwise if the market is saturated heavy promotion may be needed to entice customers away from competitors.

Market development (existing products, new markets)

This is a good strategy for a business with a well-established brand name such as Starbucks or Coca-Cola. The product is already proven and the business remains focused on its core function, which should make entry to new markets easier. It avoids the development of new products, which can be costly. However, such a strategy depends on markets being accessible and could be costly if modifications are required to suit the new market.

New product development (new products, existing markets)

This strategy is a good choice for an organisation that has a strong brand name, such as Virgin or Apple. Businesses adopting this strategy benefit from knowing their customer base, making market research and promotion easier. Such a strategy is required if an existing product has become obsolete and may also be used if there is potential for new segments of the market to be targeted or if complementary products can be produced. There is also the possibility of new innovative products being developed for the market, as Apple has done with its products. However, this approach may involve producing and selling products it has limited expertise with, and where there may be already established producers.

Diversification (new products, new markets)

This might be related diversification (e.g. an alcoholic drinks business moving into soft drinks) or unrelated diversification (where there is no previous industry experience). This strategy may be chosen if the existing industry is in decline or has become saturated. As a result, it can enable further growth for a business and spread risk. However, it does involve greater risk as a business is moving into an area in which it has no experience.

> **Typical mistake**
>
> Diversification is rightly considered the most risky strategy, but do not dismiss such a strategy without studying all other information. For some businesses, diversification has been hugely successful.

> **Now test yourself**   TESTED ☐
>
> 1 What do you understand by the term 'strategic direction'?
> 2 List four factors that might affect strategic direction.
> 3 Distinguish between market and product development in the Ansoff matrix.
> 4 For what reasons might a business choose a strategy of diversification?
>
> **Answers on p. 211**

> **Exam tip**
>
> Remember that all strategies have some risk and that the degree of risk varies according to the circumstance of the business involved. Any judgement made needs to be set in the context of the business as a whole, not just the strategy adopted.

Strategic positioning: choosing how to compete

Once the strategic direction of an organisation has been determined, the business needs to decide how it wishes to be perceived in the market. This is referred to as its **strategic positioning** and it influences how it competes in terms of benefits and price.

> The **strategic positioning** of a business relates to how that business is perceived relative to other businesses in the same industry.

How to compete in terms of benefits and price   REVISED ☐

In many markets customers are faced with a tremendous amount of choice. It is the job of individual companies within the market to find their competitive edge and position in the market in order to meet customer needs better than the next company. How companies do this is a crucial question and the specification suggests that strategic positioning and how to compete are examined in terms of two models: Porter's three generic strategies of low cost, differentiation and focus strategies and Bowman's strategic clock.

Exam practice answers and quick quizzes at **www.hoddereducation.co.uk/myrevisionnotes**

Porter's generic strategies

Porter's generic strategies are ways of gaining a competitive advantage that can be applied to all industries and organisations. The three strategies are illustrated in Figure 8.2.

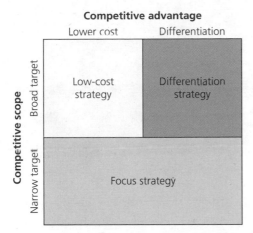

Figure 8.2 Porter's generic strategies

Low-cost strategy

This is not just having low costs but being the leader in terms of cost in your industry. In pursuing this strategy, an organisation needs to be confident it can maintain its leadership. It must have a sustainable low-cost base and access to capital to invest in technology that can further reduce costs.

Differentiation strategy

This involves making products different from and more attractive than your competitors. Methods of achieving this may be through quality, durability, functionality, customer service or a brand image that is valued by customers. A successful differentiation strategy requires research and development, innovation and effective sales and marketing.

Focus strategy

With a focus strategy, an organisation focuses on a particular niche in the market. However, within that niche it is still important to decide how to achieve a competitive advantage and whether a low-cost or differentiation strategy will be chosen. For example, Baxters soups focuses on a small segment of the soup market, providing highly differentiated products. It is this focus that makes Baxters soup stand out; without it, the business would be stuck in the middle, heading for failure.

Bowman's strategic clock

Developed in 1996 by Cliff Bowman and David Faulkner, **Bowman's strategic clock** looks at Porter's generic strategies in a different way. Price is used as a variable rather than cost, and rather than three strategic positions it identifies eight according to varying levels of price and value, as well as identifying the likelihood of success of each strategy. This is illustrated in Figure 8.3.

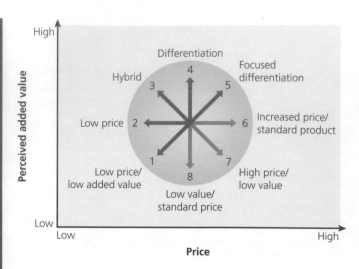

Figure 8.3 Bowman's strategic clock

The eight positions on the clock are outlined below:

1 **Low price/low added value.** Offers bargain basement — not a popular choice as there is a lack of differentiated value and profit is achieved only by selling high volume (e.g. Poundland).

2 **Low price.** Companies operating in this area are low–cost leaders selling everyday products on low margins but in high volume (e.g. Aldi and Lidl).

3 **Hybrid (moderate price/moderate differentiation).** Offers products at a low cost but a higher perceived value and gains a reputation and consumer loyalty for fair prices and reasonable goods (e.g. IKEA).

4 **Differentiation.** Offers customers high perceived value at a reasonable price. Branding is important with this strategy as it allows companies to become synonymous with quality and can enable higher prices to be charged (e.g. Nike, BMW).

5 **Focused differentiation.** Offers high perceived value and price, such as where markets are highly targeted and margins are high, as with designer products (e.g. Gucci, Armani and Rolex).

6 **Increased price/standard product.** This can only be a short-term strategy as a premium price cannot be justified in a competitive market and will not survive.

7 **High price/low value.** A classic monopoly position that fortunately for consumers is unlikely to exist in a market economy.

8 **Low value/standard price.** Such a strategy involves a business losing sales.

In situations where price is greater than the perceived value, there are always competitors offering better-quality products at lower prices, making positions 6, 7 and 8 unviable as competitive strategies.

By looking at different combinations of price and perceived value, it is possible to identify and choose a position of competitive advantage. This can be useful and certainly helps in the understanding of how companies compete in the market place. Compared to Porter's generic strategies, however, Bowman's strategic clock is overcomplicated and little used in business today.

> **Exam tip**
>
> Porter and Bowman are useful in strategic decision-making. Porter is a good starting point, but once a choice has been made there are a number of options available and Bowman enables these options to be looked at in more detail.

Influences on the choice of a positioning strategy

REVISED

Where a business chooses to position itself is influenced by a number of factors:

- **The business itself.** This relates to the size, skills, assets and culture of the business and its resulting strengths, what it is good at, what it is known for and where it wishes to go.
- **The competition.** This relates to the strengths and weaknesses of competitors. Customer perception of their value brand and quality may influence positioning, e.g. Aldi and Lidl are positioned in order to appear different from Tesco and Asda.
- **Customer.** This relates to customer needs and current trends and may be analysed in terms of existing and potential customers, demographics or satisfaction and brand perception.
- **External environment.** This includes political and economic factors.

The value of different strategic positioning strategies

REVISED

The correct positioning of a product or service is essential to the generation of revenue and profit. As a result, knowledge of different positioning strategies has some value. Although the model produced by Bowman is complex, it gives an insight into the possibilities available to a business in terms of price and perceived value. Although little used by businesses today, it enables students to more easily understand positioning. Porter's generic strategies of low cost versus differentiation are perhaps easier to use and may provide a better insight into the business world. However, the message that comes from both these models is that any business needs to treat positioning seriously, ensuring that the strategy chosen fits clearly with its mission and objectives and with how consumers perceive the organisation and their expectations.

> **Exam tip**
>
> Positioning strategies can be linked to market mapping. Identifying a particular gap in the market leads to the correct positioning strategy being adopted.

The benefits of having a competitive advantage

REVISED

A competitive advantage is gained by an organisation when it provides the same value as its competitors but at a lower price, or charges a higher price than competitors due to greater value through differentiation. This has a number of benefits for the organisation:

- **Sales:** a competitive advantage should lead to greater sales.
- **Brand loyalty:** this should be achieved due to the competitive advantage.
- **Profit:** this could be achieved through higher volume in a cost leadership strategy or from higher margins in a differentiation strategy
- **Shareholder value:** if the three benefits above are achieved, greater shareholder value is generated.

However, these benefits are dependent on having a competitive advantage that is not easy for competitors to duplicate or beat: in other words, it needs to be sustainable. As a result, it may be dependent on an organisation's willingness and ability to invest in research and development in order to innovate products and production processes, as well as investing in the skills and development of its workforce and marketing processes.

The difficulties of maintaining a competitive advantage

Maintaining a sustainable competitive advantage is a challenge faced by all organisations and one that some, such as Kodak, Nokia and BlackBerry, have failed to achieve. Difficulties include:

- **Developments in technology.** An organisation may fail to see or embrace new technologies, e.g. Blockbuster failed to foresee the advent of Netflix and Kodak failed to embrace digital technologies.
- **Investment.** Investment in new plant and equipment as well as research and development is expensive, and a failure to constantly update products and processes could lead to cost and differentiation advantages being lost.
- **Human resources.** Having a highly skilled and loyal workforce provides advantages, but if this is not maintained any competitive advantage might be lost. This might also be true of the leadership of an organisation, which can sometimes lose direction when there is a change.
- **Financial constraints.** These can lead to a lack of investment.
- **Short termism.** A focus on short-term profit could lead to a lack of focus on sustaining a long-term competitive advantage.

Now test yourself

5 What do you understand by the term 'strategic positioning'?
6 With the use of an example, explain what is meant by a low-cost strategy.
7 In Porter's generic strategies, distinguish between a differentiation and a focus strategy.
8 Why are positions 6, 7 and 8 on Bowman's strategic clock unlikely to be adopted?
9 Explain the importance to a business of having a competitive advantage.
10 Identify three reasons why it may be difficult to maintain a competitive advantage.

Answers on p. 211

Exam practice

Flyfast plc

After 10 years of rising profit, Flyfast plc, the no-frills budget airline, has just announced a significant and worrying fall in profit. Up to now its core competencies of low price and a cost-conscious culture have served the company and its shareholders well. However, for a number of years the City has been questioning the sustainability of its growing profit levels, with some now even questioning the long-term future of the business.

Although economic conditions have not been great, other budget airlines have been able to post modest increases in profit. As a result, Flyfast's directors were beginning to question the strategic position of the business. Were its low-price, cost-conscious competencies beginning to be seen as low price and low value? It is all very well being no-frills, but other budget airlines were perhaps better at looking after their customers. A change in strategic direction appeared to be on the cards and the next board meeting was likely to be an interesting one.

Questions

a Analyse how Flyfast's core competencies enabled it to both enter and achieve 10 years of rising profit. [9]
b Evaluate the extent to which Flyfast needs to change its strategic positioning. [16]

Answers and quick quiz 8 online

Summary

You should now have an understanding of all the points below.

Strategic direction: choosing which markets to compete in and what products to offer

- the factors influencing which markets to compete in and which products to offer
- the Ansoff matrix and the value of market penetration, market development, new product development and diversification
- the reasons for choosing and value of different options for strategic direction

Strategic positioning: choosing how to compete

- how to compete in terms of benefits and price including the positioning models of Porter (low cost, differentiation and focus strategy) and Bowman (strategic clock)
- influences on the choice of positioning strategy
- the value of different strategic positioning strategies
- the benefits of having a competitive advantage
- the difficulties of maintaining a competitive advantage

9 Strategic methods: how to pursue strategies

Assessing a change in scale

A change in scale is a change in the size of a business. We most often think of this in terms of businesses growing, but it is also possible for businesses to shrink, usually because of a strategy of **retrenchment**.

The reasons why businesses grow or retrench

REVISED

> **Retrenchment** is a strategy used by a business to reduce its overall size or diversity of operations.

Growth may be achieved either internally (organically) or externally through **takeovers** or **mergers**. Growth is an important objective and there are a number of reasons for this:

- **Increased profit.** Growth brings with it increased sales and revenue and hopefully profit. This is likely to lead to an increase in share price and greater returns to shareholders. In turn, this leads to positive media attention and greater security for the CEO and board members.
- **Survival.** Sometimes growth is essential for the survival of a business. By remaining small, a business may not be able to benefit from economies of scale, resulting in high costs and a lack of competitiveness. Small businesses could more easily be taken over by larger rivals.
- **Reduce risk.** Growth in the form of diversification or moving into new markets can be used to reduce risk.
- **Increase market share.** Growth in market share may give a business a more dominant position in the market, thereby giving it greater power over both suppliers and perhaps prices.

> **Takeovers**, also known as acquisitions, are where one business acquires control of the assets of another business either by a formal offer that is accepted (a friendly takeover) or by the purchase of a controlling interest of shares (a hostile takeover).
>
> **Mergers** are where two or more businesses join together by mutual consent.

Retrenchment is the opposite of growth and means cutting down or reducing the size of a business, usually with the aim of becoming a more financially stable business. It is likely to involve job losses and reductions in output and capacity. Some areas of the business may be sold off or demerged. There are a number of reasons why a business might pursue a strategy of retrenchment:

- **Changes in the market.** This might be because of changes in taste and fashion, technological development or the arrival of new more competitive businesses.
- **Failed takeover.** It is not unusual for a takeover to fail and for a business to demerge part or all of the business taken over.
- **Economic downturn.** Sometimes an economic downturn leads to a business retrenching in order to better cope with the changed economic environment.

> **Exam tip**
>
> Sometimes a business might retrench in order to focus more closely on core competencies, so make sure you read carefully any case study material in an exam to see if this is the case.

The difference between organic and external growth

Organic growth (or internal growth) is when an organisation expands by selling more of its existing products/services or develops new products/services. It may be achieved by targeting a wider market or moving into new markets. This type of growth is often financed from retained profit and, as a result, tends to be slower and less risky than external growth.

External growth is achieved through takeovers or mergers. It may also be termed as growth by acquisition or integration. This type of growth is much quicker than internal growth, but it brings much greater risk on account of the problems of integrating two different businesses.

How to manage and overcome the problems of growth or retrenchment

Issues with growth

Economies of scale

Economies of scale are the reduction in unit costs as a result of increased size. If a business can increase output from existing plant and equipment without further investment in fixed costs, the unit cost of production declines as the fixed costs are spread over more units of output. Economies of scale also occur in other areas such as finance, technical, purchasing and managerial:

> **Economies of scale** are the proportionate saving in costs as a result of an increase in the size of an operating unit.

- Financial economies stem from the fact that financial institutions see bigger businesses as a safer bet because of their greater assets, and as a result they are more willing to lend and often at lower interest rates.
- Technical economies stem from the fact that larger businesses are more able to invest in technology, they are more likely to have the finance to do so and they can use the technology more efficiently and productively, producing a greater return on investment.
- Purchasing economies result from the greater power that can be exerted by large businesses over suppliers.
- Managerial economies result when a business grows as there is greater scope to employ specialists in all parts of the business.

Economies of scope

Economies of scope are the reduction of unit costs because of producing a wider variety of goods and services. This may result from the joint use of production facilities and other inputs, joint marketing or administration, or a particular product might provide a by-product, e.g. a bread manufacturer could also produce sandwiches. Cadbury, Kleenex and Procter & Gamble are all examples of companies that benefit from economies of scope because of the wide range of products they produce.

> **Economies of scope** are the proportionate saving gained by producing two or more distinct products, when the cost of doing so is less than that of producing each separately.

Diseconomies of scale

Despite the benefits, growth can result in problems for a business, such as **diseconomies of scale**. This is when a business grows so large that costs per unit increase. Diseconomies may occur because of the following reasons:

- **Poor communication.** Larger firms often face communication problems because of the greater complexity involving more people, layers, divisions, etc. This may slow the whole decision-making process and result in a less responsive and flexible business. It may be a big problem in markets where tastes and fashion change regularly or in industries where technology is subject to rapid change.
- **Lack of control and coordination.** A larger business is more complex, making it harder to monitor and making coordination between departments and divisions increasingly difficult.
- **Alienation of the workforce.** The workforce of larger businesses can sometimes become alienated because of job losses as a result of greater investment in technology, or it may stem from poor communication and a feeling of no longer being valued. Whatever the cause, workers become less engaged and motivated, leading to lower productivity and increasing unit costs.

Diseconomies of scale refer to a situation where economies of scale no longer occur and unit costs begin to increase rather than decrease.

The experience curve

The Boston Consulting Group in the mid 1960s developed **the experience curve** when they noted that unit costs of production of a semi-conductor manufacturer fell by 25% for each doubling of volume produced. Put simply, the more often a task is performed, the lower the cost of performing it. This is because of the greater experience of those performing the task. This then implies that, as a business gets bigger, it should gain a competitive cost advantage. The experience curve can therefore be linked to a cost leadership strategy.

The experience curve is the idea that the more you do something, the better you get at it, enabling quicker and cheaper production.

Exam tip

Make sure you have a clear understanding of economies of scale, economies of scope and the experience curve so that they can be correctly applied in an exam.

Overtrading

A further problem of growth is **overtrading**, which may occur when a business grows too quickly. Cash often has to leave the business before more cash comes in — not only everyday costs such as paying wages but also the cost of expansion itself — and this can quickly lead to liquidity problems.

Synergy

Organisations that undertake external growth expect to achieve synergy from the combination of two businesses. **Synergy** is the idea that 2 + 2 = 5 — in other words, the cost savings resulting from the combination of two businesses should lead to greater profit.

Overtrading is the situation where a business grows too quickly, undertaking more business than its working capital can cope with.

Synergy is the idea that the value and performance of two businesses combined will be greater than the sum of the two parts.

Greiner's model of growth

Growth needs to be managed carefully to avoid problems occurring, and if growth is an important objective, it is important to have a scalable management model that evolves and develops with the business. This can be illustrated by **Greiner's model of growth**.

In Figure 9.1, the horizontal axis shows the age of the business and the vertical axis gives the business size. As a company grows and develops, it goes through a series of phases, with each one bringing its own problems:

Greiner's model of growth describes different phases of a business's growth and provides a framework to help understand different organisational structures and coordination methods.

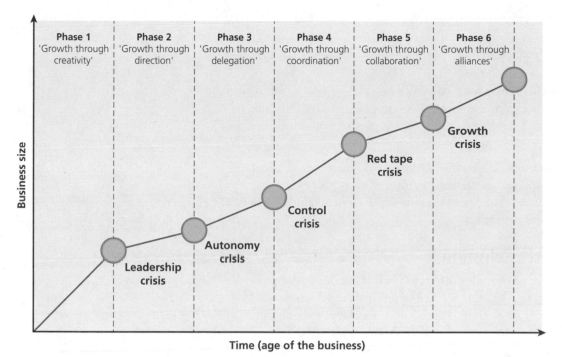

Figure 9.1 Greiner's model of growth

- **Phase 1: Growth through creativity.** When companies first form, they are driven by a creative force and do whatever is needed to make things work. There are likely to be few workers and initially the founder can cope with the demands. However, as the company grows, the increasing complexities present challenges and a leadership crisis that requires a much clearer direction to be formulated with distinct management roles.
- **Phase 2: Growth through direction.** As a result of the leadership crisis, professional managers are brought in who know more about planning and tactics and can help with strategic thinking. Although there may be some separation of roles such as budgeting and marketing, this may not yet be as separate departments. As the company continues to expand with more employees and more markets, there is more pressure from managers for greater autonomy and control over individual areas of the business.
- **Phase 3: Growth through delegation.** The response to the autonomy crisis is to create a greater structure with a clear hierarchy, including individual departments and divisions with their own managers who have greater autonomy. In this phase, middle managers also begin to appear. As delegation gets more complex in a growing business, there may arise a control problem where senior managers at the top do not know what is really going on at the bottom of the organisation and lose touch and control of the everyday operations
- **Phase 4: Growth through coordination.** To try to solve these control problems, greater effort is put into reporting and communicating about all aspects of the business. This becomes centralised with clear budgets and targets, but can become burdensome and bureaucratic with too much paperwork causing a crisis of red tape.
- **Phase 5: Growth through collaboration.** The business now tries to encourage greater collaboration, bureaucracy is simplified and there is a greater focus on organisational goals. Structures may be implemented to enable managers to move around the business and reward systems

may be formed to promote team and organisational success rather than individual performance. Although this may be better than previous forms, it presents a growth crisis, i.e. how to grow further without overloading the current system.

● **Phase 6: Growth through alliances.** The final stage is to address the problem of growing internally by looking externally. This may be through mergers or takeovers or by forming partnerships and alliances with businesses.

Greiner through his model illustrates the need for businesses to adapt and evolve as they grow. Although the timing of each phase may vary, a business needs to expect and prepare for each crisis in order to successfully manage its growth.

Issues with retrenchment

Managing retrenchment provides different challenges. It typically involves downsizing, resulting in inevitable job losses and redundancy, which leads to the biggest potential problem of workforce alienation. However, the key to a good outcome is the development of a retrenchment procedure that achieves objectives while minimising workforce impact. This requires careful consideration, with early consultation and collaboration with trade unions and worker representatives in order minimise potential issues.

The impact of growth or retrenchment on the functional areas of business

REVISED

Both growth and retrenchment impact on decision-making in the functional areas of a business:

● **Marketing.** This relates to decisions regarding changing marketing objectives in a growing or declining market and the impact on the marketing mix.
● **Finance.** This may include decisions regarding the finance of growth in terms of both working capital and capital investment. Alternatively, it might relate to achieving financial stability in a declining market, including the finance of redundancy payments.
● **Operations.** Whether increasing or decreasing scale, the impact here is likely to be in relation to unit costs, capacity and how to use technology.
● **Human resources.** Again, whether increasing or decreasing scale, the impact of a change in size is likely to be in relation to organisational structure and responsibilities, the need for recruitment, selection and training as well as how to approach redundancies.

Assessing methods and types of growth

REVISED

Mergers and takeovers

Mergers occur when two or more businesses agree to join together, whereas takeovers are when one business gains control of another business through the purchase of a controlling interest. Takeovers are usually hostile in nature and can be met with resistance. The different types of mergers and takeovers are shown in Figure 9.2.

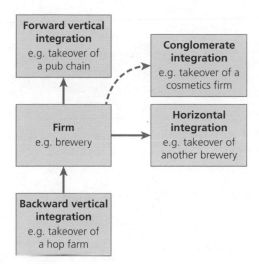

Figure 9.2 Types of mergers and takeovers

- **Vertical.** This is when a business merges or takes over another business in the same production chain but at a different stage. This could be an earlier stage (backward vertical integration) or a later stage (forward vertical integration). Backward results in greater control over suppliers and prices whereas forward helps guarantee access to markets. Using the brewery example, taking over a hop farm is backward and gaining control of a series of public houses is forward. One reason for undertaking a backward vertical merger is that it gives control over supplies. However, sometimes *more* control — particularly over quality and price — can be exercised when not owning the supplier, especially if the business is a major customer of the supplier.
- **Horizontal.** This is when a business merges with or takes over another in the same stage of the same production chain. It results in a larger presence and perhaps greater power in the market, e.g. a brewery merges or takes over another brewery.
- **Conglomerate.** This occurs when a business merges or takes over a firm in a totally unrelated business area. It is also described as diversification and an example is a brewery taking over a cosmetics business.

Businesses undertake mergers and takeovers because they expect to achieve some synergy, but in practice this is often not achieved and it is estimated that 65% fail to benefit the acquiring business. Failure may occur for a number of reasons:
- an over-optimistic assessment of the benefits
- a lack of detailed research
- resistance from employees
- clashes of culture
- a lack of experience and expertise in the case of conglomerate mergers and takeovers
- financial pressures including paying too high a price

Ventures

A method of combining two businesses without undertaking a full takeover or merger is to form a **joint venture** with another business. This is where two separate organisations work together and agree to pool resources for the purpose of achieving a specific task. For a number of businesses, such as Jaguar Land Rover and Tesco, this has provided easier access to emerging markets. It enables the established business to benefit from the local knowledge and expertise of a business already in the market.

> A **joint venture** is a business arrangement where two or more businesses agree to pool their resources for the accomplishment of a specific task.

Franchising

Franchising is a form of growth that enables a business to grow relatively quickly. It occurs where an existing business (the franchisor) grants the right for another party (the franchisee) to use its trade name and sell its products or services. The franchisee usually has to pay an upfront fee and a percentage of sales revenue as a royalty each year. However, the franchisee benefits from a recognised trade name, together with help setting up and ongoing promotion and upgrading of products. For the franchisor this method of growth has the following benefits:

- It is relatively quick.
- Finance is provided by the franchisee.
- The franchisee is likely to be highly motivated.
- The organisational structure is less complex.

> **Franchising** is a method of growth where an existing business (the franchisor) grants another party (the franchisee) the right to use its trade name and sell its products or services.

Now test yourself

TESTED

1 Identify three reasons why businesses grow.
2 What do you understand by the term 'synergy'?
3 Briefly explain why a business might undertake a strategy of retrenchment.
4 With the use of an example, describe what is meant by the term 'economies of scope'.
5 How does the experience curve differ from economies of scale?
6 Distinguish between organic and external growth.
7 List three reasons for diseconomies of scale occurring.
8 Describe briefly Greiner's model of growth.
9 Distinguish between horizontal, vertical and conglomerate mergers and takeovers.
10 Identify three reasons why a business might undertake franchising as a form of growth.

Answers on pp. 211–212

Assessing innovation

Innovation refers to the creation of more effective processes, products and ideas, and can increase the probability of a business succeeding. An innovative business is likely to have better products and more efficient processes.

> **Innovation** is the process of converting an invention into a good, service or process that creates value for a business.

The pressures for innovation

REVISED

When examining innovation, it is possible to distinguish between product innovation (the creation of new or improved products) and process innovation (the development of new ways of making or providing a product or service). The world we live in is constantly changing and consumers have come to expect new products, new services and new ways of doing things. The competitive market environment means businesses are looking for more efficient ways of producing and providing goods and services, resulting in new processes and a greater use of technology in production. As a result, it is necessary for businesses to undertake research and development (R&D). The budget set aside for R&D varies from industry to industry, with computing, electronics and pharmaceuticals having by far the biggest budgets in the UK.

The pressures for change include the following:

- **Survival.** There are a number of examples of companies that have fallen on hard times because of a failure to innovate, such as BlackBerry, Nokia and Kodak. Apple must continue to innovate to maintain market share and even chocolate manufacturers are looking for new products and processes to maintain their competitive position.
- **Shareholders and the City.** Businesses are under pressure from shareholders and City analysts to perform well in order to increase revenues and profit. Innovation is one way of achieving this.
- **Competitive environment.** The market economy means competition and, in order to stay ahead of competitors and maintain and perhaps improve market share, innovation is essential.
- **Social and ethical.** Pressures for change and innovation may come from a change in social attitudes, particularly with regard to the environment.

The value of innovation

Innovation results in a number of benefits for a business:

- **Competitive advantage.** An innovative business is likely to achieve a competitive advantage, enabling it to maintain competitiveness or capture and increase market share.
- **Aligned to strategic positioning.** Innovation is likely to be aligned to and reinforce strategic positioning, whether this is a differentiation or low-cost strategy.
- **Stakeholder value.** Innovation can result in greater value for stakeholders through greater returns for shareholders, better value for customers and an improved environmental position.

However, despite its value, innovation is not without its challenges. It comes with a high cost and a high risk. For every success there are untold failures and the pressures of short termism can deter some CEOs from making the necessary investment in R&D.

The ways of becoming an innovative organisation

Innovative organisations usually have an environment or culture that fosters innovation. In such an environment, innovation is likely to be promoted as an organisational value and there will be an acceptance that some ideas will fail. Finance will be available for innovation and there will be encouragement for employees to 'think outside the box' and share ideas. This type of culture inevitably starts from the top of the organisation and requires leadership that embraces innovation and the recruitment of employees who have talent and share the organisation's values. Organisations such as Google and Apple have this type of culture, but for those that do not, the following may help in becoming innovative.

Kaizen

Originating in Japan, **Kaizen** is the philosophy and practice of continuous improvement. It focuses on making continuous small improvements that help keep a business at the top of its field. This philosophy involves everyone in the business from the top down and urges all to strive for improvement. Kaizen recognises there is always room for improvement and wants workers to be confident about offering suggestions. It relies on teamwork and quality circles, and worker groups meet and work together to solve problems and come up with innovative changes.

> **Kaizen** is a Japanese business philosophy of continuous improvement in working practices and efficiency.

> **Exam tip**
>
> As well as bringing innovation, the introduction of Kaizen is likely to lead to a more motivated and engaged workforce with improved overall performance.

Research and development

R&D is at the heart of innovation: it is about developing new products and processes. The amount spent on R&D varies from industry to industry and business to business, but there is no doubt it is essential for new product development.

> **Typical mistake**
>
> Do not assume that just because a business spends a large amount on R&D it is more innovative than a business with a smaller budget. What is key is how well the budget is spent and the success rate in developing new products and processes.

> **Typical mistake**
>
> Students often confuse research and development (R&D) with market research, but they are two completely separate business areas.

Intrapreneurship

Entrepreneurs are individuals who are prepared to take the risk of developing their own ideas as a business. **Intrapreneurship** is the act of behaving like an entrepreneur but within an existing business organisation. By embracing an intrapreneurial approach, a business can tap into the entrepreneurial talent of its workforce and thereby stimulate innovation.

Benchmarking

Benchmarking is a tool for continuous improvement. It is the process of measuring the performance of an organisation against the best in an industry (best practices). It means learning from others, using their knowledge and experience to improve. The benefits of benchmarking are that it is a more efficient, cost-effective and quicker way of making improvements. However, it is not about copying other organisations; it is about adapting the best practices to the needs, culture and systems of your organisation in order to establish the best way of doing things.

> **Intrapreneurship** is the practice of entrepreneurship that exists within an established business.
>
> **Benchmarking** is a strategic and analytical process of continuously measuring an organisation's products, services and practices against a recognised leader.

> **Exam tip**
>
> Kaizen and intrapreneurship are both part of the culture of an individual business.

How to protect innovation and intellectual property

REVISED

Intellectual property (IP) is an intangible asset belonging to the owner or organisation. It may be in the form of inventions, symbols, artistic or literary work and stems from innovation. Having created intellectual property, it is important to protect it so that others cannot simply copy and benefit from it. Protection of IP can be achieved in the following ways.

Patents

A **patent** gives the inventor exclusive rights to use their invention for 20 years and prevents other parties from copying or selling the invention without the permission of the inventor. The objective of a patent is not only to protect the inventor but also to encourage innovation. The exclusivity associated with a patent enables a business to charge higher prices and recoup the R&D costs. However, a patent does not prevent firms from introducing their own version of a product so, in time, prices tend to fall. For example, Dyson was the first producer of bagless vacuum cleaners but, over time, competitors have introduced their own versions.

> A **patent** is a government licence that gives the holder exclusive rights to a process, design or new invention.

Trademarks

A **trademark** is something that distinguishes your products or business from others in the market. It might be a name, a logo, a slogan or a design. Trademarks must be registered and go through a rigorous process before acceptance. Once registered, however, a trademark gives exclusive rights to its use.

Copyrights

A **copyright** is an author's legal ownership of a creative work such as a literary or musical work. From a business point of view, a copyright might be used for computer programs or blueprints.

Businesses can spend large amounts of money protecting their inventions and names. Trying to associate a product or service with Rolls-Royce, for example, could give a business an unfair advantage or indeed, if it were poor quality, tarnish the high-quality reputation of Rolls-Royce. Intellectual property theft has become a big issue especially in China, where indigenous businesses copy the inventions of many Western companies, resulting in expensive lawsuits.

> A **trademark** is a recognisable name, logo, slogan or design that denotes a specific product or service and legally differentiates it from others.
>
> A **copyright** is the legal protection provided for the work of authors, composers and artists.

The impact of an innovation strategy on the functional areas of the business

REVISED

Innovation has an impact on the functional areas of a business in the following ways:

- **Finance.** Innovation requires funding with no guarantee of a return.
- **Marketing.** Innovation may stem from market research or require market research to ascertain consumer reaction to new ideas and products. New products or services also require promotion, which adds to the costs of a business.
- **Operations.** Process innovation directly affects operations and the way a product is made. New products may also require new processes or perhaps even new capacity.
- **Human resources.** Innovation is likely to involve human resources in terms of the skills and training required for new products and processes. It may also be affected through the culture of the business, as the introduction of a more innovative culture may lead to a more engaged and productive workforce.

Now test yourself

TESTED

11 Distinguish between product and process innovation.
12 Briefly outline why R&D is necessary in a competitive business environment.
13 How does an intrapreneur differ from an entrepreneur?
14 Define the term 'benchmarking'.
15 What is meant by the term 'intellectual property' and how might it be protected?

Answers on p. 212

Assessing internationalism

Internationalism is the ideal of countries working together politically, economically and socially to achieve common goals. This has resulted in the internationalisation of business, which is the process of increasing involvement of organisations in international markets.

Reasons for targeting, operating in and trading with international markets

REVISED

- **Growth and profit.** No matter how attractive a product, a national market will always have a finite capacity. More overseas trade enables further growth of a business, satisfying a key objective and benefiting its shareholders and the economy as a whole.
- **Economies of scale.** By moving into overseas markets, more will be produced. This may enable the better use of capacity, particularly in a seasonal business, improve productivity and reduce unit costs. Greater production may also enable the business to benefit from further economies of scale, such as purchasing, managerial and technological.
- **Diversify risk.** An organisation's home market may be saturated or struggling due to economic pressure. Moving into overseas markets provides an almost unlimited range of customers. As different cultures have different wants and needs, it may also be possible to diversify the product range to satisfy these differences.
- **Trade liberalisation.** International trade barriers have decreased massively over recent decades, enabling greater international trade. The World Trade Organization (WTO) has helped achieve greater cooperation between nations, making markets more accessible. Costs of trading have also reduced. For example, the use of shipping containers and **e-commerce** has made shopping accessible to people anywhere in the world.
- **Tax.** This is a controversial topic at the moment as a number of organisations such as Starbucks and Amazon have been able to gain significant tax advantages through trading internationally. This may be as a result of **transfer pricing** or by declaring profit in the country with the lowest corporation tax.

> **E-commerce** is the buying and selling of goods and services through an electronic medium.
>
> **Transfer pricing** is the setting of the price for goods and services sold between related legal entities within an organisation. For example, if a subsidiary sells goods to a parent company, the cost of those goods paid by the parent to the subsidiary is the transfer price.

Factors influencing the attractiveness of international markets

REVISED

There are a number of factors to consider when looking to enter international markets:

- **Risk.** Entering any new market presents a risk and the risk is potentially greater in an overseas market. These risks include dealing with different languages and cultures, the potential for intellectual property (IP) theft, problems assessing the creditworthiness of customers and potential transport and delivery issues.
- **Competition.** This includes both current and potential future competition. Information related to the number and size of competitors as well as their market strategies needs to be considered.
- **Market potential.** This relates to the size and growth of the overseas market. Aspects that might be assessed are population size and GDP growth rate, as well as product-specific market data.
- **Legal and political environment.** It is important to understand an overseas country's policies towards trade as well as the legal environment. Do any trade barriers exist, what are the tax policies and how stable is the political regime?
- **Economic factors.** These include factors such as exchange rate stability and GDP growth.
- **Cost.** This includes both the direct cost of entering a foreign market and the opportunity cost that might result from investing in overseas markets.

- **Culture.** This is a factor that needs to be considered carefully as it impacts on the ways messages concerning the ability of a product to satisfy wants and needs are interpreted and received.
- **Methods of entry.** A business needs to consider the most appropriate method of entry (see below).

Reasons for producing more and sourcing more resources abroad

Cost is the primary reason for organisations to source materials from abroad. If resources of the desired quality, quantity and reliability can be obtained overseas, it makes economic sense to purchase them. Cost is also a big factor in an organisation's decision to produce abroad or to **off-shore** production.

> **Off-shoring** is the movement of the operations of a business to another country.

Ways of entering international markets and value of different methods

There are a number of ways of entering international markets and the following four methods are identified in the specification.

Exporting

A business may engage in exporting, either indirectly through agents where there is no direct contact with customers or markets, or directly where customers and markets are dealt with and a relationship is developed with the business. The benefits of exporting are that relatively little investment is required, entry may be gradual which allows local knowledge to be acquired and it avoids any restrictions imposed on foreign investment. However, it suffers from vulnerability to tariffs and other trade barriers, costs of transport and lack of local knowledge.

Licensing

This occurs when a business grants a licence or the right to a business in another country to produce its product. This provides a quick, low-cost method of entering a foreign market that avoids tariffs and other trade barriers as well as benefiting from knowledge of the local producer. However, it is dependent on the local producer who, in time, could become a competitor, resulting in limited long-term market opportunities and profit.

Alliances

Sometimes known as strategic alliances, these involve a cooperative agreement between a company and an overseas business. Such alliances provide access to a foreign market as well as benefiting from the knowledge and expertise of the local business. However, this method involves sharing the knowledge and technology of the products concerned and the local business may later use this as a direct competitor rather than as a partner.

Direct investment

A business might choose to make direct investment in the foreign market, setting up its own production facilities (off-shoring). This method gives direct control over operations while avoiding tariffs and trade barriers.

It also reduces transportation costs and possibly labour costs. However, it has a high initial cost, results in greater exposure to economic and political risk and may create problems in terms of management and control of the overseas operation. A business that has production facilities in more than one country is known as a **multinational company.**

Other methods of entering foreign markets are mergers and takeovers, ventures and franchising, which are looked at on pp. 166–168.

> A **multinational company** is a business that has facilities and other assets in more than one country.

Influences on buying, selling and producing abroad

REVISED

The main reasons for buying resources from overseas revolve around quality and price. If reliable suppliers can be found that can produce at the right quality and price, it makes economic sense to purchase from them. Although cost is seen as a prominent reason for producing or off-shoring production, particularly in the area of wage costs, this is not the only reason. Other factors include:

- **Skills.** An organisation might off-shore as the necessary skilled staff cannot be found at home. For example, India and China produce far more IT graduates than the UK and the USA. In a knowledge society, human capital can be a scarce resource and lead to off-shoring of production.
- **New markets.** Sometimes it is a good idea to produce locally in a market benefiting from local knowledge and expertise. It may be that the host government makes it a requirement that local production facilities are built up.
- **A business-friendly framework.** It may be that the overseas country has a more friendly framework with more liberal labour and employment rules, subsidies, tax breaks and less regulation.
- **Overcome trade barriers.** Off-shoring and producing abroad overcomes the problem of trade barriers such as tariffs and quotas.
- **Natural resources.** For primary industries such as mining and oil producing, it has always been necessary to locate production where the resource is found.

However, off-shoring has its problems, including:

- **Ethical issues.** The problem here is twofold. First, if production is moved overseas there are likely to be job losses in the home country. Second, it may be that production is moved to an area where labour costs are cheaper but where employees are exploited. Either way, the reputation of the business could be damaged.
- **Control and quality.** Off-shoring can cause difficulties in terms of communication and control because of the distance involved. Quality can also become an issue, which will be much harder to address from a distance.
- **IP theft.** This has become an increasing problem over recent years, e.g. Dyson.
- **British reputation.** Having a 'made in Britain' label carries with it a certain reputation which, if it is a key strength of the business, is lost by off-shoring.

As a result of these problems, a number of UK businesses have now **re-shored** back to the UK, including Hornby and the producers of Trunki suitcases.

> **Re-shoring** is when businesses bring back to their home country operations which had been moved overseas.

Managing international business including pressures for local responsiveness and pressures for cost reduction

When examining the management of international business, the specification makes specific reference to pressures for local responsiveness and pressures for cost reduction. Pressures for local responsiveness relate to the tastes and preferences of the local market, which may be different because of differences in culture, or where a business has to be responsive to the political demands of the government. Pressures for cost reduction are likely to stem from the competitive environment.

Bartlett and Ghoshal's international strategies

Bartlett and Ghoshal's matrix was first put forward in *Managing Across Borders: The Transnational Solution* published in 1989. It addressed the issues of the pressures for local responsiveness and cost reduction, formulating a strategies matrix. As shown in Figure 9.3, the *x*-axis depicts the pressure for local responsiveness and the *y*-axis the pressure for global integration, the latter being the extent to which an organisation needs to standardise its products to benefit from economies of scale (cost reduction).

> **Bartlett and Ghoshal's matrix** identifies four international strategies according to the pressure for local responsiveness (high or low) and the pressure for integration (high or low).

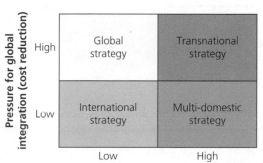

Figure 9.3 Bartlett and Ghoshal's matrix

The matrix depicts four different strategies according to the importance (high or low) of the two forces:

- **International strategy (low-pressure integration, low-pressure responsiveness).** This strategy is based on the home country's expertise with the concentration of activities in that country. Products are manufactured with little adaptation and only marketing, pricing and distribution are decided at the local level.
- **Multi-domestic strategy (low-pressure integration, high-pressure responsiveness).** Each market is treated independently, with products adapted to local needs and production, marketing and product development taking place in the overseas country. The business is essentially a collection of separate units.
- **Transnational strategy (high-pressure integration, high-pressure responsiveness).** This strategy tries to maximise both integration and responsiveness, where knowledge and innovation are sought, developed and dispersed throughout the organisation.
- **Global strategy (high-pressure integration, low-pressure responsiveness).** This involves a highly centralised business based on scale economies where the pressures for efficiency and cost reduction are high. Although products are made overseas, there will be little adaptation.

As a result of intense globalisation over the last two decades and increased competitive forces in almost every industry, Bartlett and Ghoshal recognised that many organisations need to adopt a transnational strategy. In other words, they need to master both cost reduction and local differentiation in order to maintain a competitive edge.

Exam tip

It might also be possible to use the Ansoff matrix (see p. 154) when analysing the possibility of entering international markets.

The impact of internationalism on the functional areas of the business

REVISED

Decisions related to internationalism, such as selling in overseas markets, off-shoring and re-shoring, have an impact on all areas of a business:

- **Marketing.** The marketing function has a key role to play in researching the market and developing appropriate promotional strategies.
- **Finance.** Any decision related to internationalism needs financing, on top of which the increasing competitiveness of these markets may lead to pressure for cost reductions.
- **Operations.** Sourcing materials, adaptation of products, quality and capacity are all issues the operations function needs to examine. There may be increased pressure to reduce unit costs.
- **Human resources.** Recruitment and training are key issues and, if off-shoring, redundancy strategies may be needed as well as consideration of management styles when working with different cultures.

Now test yourself

TESTED

16 Identify four reasons why a business might target international markets.
17 Briefly outline two factors that might affect the attractiveness of international markets.
18 What do you understand by the term 'off-shoring'?
19 Why might a business decide to re-shore production back to the UK?
20 What are depicted on the two axes of Bartlett and Ghoshal's matrix?

Answers on p. 212

Assessing greater use of digital technology

It has been claimed that every company today is a tech company, suggesting that technology reaches into every sector of industry. **Digital technology** is increasingly becoming a pivotal part of business, no longer just a facilitator of everyday practices but more likely to be at the heart of a business's strategy.

Digital technology describes the use of digital resources to find, analyse, create, communicate and use information effectively in a digital context.

The pressures to adopt digital technology

REVISED

The pressures to introduce digital technology include:

- **Improved performance.** Essential in a competitive market, digital technology can lead to lower costs and quicker and more efficient decision-making, enabling an organisation to stay one step ahead of the competition.
- **Keep up with consumer and market trends.** Digital technology means a more flexible business that can quickly respond to changes in consumer tastes, fashion and market trends.

Businesses today are experiencing a minor revolution in the way they operate, harnessing digital technologies to redesign the way they function. These technologies include the following.

E-commerce

E-commerce relates to buying and selling goods and services through an electronic medium. It might be business-to-business (B2B), business-to-consumer (B2C) or consumer-to-consumer (C2C) such as on eBay. This has benefited both consumers and businesses. Consumers have access to more products and services at cheaper prices, information is available instantly and it enables participation at auctions. For a business, it provides opportunities 24/7 and 365 days a year, and offers a global reach, potential cost reductions and supply chain improvements.

Despite the benefits, there are disadvantages to e-commerce. Consumers are unable to examine products personally, they are dependent on system reliability, personal information can be stolen through hacking and even today some people are not connected to the internet.

Related to e-commerce, m-commerce is the buying and selling of goods and services through wireless technology using mobile phones and tablets.

Big data

Big data refers to the ever-increasing amounts of structured, semi-structured and unstructured data that have the potential to be mined for information. It can be characterised by four Vs, as shown in Figure 9.4.

- **Volume:** the almost inconceivable amount of data generated every second, such as from market research, business transactions and social media, which can be stored and analysed through new technology.
- **Velocity:** the speed at which new data is generated and moves around. For example, social media messages and pictures can go viral in seconds. Technology provides the ability to analyse this data while it is being generated.
- **Variety:** the different types of data that can be used: text, images, videos, voice messages, etc. Technology allows all types of data to be brought together and analysed.
- **Veracity:** the 'messiness' or trustworthiness of data, particularly that on social media. Technology increases the ability to work with this type of data.

> **Big data** refers to the ever-increasing amounts of structured, semi-structured and unstructured data that have the potential to be mined for information.

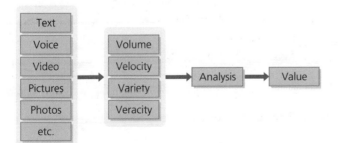

Figure 9.4 Big data

Having all this data is one thing, but turning it into value is another. The use of technology has enabled the analysis of all data, leading to insights and the ability to add value. It can create a better understanding of customers and purchasing habits, allowing businesses to target consumers more directly with promotions. Business processes such as stock levels, supply chains and delivery routes can be optimised. Big data can also be used to improve sports performance, national security and health.

Data mining

Data mining is the process used by organisations to turn large amounts of data (big data) into useful information. It has come about as a result of the vast amount of data available, so much so that organisations are 'drowning in data yet starving in knowledge'. It can be used in market analysis and management such as customer profiling and promotion and financial planning (e.g. cash-flow analysis, resource planning and fraud and detection management).

> **Data mining** is the process used by organisations to turn large amounts of data (big data) into useful information.

Enterprise resource planning

Enterprise resource planning (ERP) is the business management software system by which an organisation manages and integrates the important parts of its business. Before the introduction of ERP, organisations had separate systems for different functions and processes, which resulted in duplication, a lack of sharing of data, inconsistency, isolated decisions and increased expenses. However, ERP uses one software system that eliminates duplication, integrates all functions and processes, and provides greater accuracy. It brings with it a number of advantages — improved speed, efficiency, integration and flexibility — that may result in better analysis and planning capabilities, better management of resources, better customer satisfaction and lower costs. An illustration of how this can benefit both customers and a business is the ease with which orders can now be tracked both for resources and for finished products.

> **Enterprise resource planning (ERP)** is the business management software system by which an organisation manages and integrates the important parts of its business.

However, ERP can be costly. It needs to be adapted to each individual organisation and takes time to set up and test. It also requires dedicated staff and training.

The value of digital technology

REVISED

The value of digital technology has been touched on above. It can help reduce costs, create efficiencies, enable entry into new markets, maintain competiveness and improve overall living standards. It can also be used in planning, and results in more integrated and quicker decisions being made. However, it is not without its problems. There is likely to be a high initial investment, and change within an organisation can lead to stress and lower morale.

The impact of digital technology on the functional areas of the business

REVISED

Digital technology impacts all areas of business:
- **Financial.** Financial monitoring and analysis are both quicker and easier to undertake.
- **Marketing.** Digital technologies have opened up new markets, enabled more targeted promotions and significantly reduced marketing costs. E-commerce and social media have transformed the way businesses operate.

- **Operations management.** Digital technology has enabled greater automation of production and more efficient inventory control, leading to lower costs, better quality, greater flexibility and reduced waste.
- **Human resources.** Digital technology has enabled the development of more flexible, multi-skilled workforces who work under better conditions and who can be more closely monitored. Such change comes with a cost in terms of recruitment and training and in some cases can lead to industrial relations problems.

> **Exam tip**
>
> Digital technology can bring many benefits, but it can also cause problems for a business. Do not automatically assume it is right for every business.

Now test yourself

TESTED

21 Define the term 'digital technology'.
22 Distinguish between the terms 'big data' and 'data mining'.
23 What is enterprise resource planning (ERP) and what benefits does it bring?
24 Briefly outline two possible problems associated with introducing greater digital technology.

Answers on p. 212

Exam practice

Essays

a Despite the attractiveness of international markets, a number of businesses have experienced considerable difficulties when operating internationally. To what extent do you believe targeting international markets is the best strategy for growth for UK businesses? [25]
b Growth brings with it the promise of numerous economies, but it also leads to a variety of new challenges and problems. Evaluate how a business might overcome these challenges and problems. [25]

Answers and quick quiz 9 online

ONLINE

> **Exam tip**
>
> Students' answers are often too narrowly focused. Business is an integrated subject and questions require you to demonstrate this interrelated nature. Read the questions carefully to spot when this is required so that you can expand beyond what appears to be the focus of a question. A question that asks, for example, 'To what extent are cultural clashes the most important reason for takeover failures?' requires you to address other factors such as price paid and lack of experience as well as culture in order to draw a fully justified conclusion.

Summary

You should now have an understanding of all the points below.

Assessing a change in scale

- the reasons why businesses grow and retrench
- the difference between organic and external growth
- issues with growth including economies of scale, economies of scope, diseconomies of scale, the experience curve, synergy and overtrading
- Greiner's model of growth
- how to manage and overcome the problems of growth or retrenchment
- the impact of growth or retrenchment on the functional areas of the business
- methods of growth including mergers and takeovers, ventures and franchising
- types of growth including vertical (backward and forward), horizontal and conglomerate integration

Assessing innovation

- product and process innovation and the pressures for it
- the value of innovation
- the ways of becoming an innovative organisation including Kaizen, research and development, intrapreneurship and benchmarking
- how to protect innovation and intellectual property including patents and copyrights

- the impact of an innovation strategy on the functional areas of the business

Assessing internationalism

- reasons for targeting, operating in and trading with international markets
- factors influencing the attractiveness of international markets
- reasons for producing more and sourcing more resources abroad
- ways of entering international markets and value of different methods including exporting, licensing, alliances and direct investment; also including multinationals
- influences on buying, selling and producing abroad including off-shoring and re-shoring
- managing international business including pressures for local responsiveness and pressures for cost reduction as shown in Bartlett and Ghoshal's matrix
- the impact of internationalisation on the functional areas of business

Assessing greater use of digital technology

- the pressures to adopt digital technology including e-commerce, big data, data mining and enterprise resource planning (ERP)
- the value of digital technology
- the impact of digital technology on the functional areas of the business

10 Managing strategic change

Strategic change is a restructuring of an organisation's business or marketing plan that is typically performed to achieve an important objective. For example, strategic change might include shifts in an organisation's policies, target market, mission or organisational structure. It is a change in the fundamental strategy of an organisation that is likely to create issues of identity, culture and direction that need careful management.

Managing change

Change management is the process of managing change in a structured way in order to meet organisational goals, objectives and mission.

Causes of and pressures for change

Types of change

Internal change

Internal change happens within a business. This is sometimes identified as a result of a SWOT analysis of the internal strengths and weaknesses, such as:
- employee attitudes
- change of leadership
- restructuring

External change

External change happens because of forces outside a business. They might be identified as a result of a SWOT analysis of the opportunities and threats posed by any of the following:
- changing consumer tastes and fashion, e.g. the use of e-commerce
- political changes, e.g. lifting sanctions on Iran
- government action, e.g. Brexit
- economic influences, e.g. changes in the business cycle or exchange rates
- competition, e.g. due to globalisation
- technological changes, e.g. the greater use of digital technologies

Incremental v disruptive change

Change may be major one-off or disruptive changes or they may take place incrementally over a number of years:
- **Disruptive change.** This is likely to be transformational and to involve radically rethinking or redesigning a major business process with the objective of making large-scale improvements quickly. As a result, it may change the existing organisation structure and culture and it is therefore relatively high risk. Examples of disruptive change occur with new innovations and technological breakthroughs such as the bagless vacuum cleaner, mobile phones and digital cameras.

> **Disruptive change** involves radical change, often rethinking or redesigning a business or project.

● **Incremental change.** This is aimed at making many small-scale improvements to business processes. They are unlikely to challenge existing assumptions and culture, and will use existing structures and processes and cause little disruption. As a result, incremental change is relatively low risk.

> **Incremental change** involves introducing many small, gradual changes in a business or a project.

Managing change

Lewin's force field analysis

Change within business is inevitable and the management of change is a key factor in the success of the business. **Lewin's force field analysis** can help in managing change by examining the forces for and against a change. This is illustrated in Figure 10.1.

> **Lewin's force field analysis** addresses the issue of change according to the balance of driving and restraining forces.

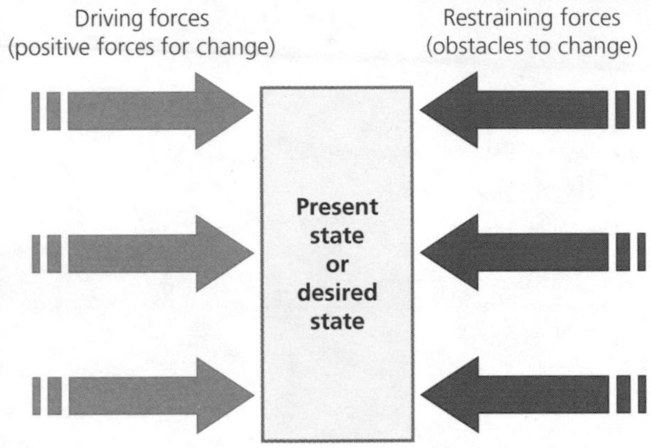

Figure 10.1 Lewin's force field analysis

Kurt Lewin was an American psychologist who, in developing his force field analysis, suggested an issue is held in balance by the interaction of two opposing forces: those seeking to promote change (driving forces) and those seeking to maintain the status quo (restraining forces). Although these forces work in opposite directions, there is normally a balance or equilibrium within a business. For a change to occur, the driving forces need to be greater than the restraining forces, thereby changing the balance or equilibrium.

Force field analysis investigates that balance of power, identifying the most important players (stakeholders) and target groups and how to influence them. In conducting a force field analysis, the following steps might be taken:

1 Identify the current situation.
2 Identify the desired situation.
3 List all the driving forces.
4 List all the restraining forces.
5 Evaluate each of the driving forces and the restraining forces, giving each one a value on a scale of 1–10, with 1 = very weak and 10 = extremely strong.
6 If change is viable, develop a strategy to strengthen the key driving forces and weaken the key restraining forces.

> **Exam tip**
>
> In a force field, any action can have an equal and opposite reaction, so strengthening driving forces may lead to a strengthening of restraining forces. Therefore, the organisation may gain more success by looking to weaken the restraining forces.

The value of change

REVISED

If something is not working, it needs to be changed. This change should be seen as a good thing that will move the organisation forward, and without it, stagnation is likely to result. Therefore, in today's fast-moving environment change should be embraced by business. The value of change can be summed up as follows:

- **Flexibility.** A business that embraces and has a culture of change is likely to have a more engaged workforce that actively seeks to instigate changes. As a result, the business is likely to be more flexible and adaptable to new ideas, enabling it to maintain a competitive edge.
- **Progress.** Without change businesses would not have been able to take advantage of new technologies. If Kodak had been a business that embraced change, it might have maintained its leading position in the camera industry.
- **Opportunities.** Change provides opportunities for business growth, not only in new markets or new products but also in the skills and abilities of the workforce.
- **Customer needs.** Over time, customer needs change and grow, creating demand for new types of product and services. Businesses that embrace change are more able to meet these needs.
- **Challenging the current situation.** Businesses that challenge current practices are more likely to develop new products and processes and gain a competitive advantage. Therefore, all employees should be encouraged to question the way things are done and to look for new ways of doing things.

The value of a flexible organisation

REVISED

A flexible organisation benefits from a number of advantages:

- **Competitiveness.** The business is able to respond more easily to change as it recognises it as inevitable and uses it to maximise competitiveness.
- **Efficiency.** New approaches are likely to be developed, even when old ones are working fine, and as a result, over time, efficiency improves.
- **Teambuilding.** Where a culture of change exists, the workforce is more likely to be engaged and motivated, which in turn leads to better-quality job applicants.

Restructuring

Organisational structure is the way in which tasks are divided, grouped and coordinated in order to achieve the most efficient way of meeting objectives. Today's rapidly changing environment demands a structure that is flexible and adaptable to changing circumstances. As a business grows and expands, it may become necessary to redesign or **restructure** the organisation. Such restructuring encompasses a fundamental internal change that alters the relationships between different components, elements or systems within that organisation to more effectively and flexibly meet its needs.

> **Restructuring** involves a fundamental internal organisational change that alters the roles and relationships of those involved.

Delayering

Delayering is the removal of levels in the hierarchical structure in order to create a leaner and more efficient business. Not only is this likely to reduce costs and improve motivation, it will also improve flexibility. This is because decision-making will be quicker and the business as a whole will be better able to respond to changing market conditions because of delegation, a better understanding of customer needs and the generation of ideas.

> **Delayering** is the process of reducing the number of levels of hierarchy in an organisational structure.

Flexible employment contracts

Flexible working covers a whole host of areas including part-time, temporary, zero hours and flexible hours contracts. It also covers areas such as self-rostering, flexible work locations and special leave availability. Some of the initiatives in this area are designed to improve the work–life balance of employees in order to improve motivation. For example, Rank Xerox introduced an extended-hour 4-day week which led to a 30% fall in absenteeism. Other measures are designed to improve the flexibility of an organisation and make it more adaptable to change, such as zero hour contracts, flexible locations and flexibility in terms of skills, which all lead to an organisation that is more adaptable to changing demand and the needs of the consumer.

Organic structures v mechanistic

The organisational structure defines how tasks are divided, grouped and coordinated. It clarifies the roles organisational members perform so that everyone understands their responsibilities to the group. An organisation must therefore develop a structure that is appropriate for its needs and one that can react to uncertainties and changes in its internal and its external environment. Although structures vary from organisation to organisation, two basic forms are organic and mechanistic.

- An **organic structure** is one that is decentralised, that has wider spans of control and in which information flows seamlessly between functional areas and departments. Organic structures are likely to be more flexible and are more suited to organisations that operate in unstable dynamic environments and that need to adapt quickly to change.
- A **mechanistic structure** is bureaucratic and based on a formal centralised network with a well-defined hierarchy, narrow spans of control and communication, and decisions flowing from the top down. This structure is the traditional form. It is easy to maintain and rarely needs to be changed when an organisation operates in a stable environment.

> An **organic structure** is one that is decentralised, with flatter and wider spans of control and likely to be flexible and able to adapt easily to change.
>
> A **mechanistic structure** is one that is hierarchical and bureaucratic with centralised authority and formal procedures and practices.

Knowledge and information management

Knowledge and information are two separate but linked areas. Information management focuses on retrieving, organising and analysing data and information, and as such creates useful knowledge. Knowledge management focuses on knowledge, understanding and wisdom, and is the process of making effective decisions and taking effective actions. The link between the two lies in the fact that effective knowledge management and resulting decisions result from a solid foundation of data and information management.

The value of managing information and knowledge

REVISED

Managing information is important to an organisation as it results in increased knowledge, decreased inefficiency and the better creation and implementation of plans, which is likely to help save and make more money. Effective knowledge and information management have become increasingly vital in a fast-changing, competitive environment. Collective experience, wisdom and know-how can be seen as the intangible assets of an organisation, and if the knowledge can be managed properly, it can lead to the creation of further wealth and value based on the information and data available. In other words, knowledge management can be a key driver in a competitive environment. This is likely to result in new products being designed and commercialised more quickly, leading to maintained market shares and the potential for increased revenue and profit.

Barriers to change

Change is difficult to implement for a number of reasons:
- **Employee resistance.** Change often means different ways of doing things, taking workers out of their comfort zone and perhaps threatening job security.
- **Management behaviour.** Sometimes management can be resistant to change or there may be a lack of clear objectives set.
- **Inadequate resources.** This might be financial in terms of budget or involve human and physical resources such as machinery and equipment.
- **Organisational culture.** The culture of the organisation may be such that it does not easily embrace change.

Kotter and Schlesinger's four reasons for resistance to change

With regard to employee resistance to change, Kotter and Schlesinger identified four key reasons for this:
- **Parochial self-interest.** This is where people feel they will lose something and so focus on their own self-interest rather than the organisation's interest.
- **Misunderstanding and lack of trust.** These occur when people do not fully understand the implications of change and perceive it might cost them more than they will gain. They are likely to happen when there is poor communication and a lack of trust between the initiator of the change and employees.
- **Different assessments.** These occur when people assess the situation differently to managers and see more costs than benefits, not just to themselves but also to the organisation.
- **Low tolerance of change.** This occurs where people feel they will not be able to develop the new skills and behaviour required of them. There is a limit to how much people can change and sometimes it might demand too much of them. It may also be a case of saving face; they resist because they view the acceptance of change as an admission that previous beliefs or decisions were wrong.

How to overcome barriers to change

Kotter and Schlesinger's six ways of overcoming resistance to change

In order for change to be successful, the barriers or resistance to change must be overcome. Kotter and Schlesinger identified six ways managers might try to do this.

Education and communication

If resistors to change are told or educated about it beforehand, it can help them see the logic or need for change. This may be a good way if resistors have a lack of or inadequate information, but it requires a good working relationship between the initiators of the change and the resistors.

Facilitation and support

If resistors are given support to help cope with change, such as training in new skills or having their problems listened to, they may be more accepting of it. This may be time-consuming and expensive, but it works well if fear of change or anxiety are the main barriers.

Participation and involvement

This is where the initiators of change involve the resistors in the process of change, seeking and often acting on their advice. Although this method can be time-consuming and can sometimes lead to poor decisions, there is no doubt that if it leads to the whole-hearted commitment of the workforce, the process of change will be easier.

Manipulation and co-option

Manipulation involves selective use of information and careful structuring of events, while co-option is giving a leading member(s) of the resistors a key role in implementing change. When co-opting, endorsement not advice is sought in the hope that other resistors can be convinced of the benefits of change. Although manipulation and co-option are relatively inexpensive, they require good relationships and trust as resistors might feel they are being tricked.

Negotiation and bargaining

This is where incentives such as higher pay rates for productivity are offered to resistors. It is a relatively easy but expensive method.

Explicit and implicit coercion

If change is always unpopular and if it needs to be implemented quickly, coercion may be the only answer. With coercion the workforce is forced to accept the change because of, for example, the threat of job losses, transfers or actual dismissal.

In summary, there is always likely to be some resistance to change and the way managers deal with this varies according to circumstances. It might depend on the nature of the change, the potential consequences of the change, attitudes toward the change and the existing state of relations between managers and workforce. What we know for sure is that change is inevitable and essential for the long-term progress and perhaps the survival of organisations.

Now test yourself

TESTED

1 Identify four external causes of change.
2 Distinguish between incremental and disruptive change.
3 In Lewin's force field analysis, what must happen to the balance of driving and restraining forces for change to occur?
4 Outline the six steps to be undertaken in a force field analysis.
5 Briefly explain the value of change.
6 What do you understand by the term 'restructuring'?
7 Identify three flexible employment contracts and briefly explain the importance to a business of such contracts.
8 Distinguish between mechanistic and organic structures.
9 Explain the link between knowledge and information management.
10 Briefly outline four barriers to change.
11 What are the four reasons for resistance to change suggested by Kotter and Schlesinger?
12 List the six ways of overcoming resistance to change given by Kotter and Schlesinger.

Answers on pp. 212–213

Managing organisational culture

Organisational culture is 'the way we do things around here'. It is the shared values and norms that characterise a particular organisation.

An **organisational culture** is a system of shared assumptions, values and beliefs that govern how a business operates.

The importance of organisational culture

REVISED

Every organisation has its own way of doing things. It has its own beliefs, values and principles that together make up its culture. Good cultures inspire, engage and motivate employees, whereas poor cultures lack collaboration, are uninspiring and lead to employees lacking passion. Therefore, culture determines how employees interact at their workplace and is important for a number of reasons:

- **Identity.** Culture defines an organisation's identity and the way it is perceived, not only by its employees but also by its stakeholders. The way we see organisations such as Apple, Amazon and Tesco is determined in part by their culture.
- **Direction.** The culture often provides a set of guidelines, roles and responsibilities that keep employees on-task and provide a sense of direction.
- **Loyalty.** If employees feel a part of and involved in an organisation and contribute to its success, they are likely to feel more engaged and loyal to that organisation. There is also a greater sense of unity among employees as they see themselves all working together for a common goal.
- **Competition.** A healthy competition among employees may exist to achieve targets and goals, increasing performance and quality of work.
- **Attitude to change.** Culture can be important in determining an organisation's attitude to change.

A clear sense of direction and a loyal workforce working in an environment of healthy competition are likely to establish a positive identity among stakeholders that can be crucial to the overall success of an organisation.

Cultural models

A corporate culture model is the organising principle behind the values, beliefs and attitudes that characterise a company and guide its practices. In other words, models are different ways in which culture can be classified. A culture might be described as bureaucratic, where behaviour is governed by formal rules and standard operating procedures, or it might be entrepreneurial and characterised by a high level of risk and creativity. The specification requires two specific models to be studied and understood, those of Charles Handy and Geert Hofstede.

Handy's cultural model

Handy described four types of culture (Figure 10.2):

- **Task culture.** This culture is job- or project-orientated, where the emphasis is on getting the job done. It seeks to bring together the right people and resources in order to do this. This type of culture is common in organisations that have a number of different projects, such as advertising agencies, and revolves around teamwork. The existence of different teams provides for greater flexibility but can sometimes be difficult to control. Handy illustrated this culture as a net due to the interaction between different departments and functions.

- **Role culture.** This type of culture is characterised by strong functional or specialised areas coordinated by a narrow band of senior management at the top. Individuals within the business have clear roles and know whom they report to. This type of culture can work well in a stable environment where economies of scale are more important than flexibility, but because of difficulties in adapting to change it may be less successful in fast-moving, innovative environments. Handy illustrated this culture as a building supported by columns with each column having a specific role to play.

- **Power culture.** This concentrates power among a small group or central figure. There tend to be few rules and little bureaucracy and decisions can be made quickly. This type of culture can be effective in smaller businesses, but in larger organisations those in the centre can become over-burdened and decision-making can become slow. It is also dependent on the person at the top, who may sometimes appear tough and abrasive, leading to low morale and motivation. Handy illustrates this as a spider's web with the all-important spider in the middle.

- **Person culture.** This type of culture is not found in many organisations. It is where the individual is the focal point and the organisation is simply there to assist and serve that individual. It may be possible for consultants, surgeons or some form of specialist such as IT specialists to operate within this type of culture, but it can be difficult to manage. Handy illustrated this culture as a loose cluster of individual dots.

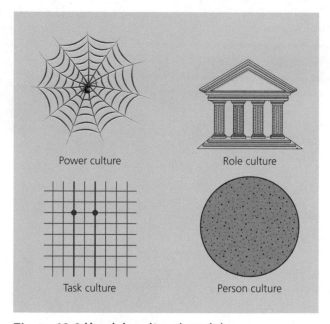

Figure 10.2 Handy's cultural model

> **Exam tip**
>
> Task cultures are often associated with a matrix organisational structure.

Hofstede's national cultures

Geert Hofstede conducted his research between 1967 and 1973 at IBM and from this research identified six dimensions of national culture that distinguish countries rather than individuals from each other, as shown in Figure 10.3. The six dimensions are as follows:

- **Individual v collectivism.** This can be looked as being 'I' or 'we'. Is society based on the importance of the individual and immediate family or is it based on the groups within that society?

- **Power distance.** This is the degree to which the less powerful in society accept and expect power to be distributed unequally and relates to how society handles inequalities. In a high power distance culture, people accept a hierarchical order where everyone has a place. In low power distance culture, people seek to equalise power inequalities and are more suited to flatter organisational structures.
- **Indulgence v restraint.** This relates to a society's attitude to gratification. Does it suppress gratification through strict social norms or does it allow free gratification related to enjoying life and having fun?
- **Long term v short term.** This relates to the value society attaches to its past and traditions. Those who value traditions are likely to be suspicious of change, whereas other societies may be more pragmatic and are more accepting of change.
- **Masculinity v femininity.** Sometimes expressed as the tough v the tender, this relates to the extent to which a society is based on male or female attributes. Is it based on achievement, assertiveness and material rewards for success (male) or is it based on cooperation, modesty and the quality of life (female)?
- **Uncertainty avoidance.** This is the degree to which members of society feel uncomfortable with uncertainty and ambiguity. It is about how a society deals with an unknown future. Those countries with a high index are governed by rules and intolerance of unorthodox behaviour and ideas, whereas those with a low index are far more relaxed in their approach.

Figure 10.3 Hofstede's national cultures

There is no doubt that different national cultures exist. This has implications for any organisation that operates globally: whether in its recruitment, marketing, approach to customer services or outsourcing, the culture of an individual country has a significant impact on the approach adopted.

The influences on organisational culture

REVISED

The age and size of an organisation affect the culture adopted. Older organisations are likely to be more traditional and power-orientated, whereas newer organisations are likely to be more flexible and offer greater consideration of employees. Smaller organisations find it easier to operate under a power culture than larger organisations. Other influences on organisational culture include:

- **Leadership style.** The role of a leader is to direct, motivate and inspire employees, and the way they approach this role affects the culture that evolves. An autocratic approach is likely to lead to a vastly different culture from a more laissez-faire approach.
- **Objectives of organisation.** An organisation looking for quick sustained growth will have a different culture from one looking for slow steady growth. Objectives in terms of ethics and the environment may also have an impact on culture.
- **Nature of the business.** Those organisations that operate within industries that revolve around creativity and innovation are likely to have a power culture, whereas those that operate in industries where economies of scale are important are more suited to a role culture.
- **Employees.** The age, sex and attitudes of employees can have an impact on the culture. Older employees may be more suited to a role culture, whereas younger employees may be more flexible and adaptable to change and therefore more suited to a power culture.

The reasons for and problems of changing organisational culture

REVISED

Reasons

Organisations evolve over time because of changing circumstances and in response to new challenges. As a result, their culture is also likely to change. It is also possible to identify a number of specific reasons or circumstances that are likely to lead to a culture change:

- **Toxic culture.** It maybe that the existing culture has become toxic, as in the banking industry at the beginning of the recession in 2008, requiring a complete reassessment of the values and norms of the industry.
- **Change of leader.** The introduction of a new leader often leads to a cultural change, particularly if that leader is brought in to rescue an ailing business where revenue and profit may be falling and customer service declining.
- **Change of ownership.** This might occur during a takeover where management may wish to align the cultures of the two organisations.
- **Changing market conditions.** This may be the result of moving into international markets and/or the growth of competition.

Other reasons include changing attitudes, such as in regard to the environment, or it may simply be the fact that the existing culture is not working that necessitates change.

Problems

Change of culture, like any change, may be difficult. This could be because of tradition and the attitude of emplyees. They may not accept the need for change, preferring existing arrangements and remaining within their comfort zone. There could also be a sense of fear of: the unknown, a loss of power and skills, break-up of work groups and a loss of income.

The scale of the change could also present a problem: for example, if there are large numbers of people involved and in different locations. This may result in high costs: to restructure the organisation and to educate and train the workforce in the new policies and practices.

Now test yourself

TESTED

13 What do you understand by the term 'organisational culture'?
14 Identify four reasons why organisational culture is important.
15 Distinguish between Handy's power and role cultures.
16 List the six dimensions of Hofstede's national cultures.
17 Explain two influences on organisational culture.
18 Identify four reasons for changing culture.

Answers on p. 213

> **Exam tip**
>
> Students often run out of time in exams. This is invariably because they spend too much time on one question or section. Get your timings right. Make sure you attempt all questions and try to develop your answers. One point with limited development, if relevant, always scores more marks than a list of points.

Managing strategic implementation

Strategic implementation refers to the activities used within an organisation to manage the execution of a strategic plan. It is critical to success and addresses the who, where, when and how of reaching the desired goals and objectives.

> **Strategic implementation** refers to the activities used within business to manage the execution of a strategic plan.

How to implement strategy effectively

REVISED

Successful strategy implementation is not easy. It is not necessarily that the strategy itself is bad, but many organisations fail to effectively motivate their employees to work enthusiastically toward corporate aims. The following factors could help in successful implementation:

- **A clear understanding of the circumstances.** If strategy is to be implemented successfully, there needs to be a clear understanding of why it is being implemented and the objectives that it is hoped will be achieved. This requires knowledge of both the internal and the external factors that influence an organisation's decision-making, such as the competitive environment and the culture of the organisation.
- **Commitment.** This includes not only the commitment of management and the workforce to the strategy but also a commitment in terms of resources. Commitment starts at the top of the organisation. If senior management are not committed to the strategy, it is unlikely the workforce will be. Such commitment from senior management can sometimes be demonstrated by their willingness to commit the financial, human and other resources necessary for the successful implementation of a new strategy.
- **The willingness to change.** Implementing new strategy requires change, which may be resented by a workforce. Some organisations embrace change whereas others are unwilling to change. For strategy to be implemented successfully, there must be an ability and a willingness to change on behalf of the whole organisation.
- **The ability to monitor and measure progress.** The implementation of a strategy does not happen overnight. It takes time, during which circumstances are likely to change, such as competitors responding to the new strategy. Continual monitoring and measuring of progress are necessary in order to undertake the refinements needed to achieve objectives.

As well as the above factors, leadership, communications and organisational structure are important in the effective implementation of strategy.

The value of leadership in strategic implementation

REVISED

Leadership plays a key role in strategic implementation. The leader is likely to have been involved in determining the strategy and will be accountable for the successful implementation. The leader must be committed to the strategy and able to involve and motivate others in its implementation. They need to be able to communicate effectively to make clear not only what is being done and why, but how it is to be achieved. Leaders are also responsible for monitoring progress and making the necessary changes to ensure the efficient implementation of the strategy.

The value of communications in strategic implementation

REVISED

Good communications are essential to the effective implementation of strategy and even the best-laid plans are unlikely to be successful if they are not communicated properly. It may even be necessary to develop a communication plan that identifies the key stakeholders and determines the correct channels and timings of any communication. It is not only employees but also shareholders, the City, the local community and consumers who need to know why a strategy has been developed and what it means for the organisation. If this can be communicated effectively, perhaps even involving key stakeholders such as employees in the process, it is likely to generate greater overall enthusiasm and commitment to the strategy.

> **Exam tip**
>
> There is a link here with stakeholder mapping and Mendelow's matrix (see pp. 28–29).

The importance of organisational structure in strategic implementation

REVISED

The organisational structure determines how roles, power and responsibility are assigned, controlled and coordinated within an organisation and how information flows between the different levels of management. From the point of view of strategy implementation, the structure is the arrangement of roles and tasks needed to implement the strategy. Sometimes when implementing strategy it may be necessary to redesign organisational structure in order to make it relevant to the strategy.

Organisational structure and the influences on organisational design, tall v flat structures and centralisation v decentralisation were covered on pp. 100–101. In addition, the specification asks for an understanding of the organisational structures shown below.

Functional structures

A **functional structure** distributes decision-making and operational authority along functional lines, with specialisation of skills according to the function, e.g. marketing, finance, and operations. As the day-to-day management is delegated, this gives senior management time to focus on strategic decisions and their implementation. Narrow specialisation within functional areas may cause difficulties to arise in coordination, which could inhibit successful strategic implementation.

> **A functional structure** is where business is organised into smaller groups based on functional areas: marketing, finance, operations, etc.

Product-based structures

A **product-based structure** is based on the product or a production line where all functions related to that product are delegated. This might be the case when a product or a group of products has high demand in the market and may be particularly relevant when expansion or diversification strategies are being implemented. Such a structure provides exclusive attention to that product or production line, increasing coordination and fixing responsibility and accountability for profit-making. However, it can only be justified if there is a high volume of sales.

> A **product-based structure** is one based on a product or a production line where all functions related to that product are delegated.

Regional structures

A **regional structure** (or geographic structure) is likely when an organisation has several factories dispersed geographically or where demand is large enough to operate on a regional basis. These structures evolve as an organisation grows and expands. They provide decentralisation to the local level, close to the market where resources and materials may be locally sourced. Regional structures require a high level of coordination and can lead to communication difficulties.

> A **regional structure** is where a business has separate structures dependent on a region or geographical area.

Matrix structures

A **matrix structure** is based around a major project or task where specialists from the various functional areas are assigned to the project. This means that for the duration of the project they report to both their project manager and their functional manager. By bringing specialists together in this way, creativity can be fostered, together with a greater understanding of the organisation as a whole. However, dual accountability may cause confusion and communications problems.

> A **matrix structure** is based around a major project or task and specialists from the various functional areas are assigned to the project.

It is not possible to identify an optimal organisation structure for a given strategy: what may suit one organisation may not suit another, and as an organisation grows and evolves its structure evolves with it. A strategy may be chosen that suits a particular organisational structure, whereas on other occasions a particular structure may be chosen to best enable strategy implementation.

The value of network analysis in strategic implementation

REVISED

Network analysis breaks down complex projects into component parts and plots them on a network diagram to show their interdependencies and interrelationships. Also known as **critical path analysis**, it acts as a basis for the preparation of schedules, resource planning and monitoring progress, and is a useful tool in strategic implementation. A network diagram shows the following:

> **Network analysis** (or critical path analysis) is a method of planning projects in order to identify the most efficient way of completing them.

- The sequence in which activities should be undertaken.
- The length of time taken by each activity.
- The earliest start time at which each activity can commence.
- The latest finish time at which each activity must be completed to avoid delaying other activities.

Understanding and interpreting network diagrams

Network diagrams consist of two elements, as shown in Figure 10.4.

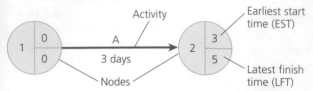

Figure 10.4 Activities and nodes in network diagrams

- **Activities.** These require resources and time and are shown by arrows. Each activity is given a letter to denote the order (written above the arrow) and a duration (written below the arrow).
- **Nodes.** These are the start or finish of an activity and are represented by circles. Each node is numbered (in the left-hand segment) and also states the 'earliest start time' (EST) and 'latest finish time' (LFT).

There are a number of simple rules in drawing a network diagram:
- It is drawn from left to right.
- It must start and end in a single node.
- Each activity is represented by a single arrow.

Additionally it is also necessary to know the order in which activities can be undertaken as some will need others to be completed before they can start (dependent activities) whilst others can be undertaken simultaneously (parallel activities).

Example

XYZ plc is planning to increase capacity by extending its factory. The expansion is expected to cause disruption and the management team is keen to complete it as quickly as possible. The building firm has listed the major activities it will carry out, as well as the expected duration of each. These are shown in the following table.

Individual activity	Expected duration (weeks)
A Design the factory extension	6
B Obtain planning permission	4
C Dig and lay foundations	3
D Order construction materials	2
E Construct walls and roof	12
F Design the interior	2
G Install production equipment	6
H Train staff in new techniques	16

The building firm has also provided the following information:
- Activity A is the start of the project.
- Activity B starts when activity A has been completed.
- Activities C, D and F follow activity B.
- Activity E follows activities C and D.
- Activity H follows activity B.
- Activity G follows activity F.

The network diagram for the factory extension is shown in Figure 10.5.

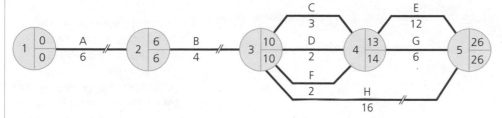

Figure 10.5 **The network diagram for the factory extension**

- **Earliest start time (EST).** This records the earliest time that a particular activity can commence. It is calculated by working from left to right and by adding the time taken to complete the previous activity. If there is more than one activity, the one with the longest duration is included in the calculation. The EST is then recorded in the top quadrant of the right half of the node. For example, in node 4 the EST is 13 days because, although activities D and F have been completed by day 12, activity E cannot commence until activity C has been completed (day 13). The EST on the final node shows the earliest date at which the whole project can be completed.
- **Latest finish time (LFT).** This records the latest time by which an activity must be completed if the whole project is not to be delayed. It is are calculated from right to left, with the activity of the longest duration being deducted. For example, the LFT at node 3 is 10 days, which is calculated as 26 days at node 5 minus the 16 days' duration of activity H. Calculating LFTs is useful as it helps to highlight those activities where there is some slack time or float.
- **Float.** This is any spare time that may exist during a project and can be calculated using the following formula:

  Float = LFT – duration of activity – EST

  For example, activity G has 6 days' float (26 – 6 – 14 = 6) and its start could be delayed until day 20 without delaying the whole project.
- **Critical path.** This shows the sequence of activities that must be completed on time if the whole project is not to be delayed. It is indicated by two small dashes across the relevant activities. In Figure 10.5, the critical path is A–B–H.

Network analysis is a valuable tool when it comes to implementing strategy:
- It encourages managers to undertake strategic planning, which helps reduce the risk of delays and other problems.
- The resources needed for each activity can be made available at the appropriate time, reducing costs and improving an organisation's cash-flow position.
- Time can be saved by operating activities simultaneously — vital in industries where time is an important competitive weapon.
- If delays or problems occur, the network can be a useful tool in finding a solution.

As with any analytical tool, there are some drawbacks:
- Much depends on how accurately the durations of activities are estimated. These can be difficult to forecast and if wrong the whole process may be of little value.
- Complex activities may be difficult to represent on a network diagram.
- The project still requires management after the initial network is drawn as external factors may change.

Typical mistake

There is often a temptation with network diagrams to focus on the calculation of EFTs and LFTs while ignoring the benefits and drawbacks of network analysis. A focus on the pros and cons will help you write both analytically and evaluatively.

Exam tip

Although you should make sure you can draw a network diagram from scratch and be prepared to draw one as this helps your understanding, you are more likely in an exam to be asked to amend a network or calculate EFTs, LFTs or the float.

Problems with strategy and why strategies fail

The successful implementation of a well-planned strategy can give an organisation a competitive advantage. A great deal of time and effort is put into strategic planning, with new strategies being launched to great fanfare and optimism. However, they are high risk and often fail. The failure rates have been estimated at anywhere between 60 and 90% by various studies.

Difficulties of strategic decision-making and implementing strategy

REVISED

Strategic decision-making and implementing strategy can present a number of challenges and difficulties to management:

● It may be that the overall goals are not sufficiently understood by the workforce or perhaps the wrong targets have been set because of insufficient analysis of data.
● There could be a lack of capability of employees or training and instruction might have been inadequate. Perhaps key personnel have left during the implementation process.
● It may be that the leadership fails to provide adequate direction, leading to an overall lack of commitment.
● There may be unforeseen events, perhaps problems with implementation that had not been anticipated or changes in the external environment.
● Difficulties may arise due to implementation taking longer than anticipated.

Planned v emergent strategy

REVISED

A **planned strategy** is the strategy managers intend to implement, where the difference between the present and the desired position is clearly seen. It assumes a smooth change from the current position to the new position, with little in the way of disruption from either internal or external forces. A planned approach assumes one type of approach to change is suitable for all organisations. It involves laying down timetables and tends to ignore the dynamic environment in which organisations operate. A planned strategy does not address the continuous need for structural adaptation and employee flexibility, and assumes common agreement can be reached among all parties.

A **planned strategy** is one that managers intend to implement using a carefully laid plan to achieve the desired position.

Exam practice answers and quick quizzes at **www.hoddereducation.co.uk/myrevisionnotes**

An **emergent strategy** is one that develops over time and is based on the belief that change should not be seen as a series of linear events. Instead, it is characterised by unforeseen events, disruptions that pose opportunities and threats that lead to strategy emerging. Advocates of emergent change stress that there can be no simple answer to managing organisational change and that change management should not be seen as one person's role but part of every manager's role within an organisation.

> An **emergent strategy** is an unplanned strategy that develops over time and is based on the belief that change should not be seen as a series of linear events.

Reasons for strategic drift

Strategic drift usually occurs when organisations that have enjoyed considerable success are unable to keep pace with changes in their external environment, which in a worst-case scenario can lead to their slow and gradual demise. Strategic drift usually happens over an extended period of time and may not be noticed until it is too late, such as in the case of Nokia and Kodak.

> **Strategic drift** occurs where a business responds too slowly to changes in its external environment and results in the strategic plan no longer being appropriate.

Figure 10.6 shows the four phases in strategic drift:
- **Phase 1: Incremental change.** The organisation remains competitive due to incremental changes in strategy that are made in line with the external environment.
- **Phase 2: Strategic drift.** Strategic drift begins to appear as the incremental changes fail to keep up with a faster rate of change in the external environment.
- **Phase 3: Flux.** A state of flux in strategy now develops, where the management recognises the existence of drift due to poorer performance and tries to make strategic changes. However, there is no clear direction and disagreements can occur, leading to poorer performance and increased drift.
- **Phase 4: Transformational change or demise.** This is the final phase where the organisation either fails completely or undertakes a transformational change to realign itself with the external environment.

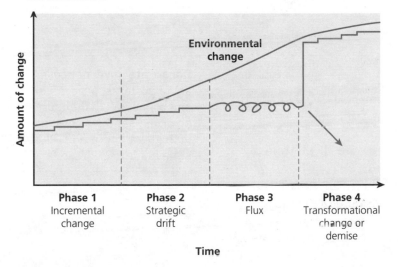

Figure 10.6 Strategic drift

Although it may be easy to see major changes with hindsight, it is not so easy to see them when they are happening. Possible causes of strategic drift include:
- **Technological environment.** This changes so quickly that it can be difficult to keep up with. We only have to look at the demise of Blockbuster and Myspace to see evidence of this.

- **Lagged performance.** The first symptoms of strategic drift may not be immediately apparent as financial results are normally reported at the end of a period and management may not instantly identify the right reasons for lower performance.
- **Culture.** The culture of the business may be quite rigid in terms of values and relationships, and attempts to change may be limited to what is familiar rather than the more radical plan that might be needed.
- **Lack of monitoring.** An organisation may have insufficient monitoring of strategy, missing changes in the environment that are taking place that require a response in terms of strategy change.

Strategic plans should not be seen as something concrete if strategic drift is to be avoided. The environment is changing all the time, meaning that the strategic plan needs a degree of flexibility and manoeuvrability to adapt to the changing needs.

The possible effect of the divorce between ownership and control

REVISED

In small businesses such as sole traders and private limited companies, the owners are likely to manage and control the business. However, if a business converts to a public limited company, the chances of the owners continuing to manage and control the business are lower. Although to begin with the original owners may hold a majority shareholding, as the business continues to grow and further capital is raised through the issue of shares this position is likely to change. This results in what has become known as a **divorce of ownership and control**, where the business owners (the shareholders) no longer control the business but elect a board of directors to control it for them. This can result in a conflict of interest where the owners may wish to see a policy of profit maximisation but the directors want a strategy of long-term growth.

> A **divorce of ownership and control** refers to the separation of the ownership (shareholders) and control (elected board of directors) in a public limited company.

Corporate governance

Corporate governance is about seeing that an organisation is run properly and involves the following:

- **Accountability:** to ensure that the management are accountable to the board of directors and in turn the board of directors is accountable to the shareholders.
- **Fairness:** to protect shareholders' rights, to ensure all are treated equitably and to provide redress for violations.
- **Transparency:** to ensure all matters related to finance, performance, ownership and corporate governance are communicated both accurately and in a timely manner.
- **Responsibility:** ensuring organisations comply with the relevant laws and regulations of a society.

> **Corporate governance** is a set of systems, processes and principles that ensures an organisation is governed in the best interest of all its stakeholders.

Good corporate governance is important in an economy as it provides a barrier to corrupt dealings, enhancing access to capital and the long-term prosperity of both individual organisations and the economy as a whole.

Evaluating strategic performance

REVISED

It is vital for an organisation to undertake **strategy evaluation** as it not only ensures that the stated objectives are being achieved but also alerts management to problems or potential problems. Evaluation may be undertaken in the following ways:

- A review of the underlying factors in an organisation's strategy.
- Comparing expected results with actual results (measuring performance).
- The analysis of any variances in performance.
- Identifying corrective actions to ensure performance conforms with the strategy.

> **Strategy evaluation** is the process of determining the effectiveness of a given strategy in achieving the organisational objectives and taking corrective action wherever required.

The value of strategic planning

REVISED

Strategic planning is about the mission of an organisation. It is about where that organisation wants to go and is crucial to its success, just as in travel plans — unless you know where you are going it is impossible to plan your journey. Strategic plans can help create value as they:

- give purposeful direction to the organisation and outline measurable goals
- identify and help build a competitive advantage
- assist in making choices where resources are limited
- save time as clear priorities are set

Remember that in a dynamic competitive environment the strategic plan is likely to be modified and changed over time and organisations should not see it as an inflexible blueprint for the future.

The value of contingency planning

REVISED

Contingency planning is about planning for the unexpected. There are no guarantees in business. Growth has risks, things can change quickly and people can make mistakes. Contingency planning helps deal with the unexpected. The type of event planned for includes:

- **natural disasters:** fires, floods, earthquakes, etc.
- **loss of data:** perhaps from a natural disaster but also from sabotage or hacking
- **loss of key personnel:** maybe due to retirement, accident or untimely death
- **product issues:** perhaps a large, unexpected order or a product fault requiring a product recall

> **Contingency planning** means planning for the unexpected, such as natural disasters or loss of data.

Although most events involving contingency planning are negative, the possibility of positive events occurring, such as an unexpectedly large order, should not be overlooked. If a contingency plan is in place it means a quicker response to the situation, saving the business both time and money and providing customer reassurance which could limit the damage in terms of lost customers. Although some people criticise contingency planning — they see planning for events that may never happen as a waste of time, effort and money — there is no doubt a well-laid plan can limit the adverse effects of an unplanned event.

Now test yourself

24 Briefly outline four difficulties of implementing strategy.
25 Distinguish between planned and emergent strategy.
26 Define what is meant by the term 'strategic drift' and briefly explain two reasons for it.
27 What is meant by the term 'divorce of ownership and control'?
28 Why is good corporate governance important in a market economy?
29 What is the importance of strategic planning and evaluation?
30 Define the term 'contingency planning'.

Answers on pp. 213–214

Exam practice

Zero plc

Over recent years, Zero plc's profit margins have declined. Profits were down 32% last year and it has encountered occasional cash-flow difficulties. However, sales in the EU have increased to 67% of production and the chocolate manufacturer is now on the verge of a major strategic decision — that of moving production from Bristol to Hungary. Study the following table.

Item	UK	Hungary
Average gross wages (£, 2014)	27,903	11,755
Tax rate on profit (%)	20–22	10
Labour productivity (value of average output per hour in £)	27.09	14.91
Average consumption of chocolate per person per year (kg, 2014)	10.3	3.5

The company's plans show that it intends to close its factory in Bristol in stages over a 3-year period as its facilities near Lake Balaton in Hungary are developed. This is a complex project as the company also intends to increase its productive capacity as part of the move. The proposed relocation is expected to cost £276m.

The leaking of the company's plans has led to storms of protest from consumer groups, trade unions and Bristol City Council. Some consumer groups have called for a boycott of the company's products by UK consumers.

Questions

a Analyse the value of network analysis to Zero plc in planning its proposed move to Hungary. [9]
b To want extent do you believe Lewin's force field analysis could help in managing the proposed change? [16]

Essay

'People are the most important element in implementing change management successfully and the strongest force opposing it.' Do you agree with this statement? Justify your answer with reference to businesses with which you are familiar. [25]

Answers and quick quiz 10 online

ONLINE

Summary

You should now have an understanding of all the points below.

Managing change

- the causes and pressures for change including Lewin's force field analysis
- the value of different types of change including internal, external, incremental and disruptive change
- the value of flexible organisations including restructuring, delayering, flexible employment contracts and organic v mechanistic structures
- the value of knowledge and information management
- the barriers to change and how to overcome them with specific reference to Kotter and Schlesinger's four reasons for resistance to change and six ways of overcoming resistance to change

Managing organisational culture

- the importance of organisational culture including the cultural models of Handy and Hofstede
- the influences on organisational culture
- the reasons for and the problems of changing organisational culture

Managing strategic implementation

- how to implement strategy effectively
- the value of leadership and communication in strategic implementation
- the importance of organisational structure in strategic implementation including functional, product-based, regional and matrix structures
- the value of network analysis including its interpretation and amendment and the identification of the critical path and total float

Problems with strategy and why strategies fail

- difficulties of strategic decision-making and implementing strategy
- planned v emergent strategy and the reasons for strategic drift
- the possible effect of the divorce between ownership and control including corporate governance
- the value of strategic planning and how to evaluate it
- the value of contingency planning

Now test yourself answers

1 What is business?

1 Three reasons why business exist include:

(i) to provide goods and services

(ii) to develop a good idea (enterprise)

(iii) to provide help and support to others

2 A mission statement paints the broad picture. The objectives of a business are more specific — they are targets or goals that will enable a business to achieve its overall mission.

3 Five business objectives are:

(i) growth

(ii) survival

(iii) profit

(iv) customer service

(v) corporate social responsibility

4

Type of organisation	Objectives
Public limited company	Profit, growth
Public sector organisation	Service, social and economic benefits for community
Charity	Fundraising and support for charity

5 The mission statement sets out the vision of the business and its core purpose and focus. Overall corporate and strategic planning can then be set and measured against the core purpose.

6 SMART means specific, measurable, achievable, realistic and time based. By having SMART objectives it is possible to evaluate the success in achieving them.

7 Profit = total revenue – total costs

£50,000 – £5,000 – £30,000

profit = £15,000

8 (i) Corporate businesses have limited liability, unlike non-corporate businesses.

(ii) Corporate businesses can sell shares and have shareholders.

(iii) Corporate businesses (especially plcs) are generally much larger.

9 The public sector is that part of the economy owned and controlled by the government or local authorities, e.g. NHS, fire service and rubbish collection.

10 (i) To help the local community, possibly by providing essential services.

(ii) To help people to acquire job-related skills to assist them into employment.

(iii) To buy products from overseas under fair-trading schemes offering benefits to producers in less developed countries.

11 Mutuals are owned collectively by a business's clients or members, whereas incorporated businesses are owned by their shareholders.

12 Most new businesses are set up as sole traders because they are usually small, mostly local businesses, and a sole trader is the simplest and easiest business to form.

13 (i) Changing circumstances such as growth of the business.

(ii) Capital — it may be easier to raise capital as a plc.

(iii) Takeover may cause a change of legal structure.

14 (i) To earn income resulting from a share of the profit of the business in the form of a dividend.

(ii) For capital growth — if the business does well, the share price is likely to increase, resulting in an increase in the value of an investment.

15 (i) increased profit

(ii) expectancy of increased profit

(iii) changes in the market

(iv) world uncertainty

16 Market capitalisation = share price × number of shares issued

= 57p × 2,100m

= £1,197m

17 If sales are to be achieved in a competitive market, a business must make its product or service stand out from the rest. It must make it different, i.e. differentiate it from the rest. If it can do this successfully it is likely to gain a competitive advantage and therefore increased sales and potentially profit.

18 A rise in interest rates is likely to result in lower disposable income for consumers. This is due to the fact that many will be

making higher interest payments on loans and overdrafts, whilst others may be inclined to save more. If spending is reduced, manufacturers of luxury products are likely to be the ones that suffer most.

19 A study of demographics is important as:

(i) Population affects the level of demand.

(ii) The make-up of the population, age, income, occupation etc. affects the nature of goods bought.

(iii) An understanding of the structure of the working population will have implications for employment.

20 Fair trade is a movement that strives for fair treatment of farmers in less developed countries.

2 Managers, leadership and decision-making

1 Four key aspects of a leader's role are:

(i) setting objectives

(ii) organising the way work is performed

(iii) motivating and communicating

(iv) analysing and appraising performance

2 Three influences on leadership style are:

(i) the leader's personality and skills

(ii) the nature of the industry

(iii) the culture of the business

3 A democratic leader makes the final decision but involves others in the process.

A laissez-faire leader allows team members freedom in doing their work and meeting deadlines.

4 In the Tannenbaum and Schmidt continuum, leaders are classified according to how much they tell or listen to workers.

5 A decision tree requires the following three key pieces of information:

(i) the cost of each decision

(ii) the financial outcome

(iii) the probability

6 Decision trees have the benefit that they make managers think about and quantify outcomes, which can help reduce risk in decision-making. They do, however, have the drawback that they can be open to a manager's bias — outcomes and probabilities may be made more favourable in order to have a particular decision accepted.

7 The external environment may have a big impact on decision-making. A downturn in the economy or rise in interest rates could see decisions being postponed or even abandoned altogether, whereas an expanding economy or fall in interest rates might see decisions being brought forward.

8 (i) competition

(ii) resources available

(iii) ethics

(iv) business objectives

9

Stakeholder	Interest
Employees	job security, good working conditions and pay
Customers	good customer service and value for money
Shareholders	capital growth and dividends
Suppliers	regular orders and on-time payment

10 Mendelow categorises stakeholders according to the amount of power they have and their level of interest.

11 (i) leadership style

(ii) state of the economy

(iii) business objectives

(iv) government

12 The key to managing stakeholder relations is likely to be good communication with participation and involvement in decision-making.

3 Decision-making to improve marketing performance

1 Sales volume refers to the number of units sold. Sales value represents the value in monetary terms of those sales.

2 If the actual market is increasing in size faster than an individual company's market share, then sales will rise but market share fall.

3 If a business can achieve brand loyalty, not only will it mean returning customers and maintaining market share, but these customers are also likely to recommend the product to others.

4 Internal: (i) finance available, (ii) production capacity, (iii) human resources

External: (i) economy, (ii) competition, (iii) ethics

5 Total market size = (sales/market share) × 100

30/5 = £6m × 100 = £600m total market size

6 Primary market research differs from secondary in that it is:

(i) first-hand information

(ii) specific to the purpose required

(iii) more expensive to collect

7 Qualitative market research is designed to discover the attitudes and opinions of consumers that influence their purchasing behaviour. A food manufacturer might use a consumer panel to test a new chocolate bar and receive detailed opinions on the taste and texture of the new product.

Quantitative market research is the collection of information on consumer views and behaviour that can be analysed statistically. This type of research might be used to investigate whether a new product is likely to achieve a sufficient volume of sales to make it financially viable.

8 A business is unlikely to have either the time or the financial resources to interview the whole of the population, so it will interview only a small relevant sample when undertaking market research. This saves the business both time and money.

9 Correlation is a statistical technique used to establish the extent of a relationship between two variables such as sales and advertising.

Extrapolation analyses the past performance of sales and uses this to forecast the future trend of sales.

10 The confidence interval in market research is the margin of error. In this case, if 60% of all respondents (sample) prefer a particular soap, market research analysts can be confident that between 55 and 65% of the overall population would prefer that brand.

11 A figure of –2.3 indicates elastic demand (ignore the minus sign). As a result, a price increase would result in a fall in demand and therefore a decline in revenue.

12 Spending on luxury items requires consumers to have disposable income. This means spending on luxuries will be greater when income is rising and less when it is falling as in the recession of 2008. This means spending on luxuries is responsive to changes in income, i.e. it is income elastic.

13 Market targeting results in more effective marketing as it can be directed specifically at the target group and convey a clear message relative to the positioning of the product or service. Resources will also be used more effectively as a result of the targeted marketing approach.

Market targeting may, however, result in potentially profitable segments being overlooked. It may also be the case that changes in taste and fashion are missed.

14 Mass market refers to the whole market, whereas a niche is a small part of that larger market, e.g. Ford aims its cars at the whole market, whereas Porsche targets a small section of the car market.

15 People, process and physical environment have been included in the marketing mix of 4Ps due to the growth of the service sector and the importance of these Ps to that sector.

16 A marketing manager is likely to take into consideration market research and the nature of the product when designing a marketing mix. Market research may reveal information regarding an acceptable price for consumers or details about particular functions of the product. The nature of the product is also likely to be used to determine where it is sold and the price charged.

17 The Boston matrix allows businesses to undertake product portfolio analysis based on the product's market growth rate and its market share. It classifies products into four categories and helps managers to have products in each one.

The product life cycle is the theory that all products follow a similar pattern, moving through five stages during their life. Its use can avoid circumstances where firms have a range of products all in declining popularity.

18 A cash cow is a product that has a large share of a market that is growing quickly. A problem child is a product that has a small share of a market that is growing quickly.

19 Pricing strategies are the medium- to long-term pricing plans that a business adopts. Pricing tactics are a series of pricing techniques that are normally used only over the short term to achieve specific goals such as increasing sales.

20 Price skimming may be appropriate when a new product is launched onto the market, especially if it has unique selling points that differentiate it from rivals' products.

21 The promotional mix includes advertising, public relations, direct selling and merchandising.

22 Two influences on the promotional mix are the amount of finance available and the target market. Finance is likely to be limited for a new business and will need to be carefully budgeted. The restaurant's target market will also have an impact — is it targeting low- or high-income diners? The promotional mix will be determined accordingly.

23 Tesco sells its products both in its shops and on line. It also operates a click and collect service.

24 The people selling a product and the process used can make or break the sale of that product, so they are just as important as they are for selling a service.

25 Product life cycle and positioning will affect the marketing mix in that a product in the growth stage of the product life cycle will require a different mix from one in the maturity stage. In addition, in terms of positioning, a convenience product will require a different mix from a luxury product.

26 Digital marketing has benefited businesses in that they have the ability to gather more detailed information about consumers and to build relationships with them. For example, through its loyalty card Tesco can target promotions at individual customers.

4 Decision-making to improve operational performance

1 Added value is an amount added to the value of a product or service, equal to the difference between its cost and the amount received when it is sold.

2 Operations needs to liaise with marketing as it will make forecasts from market research as to what and how much should be produced. It will also be necessary to liaise with finance as this function will determine budgets and the availability of finance for capital investment, e.g. into technology.

3 Capacity refers to the maximum (total) amount a business can produce in a set time period.

Capacity utilisation is a measure of the proportion of total capacity that is being used in that time period.

4 Capacity utilisation = (output/maximum output) × 100

(20,000/25,000) × 100 = 80%

Labour productivity = output/number of employees

20,000/75 = 266.66 units per employee

Unit costs of production = total costs of production/number of employees

£1m/25,000 = £40

5 Unit costs of production will decline when capacity utilisation and productivity increase in the short term only — variable costs will increase and the fixed costs will be spread across more units of output.

6 Two advantages of JIT production are lower costs due to the reduced need for storage space and lower wastage as there is less likelihood of products being damaged or going out of fashion.

Two disadvantages are: production may be halted if stock fails to arrive on time due to weather or other problems; and may also be higher due to missing out on bulk purchase discounts.

7

Benefits	Drawbacks
If achieved by introduction of technology, quality and reliability may improve.	Resistance of employees.
Job redesign and training may improve motivation.	Cost.
	Quality may fall, e.g. if piece rate is used.

8 A capital-intensive approach to production puts a greater emphasis on capital than labour in production. This will benefit a UK manufacturing business as labour is expensive in the UK, so such an approach will help reduce overall costs of production and increase competitiveness.

9 Excess production capacity occurs when a business is producing below maximum capacity.

A lack of production capacity occurs when demand is greater than the maximum capacity level.

10 Capacity utilisation may be improved by increasing sales or reducing the maximum capacity. Increasing sales might be achieved through better marketing or targeting new markets. Reducing capacity involves selling off unwanted production capacity but this should only be done if a business is sure that the capacity is no longer needed.

11 Some examples of the implications of a decision to use new technology:

(i) Marketing	(ii) Finance
New production processes allowing lower prices or new products increasing sales.	Initial costs but possibly resulting in increased profits in the long term.
(iii) Operations management	**(iv) People in business**
The use of technology may assist a business in meeting its quality targets.	Production line technology may increase productivity.

12 Quality is important as it may provide a USP for a business. This could enhance its reputation with consumers and lead to word-of-mouth promotion.

13 Total quality management instils a culture of quality throughout the business. Quality issues should be spotted at an early stage as everyone is responsible, thereby reducing costs and wastage.

14 Poor quality is likely to lead to increased costs as a result of wastage and the cost of replacing or repairing returned goods.

15 If the product is perishable, less inventory will be held. If demand is seasonal, the level of inventory is likely to be higher than for products that have regular demand.

16 Four key features of an inventory control chart are:

(i) maximum inventory level

(ii) reorder level

(iii) buffer inventory level

(iv) lead time

17 Payment terms may be more important when a business has concerns over cash flow and a longer payment period may be beneficial.

18 Mass customisation is the tailoring of goods to specific customer requirements. In other words, customers build their own products. This is likely to give a business a competitive advantage and greater customer satisfaction. For example, in the car industry customers can build their own vehicle in terms of colour, trim and accessories.

19 Demand is likely to be higher during school holidays, therefore prices can be higher during these periods and lower at other times. In addition, at the start and end of the season when snow is less reliable, prices are likely to be lower and there may be more promotions.

20

Advantages of outsourcing	Disadvantages of outsourcing
Respond quicker to increases in demand.	Likely to be more expensive.
Dependability for consumers.	Quality may not be as good.
Lower costs as do not have to invest in capacity.	

5 Decision-making to improve financial performance

1 A profitable business may fail due to cash-flow problems. Although sales may have been generated to make a profit, not all money from these sales may have been received, causing cash-flow problems and in the worst case failure.

2 **Gross profit** is the difference between sales revenue and the direct costs of production.

Operating profit is the difference between gross profit and the indirect costs of production (expenses).

Profit for the year takes into consideration other expenditure such as tax and interest payments, and other income, such as interest, to arrive at a final profit figure.

3 Return on investment = (return from investment (or profit)/capital invested) × 100

4 A rise in interest rates is likely to both increase costs and reduce demand. Costs will rise due to higher interest payments on loans, and demand fall due to lower disposable income of consumers.

5 A business might not be able to achieve financial targets in favourable market conditions due to a lack of resources, e.g. production capacity or skilled labour.

6

Favourable variances	Response
Higher sales than expected.	Increase production.
Lower fixed costs.	Possibly reduce prices.
Reduced fuel costs.	Enjoy increased profits.
Reduced material costs.	Lower prices or enjoy higher profits.

Adverse variances	Response
Sales below forecast.	Increase advertising.
Wage costs higher than forecast.	Use more technology in production.
Material costs higher than forecast.	Seek new suppliers.
Profits below forecast.	Seek new markets.

7 Three benefits of budgeting are:

(i) Budgets mean that targets can be set and monitored for each part of the business.

(ii) Budgets may improve financial control by preventing overspending.

(iii) They bring focus to decision-making as a result of individual managers having to think about the financial implications of decisions.

8 Breakeven = fixed costs/contribution per unit

9 Contribution = sales revenue – variable costs

Sales revenue = £100,000 × 2.50 = £250,000

Variable costs = £100,000 × 1.50 = £150,000

Contribution total = £250,000 – £150,000 = £100,000

10 (i) Breakeven = fixed costs/contribution per unit

Fixed costs = £15,000

Contribution per unit = 5 – 3 = 2

Breakeven output = 15,000/2 = 7,500 units

(ii) Profit = total revenue – total costs

Total revenue = £10,000 × 5 = £50,000

Total costs = £15,000 + £10,000 × 3 = £45,000

Profit = £50,000 – £45,000 = £5,000

11 A rise in fixed costs will cause the breakeven output to increase.

An increase in price will lead to a fall in the breakeven output.

12 Breakeven analysis assumes that all output is sold and that it is all sold at the same price, neither of which is likely in practice.

13 Gross profit margin might be improving as a result of falling direct costs of production but, if the indirect costs are increasing at a higher rate, the operating profit margin could be falling.

14 Payables: money owed for goods and services that have been purchased on credit.

Receivables: money owed by a business's customers for goods or services purchased on credit.

15 A cash-flow forecast is important because:

(i) It can be used in support of loan applications.

(ii) It may identify periods when a business might be short of cash so corrective action can be taken.

(iii) It may help in the planning for items of capital expenditure.

16 An overdraft is flexible as the business only pays interest on the amount that it borrows, but it is repayable on demand.

A bank loan is normally for a fixed amount and repayable over a period of time.

17 Retained profit and equity may be preferable sources of finance due to the fact they do not have to be paid back and there are no interest charges.

18

Cause	Solution
Poor management	Training or recruiting skilled managers.
Giving too much trade credit	Offer shorter periods or negotiate more favourable terms from suppliers.
Overtrading	Plan the financial aspects of growth thoroughly.
Unexpected expenditure	Have a contingency fund to meet such demands.

19 Two ways of increasing profit are:

(i) increasing prices

(ii) reducing costs

20 Increasing prices could lead to a fall in demand and revenue unless the product is price inelastic.

Costs might be reduced at the expense of quality, which might damage reputation.

6 Decision-making to improve human resource performance

1 Human resource objectives are the targets set specifically by and for the human resources function and might include targets for labour productivity and labour turnover.

2 Potential benefits of a fully engaged workforce are:

(i) higher productivity

(ii) lower labour turnover

(iii) greater labour retention

3 Two internal influences on human resource objectives: style of management used and the type of product produced.

Two external factors: the economy and technology.

4 A hard human resource approach treats employees as just another asset that must be used as efficiently as possible.

A soft human resource approach treats employees as a valuable asset that needs to be developed.

5 Labour turnover is a measure of the proportion of a business's staff leaving their employment during the course of a year.

Labour retention is the proportion of employees with one or more years of service in the business.

6 (i) Unit labour costs = labour costs/number of employees = £7.5m/300 = £25,000

(ii) Labour costs as a percentage of turnover = (labour costs/turnover) × 100

(7.5m/15m) × 100 = 50%

7 A knowledge of labour turnover and market trends will help in human resource planning as it will help identify needs in terms of recruitment, training, and redundancy or redeployment.

8 Job rotation simply allows employees to move around the factory floor undertaking different jobs at the same level. Job enrichment, however, provides more challenging tasks which are likely to be more motivating for employees.

9 The Hackman and Oldham model identifies five core characteristics (skill variety, task identity, task significance, autonomy and feedback), which impact on three critical psychological states (experienced meaningfulness, experienced responsibility for outcomes and knowledge of actual results), in turn influencing work outcomes (motivation, performance, job satisfaction and absenteeism).

10 A flatter organisation structure may be introduced in order to reduce costs and to give greater responsibility to employees in their work environment.

11 Delegation is the granting of authority by one person to another for agreed purposes. It is important in that it allows managers to concentrate on the more important strategic decision-making and it gives subordinates valuable experience.

12 Centralisation is the concentration of management and decision-making power at the top of an organisation hierarchy.

Decentralisation is the process of redistributing decision-making power away from a central location or authority.

13 Four possible influences on organisational design are:

(i) size of the business

(ii) life cycle of the organisation

(iii) corporate objectives

(iv) technology

14 McDonald's relies on the uniformity of its product and service which customers trust and enjoy and it cannot afford to allow individual managers to change that. Tesco, however, can allow individual store managers to respond to both the nature of demand and changes to demand in different parts of the country.

15 Changing organisational and job design is likely to make jobs more interesting and challenging which in turn may improve employee motivation. As a result, workers may become more engaged, thus increasing productivity, lowering labour turnover and increasing labour retention.

16 Effective workforce planning enables a business to have the right employees in the right place and with the right skills, making it more likely a business will achieve both its human resources and corporate objectives.

17 The scientific school of management is concerned with the needs of the organisation and the way the job is done rather than the needs of the individual, simply believing employees are motivated by money. The human relations school recognises that the needs of the individual employee are also important in improving motivation and efficiency.

18 The non-financial methods of motivation revolve around making work more challenging and interesting, achieved by giving greater responsibility and involvement in the decision-making process. Responsibility and involvement are key motivators in Herzberg's theory and are essential in achieving self-actualisation in Maslow's theory.

19 Trade union membership has declined since 1979 due to the changing nature of employment. Traditional industries. such as coal and steel, have declined and employment has fallen in

manufacturing — both these areas tended to be highly unionised. The service industry has seen a growth of employment but is less unionised. In addition, there has been a growth in self-employment and small businesses, which are less unionised.

20 ACAS's main responsibility is to prevent or resolve industrial disputes.

7 Analysing the strategic position of a business

1 The philosophy and values of a business are the set of beliefs and principles that a business works toward that explain its overall goals and purpose.

2 Mission, corporate objectives and corporate strategy are linked by the fact that the objectives set lead to a strategy that enables the mission to be achieved.

3 Short termism refers to the excessive focus of decision-makers on short-term goals at the expense of longer-term objectives.

4 Strategy is about choosing the best plan for achieving long-term goals whereas tactics are the short-term actions or means of achieving those goals.

5 A SWOT analysis identifies internal strengths and weaknesses and external opportunities and threats, which can lead to strategies focusing on the strengths and opportunities while alleviating the weaknesses and threats.

6 Profit quality is the degree to which profit is likely to continue in the future — the sustainability of profit. It is important because it provides an indication of the financial stability of a business.

7 Gross profit is calculated by deducting the cost of goods sold from the sales revenue.

Operating profit is the gross profit minus the expenses and overheads of the business.

Profit for the year is the operating profit after adjustments for interest paid and receivable and minus tax paid.

8 Liabilities are what a business owes (money) whereas assets are what it owns. Liabilities show where the money has come from and assets show what the business has done with this money.

9 Too little working capital could lead to a business struggling to make payments and cash-flow problems. Too much working capital is an inefficient use of money if cash is sitting in a bank account rather than being invested lucratively.

10 Two ratios include return on capital employed and the current ratio. In order to make a judgement regarding performance, comparisons could be drawn with previous years or competitors' businesses.

11 An understanding of gearing is useful when deciding how to finance a major capital investment as a high-geared firm may find it difficult to raise finance through borrowing.

12 Three limitations of ratio analysis are:

(i) They are based on past results.

(ii) They may be 'window dressed'.

(iii) They are of limited focus.

13

Functional area	Performance measure	Formula
Marketing	● Market share ● Market growth	● (Sales of firm/total market sales) × 100 ● (Difference in sales/earliest year) × 100
Operations	● Unit costs ● Capacity utilisation	● Total cost/units of output ● (Actual output in time period/maximum possible output per period) × 100
Human resources	● Labour turnover ● Labour productivity	● (Number leaving/total number of employees) × 100 ● Output per time period/number of employees

14 Core competencies are the combination of pooled knowledge and technical capacities that allow a business to be competitive in the market place.

15 Kaplan and Norton's Balanced Scorecard model provides a broader view that might detect weaknesses early but it is complex and some areas are difficult to quantify.

16 (a) The four elements of the Balanced Scorecard model are financial, customer, internal business process and learning/growth.

(b) The three aspects of the Triple Bottom Line are Profit, People and Planet.

17 Anti-competitive practices are where businesses exploit consumers by unfair means such as price fixing and cartels.

18 The Competition and Markets Authority (CMA) is a non-ministerial government department responsible for strengthening business competition and preventing and reducing anti-competitive activities.

19 Discrimination in the workplace is bias or prejudice resulting in the denial of opportunity or unfair treatment regarding the selection, promotion or transfer of employees. It may be on the grounds of age, sex, race, religion, etc.

20 Closed shops, open ballots and picketing.

21 The Environment Act 1995, the Climate Change Act 2008 and the Energy Act 2013.

22 Enterprise is encouraged by the reduction of red tape and lower taxes.

23 Ofwat, Ofcom and the Civil Aviation Authority.

24 Infrastructure is important for economic development and quality of life and therefore investment in education, health and transport is a key determinant of inward investment.

25 GDP is a measure of the value of all goods and services produced within a country over a specific time period.

26 A downturn in the business cycle will result in lower demand for a car manufacturer because of rising unemployment and falling consumer confidence.

27 Direct taxation is on income (e.g. income tax) whereas indirect taxation is on spending (e.g. VAT).

28 Fiscal policy is the means by which the government controls the economy through its spending and taxation whereas monetary policy is the control of the economy through the use of interest rates and other means to control the money supply.

29 (a) Lower disposable income and a greater incentive to save.

(b) Higher interest payments and lower demand.

(c) More value or budget items being bought and fewer luxury items because of less consumer disposable income.

30 A stronger £ is likely to lead to higher export prices and therefore lower demand.

31 Protectionism refers to the policies and actions by governments to restrict or restrain international trade, such as import tariffs, quotas or subsidies to local businesses.

32 Improved transport with bigger ships and containers making transport cheaper and easier.

Improved technology making it easier and quicker to communicate and share information.

33 An emerging market describes a national economy that is progressing toward becoming more advanced through rapid growth and industrialisation.

34 Immigration provides valuable human capital and vital skills, it increases aggregate demand and real GDP, and without it the NHS would have to spend millions on recruitment.

35 People have more leisure time, taking more holidays and to places further afield.

People are generally more affluent and eat out more frequently. When eating in, they often opt for a ready meal.

36 Online shopping opens a wider market, increases sales and can reduce costs.

37 The shareholder concept sees the role of a business as one of making a profit for its owners (shareholders) whereas the stakeholder concept views the role of a business as one of looking after the interests of all stakeholders not just shareholders.

38 Corporate social responsibility (CSR) is a business approach that contributes to sustainable development by delivering economic, social and environmental benefits to all stakeholders. It can result in brand differentiation, customer and employee engagement as well as in some cases cost savings.

39 Carroll's pyramid of corporate social responsibility illustrates the four layers of corporate responsibility (economic, legal, ethical and philanthropic). It provides the framework for a business to understand the necessary principles of social responsibility, enabling practices and strategies to be developed to achieve it.

40 The action of pressure groups and the resulting unwanted media attention which may impact adversely on sales have led to greater pressure for CSR, as well as increased consumer awareness and action through social media which may impact on a business, reputation.

41 The forces in Porter's five forces model are entry threat (barriers to entry), buyer power, supplier power, rivalry and substitute threat.

42 A differentiation strategy calls for the development of a product or service

offering unique attributes that are valued and perceived to be different from competitors by customers, whereas a cost leadership strategy is one that aims to gain a competitive advantage from having the lowest costs in the industry.

43 Payback, average rate of return and net present value.

44

$$\text{Payback} = \frac{100,000}{12,500}$$

$$= 8 \text{ years}$$

45

$$\text{Average annual profit} = \frac{1,000,000}{4}$$

$$= 250,000$$

$$\text{Average rate of return} = \frac{250,000}{2,000,000} \times 100$$

$$= 12.5\%$$

46 The discount factor is the percentage rate used to calculate the present value of a future cash flow.

47 Net present value is considered better than payback or average rate of return as it takes into consideration the timings of cash flows.

48 The state of the economy may impact on investment decisions, for example a downturn might lead to a postponement because of deteriorating environment.

Industrial relations could have an impact, particularly if job losses may be involved.

49 Sensitivity analysis is a 'what if' tool that enables a change in a variable to be examined and allows more informed decisions to be made.

8 Choosing strategic direction

1 Strategic direction refers to a course of action or plan that it is hoped will lead to the achievement of long-term goals.

2 Cost, barriers to entry, competitors' actions and the ethics involved.

3 Market development involves finding new markets for existing products, using market research and segmentation to identify new groups of customers. Product development involves producing new products for existing markets.

4 Diversification may be chosen if the existing industry is in decline or has become saturated, thereby enabling further growth for a business and the spreading of risk.

5 The strategic positioning of a business relates to how that business is perceived relative to other businesses in the same industry.

6 A low-cost strategy involves not only being the leader in an industry in terms of costs but also being able to sustain this leadership (e.g. Aldi and Lidl).

7 A differentiation strategy involves gaining a competitive advantage by being different from competitors in some way, whereas a focus strategy involves concentrating on a particular niche in a market which may be either through a differentiation or a cost focus.

8 They are uncompetitive because price is greater than perceived value.

9 A competitive advantage is likely to lead to brand loyalty, greater sales and therefore greater profit for a business.

10 Financial constraints, short termism and developments in technology.

9 Strategic methods: how to pursue strategy

1 Survival, increased profit and reduced risk.

2 Synergy is the idea that the value and performance of two businesses combined will be greater than the sum of the two parts, e.g. 2 + 2 = 5.

3 This involves reducing the size of a business and may be undertaken in an economic downturn or a declining market in order to reduce the costs of a business.

4 Economies of scope is an economic theory stating that the average total cost of production decreases as a result of increasing the number of different products produced, e.g. Cadbury.

5 The experience curve is the idea that the more you do something, the better you get at it, enabling quicker and cheaper production. Economies of scale refer to a reduction in cost as a result of an increase in size of an operating unit.

6 Organic growth (internal growth) is the expansion of a business from its own internally generated resources whereas external growth is achieved through mergers or takeovers.

7 Poor communication, lack of control and coordination, alienation of the workforce.

8 Greiner's model of growth describes six different phases of a business's growth from creativity to alliances and provides a framework to help understand different organisational structures and coordination methods.

9 Horizontal is the same stage of the same production chain, vertical is a different stage of the same production chain and conglomerate is merging or taking over a totally different business.

10 It is a quick method of growth, finance is provided by the franchisee and the franchisee is likely to be highly motivated.

11 Product innovation is the development of new products whereas process innovation is the development of better methods of production.

12 R&D is necessary to stay one step ahead of competitors and therefore for the survival and growth of the business. Failure to innovate can lead to failure, e.g. Nokia and BlackBerry.

13 An intrapreneur is an entrepreneur who exists within an established business.

14 Benchmarking is a strategic and analytical process of continuously measuring an organisation's products, services and practices against a recognised leader.

15 Intellectual property (IP) is an intangible asset belonging to the owner or an organisation that may be protected by patents, copyrights or trademarks.

16 Growth, profit, economies of scale and to diversify risk.

17 Risk in terms of dealing in different cultures and languages, political stability and IP theft. Competition in terms of local businesses as well as other foreign businesses.

18 Off-shoring is the moving of the operations of a business to another country.

19 Cost advantages may no longer be so great and the benefits include 'made in Britain' and control of IP theft.

20 The pressure for local responsiveness and the pressure for global integration (cost reduction).

21 Digital technology is used to describe the use of digital resources to find, analyse, create, communicate and use information effectively in a digital context.

22 Big data refers to the ever-increasing amounts of structured, semi-structured and unstructured data that have the potential to be mined for information, whereas data mining is the process used by organisations to turn large amounts of big data into useful information.

23 Enterprise resource planning (ERP) is the business management software system by which an organisation manages and integrates the important parts of its business. It has a number of advantages including improved speed, efficiency, integration and flexibility that may result in better analysis and planning capabilities, better management of resources, better customer satisfaction and lower costs.

24 With digital technology there is likely to be a high initial investment and change within an organisation can lead to stress and lower morale.

10 Managing strategic change

1 Changing consumer tastes and fashion, competition, technology and the economy.

2 Incremental change involves introducing many small, gradual changes in a business or a project, whereas disruptive change involves radical change, often rethinking or redesigning a business or project.

3 For a change to occur, the driving forces need to be greater than the restraining forces.

4 The six steps are:
(i) Identify the current situation.
(ii) Identify the desired situation.
(iii) List all the driving forces.
(iv) List all the restraining forces.
(v) Evaluate each of the driving forces and the restraining forces, giving each one a value on a scale of 1–10, with 1 = very weak and 10 = extremely strong.
(vi) If change is viable, develop a strategy to strengthen the key driving forces and weaken the key restraining forces.

5 The value of change lies in the fact that a business which embraces change is likely to be more flexible and more able to take advantage of new opportunities to take advantage of consumers' changing needs and therefore progress and grow.

6 Restructuring involves a fundamental internal organisational change that alters the roles and relationships of those involved.

7 Flexible employment contracts such as part-time, temporary and zero hours benefit a business in that they enable greater flexibility and result in the business being more adaptable to change.

8 Mechanistic structures are hierarchical and bureaucratic with centralised authority and formal procedures and practices. Organic structures are decentralised, flatter with wider spans of control and therefore likely to be flexible and adapt easily to change.

9 Effective knowledge management and the resulting decisions arise from a solid foundation of data and information management.

10 The barriers to change revolve around employee resistance and the culture of an organisation that may not embrace change. It may also be that management are unwilling to change and as a result do not provide sufficient resources for change in terms of finance or personnel.

11 Parochial self-interest, misunderstanding and lack of trust, different assessments and low tolerance of change.

12 Education and communication, facilitation and support, participation and involvement, manipulation and co-option, negotiation and bargaining, and explicit and implicit coercion.

13 The organisational culture is a system of shared assumptions, values and beliefs that govern how a business operates.

14 Identity, direction, loyalty and attitude to change.

15 Power culture concentrates power among a small group or central figure. There tend to be few rules and little bureaucracy and decisions can be made quickly.

Role culture is characterised by strong functional or specialised areas coordinated by a narrow band of senior management at the top. Individuals within the business have clear roles and know whom they report to.

16 Individualism v collectivism, power distance, indulgence v restraint, long term v short term, masculinity v feminism and uncertainty avoidance.

17 The leadership style, whether autocratic or laissez faire, has an impact on culture as well as the nature of the business, whether it is in a fast-moving technological industry or a more traditional industry dependent on economies of scale.

18 Toxic culture, change of leader, change of ownership and changing market conditions.

19 Successful strategy implementation requires a clear understanding of what needs to be achieved by all, as well as an understanding of both internal and external factors influencing the strategy. This ensures a clear focus and hopefully the commitment of all concerned. Commitment should stem from the top and involve everyone.

20 Leaders are involved with the strategy and should not only demonstrate full commitment but also communicate it effectively in order that the workforce are also fully engaged and committed to the strategy.

21 A functional structure distributes decision-making and operational authority along functional lines with specialisation of skills according to the function, e.g. marketing, finance, operations.

A product-based structure is based on the product or a production line, where all functions related to that product are delegated.

A matrix structure is where the structure is based around a major project or task and specialists from the various functional areas are assigned to the project.

22 Network analysis encourages planning, enabling resources to be ordered as needed and therefore reducing costs and potential cash-flow problems. Should anything go wrong, it can act as a starting point for making amendments.

23 Float is the spare time that may exist within a project and can be calculated using the following formula:

Float = LFT – duration of activity — EST

24 Problems occur with strategy implementation when workers or management are not fully committed to the strategy or management fail to effectively communicate the strategy to the workforce. They may also occur due to a lack of resources, both in financial and personnel terms, or it may be that there is a significant change in the external environment that prevents successful implementation.

25 Planned strategy is one that the management intends to implement using a carefully laid plan to achieve the desired position, whereas emergent strategy is an unplanned strategy that develops over time and is based on the belief that change should not be seen as a series of linear events.

26 Strategic drift occurs where a business responds too slowly to changes in its external environment and results in the strategic plan no longer being appropriate. It might occur due to a culture that is resistant to change and moves too slowly or it might occur due to a lack of monitoring, as a result of which any drift goes unnoticed.

27 Divorce of ownership and control refers to the separation of the ownership (shareholders) and control (elected board of directors) in a public limited company.

28 Good corporate governance is important in an economy as it provides a barrier to corrupt dealings, enhancing access to capital and the long-term prosperity of both individual organisations and the economy as a whole.

29 Strategic planning provides a road map and gives purposeful direction to a business, while strategic evaluation is the process of determining the effectiveness of a given strategy in achieving the organisational objectives and taking corrective action wherever required.

30 Contingency planning is planning for the unexpected, such as natural disasters or loss of data.

Acknowledgements

The publishers gratefully acknowledge the following for permission to reproduce images. Every effort has been made to trace copyright holders. However, any cases where this has not been possible, or for any inadvertent omission, the publishers will gladly rectify at the first opportunity.

p 8t iDesign/Shutterstock, p 8u MightyIsland/iStockphoto, p 8l Yuri Arcurs/Shutterstock, p 8b Murat Giray Kaya/iStockphoto, p 9t Mads Abildgaard/iStockphoto, p 9u Rido/Shutterstock, p 9l Science Photo Library, p 9b Martyn F Chillmaid/Science Photo Library, p 10t Sam Chadwick/Shutterstock, p 10c Mads Abildgaard/iStockphoto, p 10b Idris Esen/iStockphoto, p 11t Paul Maguire/iStockphoto, p 11b Image Source/Alamy, p 12 James Benet/iStockphoto, p 13 Science Photo Library, p 14t Douglas Miller/Keystone/Getty Images, p 14c Rido/Shutterstock, p 14b BSIP, Taulin/Science Photo Library, p 15c NASA/Science Photo Library, p 15b Steve Gschmeissner/Science Photo Library, p 16 Food Standards Agency, p 17 Maura Fermariello/Science Photo Library, p 18t Ian Hooton/Science Photo Library, p 18c Steve Gschmeissner/Science Photo Library, p 18b Pasieka/Science Photo Library, p 19 Eye of Science/Science Photo Library, p 22t Aaron Bunker/Shutterstock, p 22b Bob Ingelhart/iStockphoto, p 24 Pete Niesen/Shutterstock, p 28t Andrey Armyagov/Shutterstock, p 28b Andrzej Tokarski/iStockphoto, p 29t Prill Mediendesign & Fotografie/iStockphoto, p 29l David Hoffman Photo Library/Alamy, p 29c David Sucsy/iStockphoto, p 29r Drazen Vukelic/iStockphoto, p 29bl Matt Collingwood/iStockphoto, p 30 The Power of Forever Photography/iStockphoto, p 32t Colin Bell, p 32b Martyn F Chillmaid/Science Photo Library, p 34 Tony McConnell/Science Photo Library, p 35t Bochkarev Photography/iStockphoto, p 35b Russell D Curtis/Science Photo Library, p 36 Michael Braun/iStockphoto, p 38l Lya_Cattel/iStockphoto, p 38r Andris Daugovich/iStockphoto, p 38b Iain Sarjeant/iStockphoto, p 39 paul prescott/Shutterstock, p 41 Science Photo Library, p 44 jo unruh/iStockphoto, p 49 Bob Ingelhart/iStockphoto, p 51 John Radcliffe/Science Photo Library, p 52t Eduardo Rivero/Shutterstock, p 52u Franz Metelec/iStockphoto, p 52l Tom C Amon/Shutterstock, p 52b Villiers Steyn/Shutterstock, p 53t Louise Smiles, p 53u Cheryl A Hogue/Science Photo Library, p 53l Louise Smiles, p 53b Francois Gohier/Science Photo Library, p 54t Louise Smiles, p 54r Eric Gevaert/Shutterstock, p 54c Andrew Penner/iStockphoto, p 54l LdF/iStockphoto, p 54b EcoPrint/Shutterstock, p 55 Wayne Johnson/Shutterstock, p 56l Eric Isselée/Shutterstock, p 56c Eric Isselée/Shutterstock, p 56r Michael Pettigrew/Shutterstock, p 56lr David Bukach/iStockphoto, p 56br Luna Vandoorne/Shutterstock, p 57 One World Images/Alamy, p 58 Chris Crafter/iStockphoto, p 59 AtWaG/iStockphoto, p 62t Ralph125/iStockphoto, p 62b Greg Nicholas/iStockphoto, p 63 jacus/iStockphoto, p 65 Alan Lagadu/iStockphoto, p 66t David Jones/iStockphoto, p 66c Emjay Smith/iStockphoto, p 66b filmlessphotos/iStockphoto , p 67t B. G Thomson/Science Photo Library, p 67c Wendy Conway/iStockphoto , p 67b Steven Cooper/iStockphoto , p 68 Hedrus/Shutterstock, p 70tl Hugh Lansdown/Shutterstock, p 70tc Todd Keith/iStockphoto , p 70tr Joy M. Prescott/Shutterstock, p 70br Brittany Courville/Shutterstock, p 70bc saiko3p/Shutterstock, p 70bl 2009fotofriends/Shutterstock, p 70c Sprada/iStockphoto , p 72t Huw Williams/iStockphoto , p 72b Louise Smiles, p 73 nito/Shutterstock, p 74 DPS/Shutterstock, p 75t Nik Niklz/Shutterstock, p 75b Maxim Petrichuk/iStockphoto , p 76tl Mauricio Anton/Science Photo Library, p 76tr Mauricio Anton/Science Photo Library, p 77 iStockphoto, p 78t Mlenny Photography/iStockphoto, p 78c Paul Nicklen/Getty Images, p 78b Michael W. Tweedie/Science Photo Library, p 79 Andrew Howe/iStockphoto, p 80t Liz Leyden/iStockphoto, p 80b Dmitri Melnik/iStockphoto, p 82tr olada/iStockphoto, p 82l Wayne Stadler/iStockphoto, p 82cr Jordan Tan/Shutterstock, p 82br David Spears/Science Photo Library, p 83 Korionov/Shutterstock, p 84t Kenneth Wiedemann/iStockphoto, p 84b Khoroshunova Olga/Shutterstock, p 85 FLPA/Alamy, p 86 Bob Krist/Corbis, p 88t JG Photo/Shutterstock, p 88b Pedro Salaverría/Shutterstock, p 94 Wayne Johnson/Shutterstock, p 96t George Clerk/iStockphoto, p 96u Schmid Christophe/Shutterstock, p 96l Laurence Gough/iStockphoto, p 96b Steven Allan/iStockphoto, p 97t visual7/iStockphoto, p 97u Pamela Moore/iStockphoto, p 97l Shutterstock, p 97b Luis Carlos Torres/iStockphoto, p 98 teekid/iStockphoto, p 100 corepics/Shutterstock, p 101t Lidian Neeleman/iStockphoto, p 101b Paul Rapson/Science Photo Library, p 102t Brian A Jackson/Shutterstock, p 102c dusko matic/iStockphoto, p 102b mathieukor/iStockphoto, p 104t Sally & Richard Greenhill/Alamy, p 104b Nathan Watkins/iStockphoto, p 105 Jostein Hauge/Shutterstock, p 106t Erin Babnik/Alamy, p 106b Paul Aniszewski/Shutterstock, p 108r Alexey Tikhonov/iStockphoto, p 108l Karol Kozlowski/Shutterstock, p 109 G. Brad Lewis/Science Photo Library, p 110tr Hulton Collection/Getty Images, p 110tl Levent Konuk/Shutterstock, p 110l Iwona Grodzka/Shutterstock, p 110c Martin Bowker/iStockphoto, p 110cr discpicture/Shutterstock, p 110r Jeanne Hatch/Shutterstock, p 111 Maximilian Stock Ltd/Science Photo Library, p 113 Andrew Lambert Photography/Science Photo Library, p 114 Daniel Gale/Shutterstock, p 115 Dr Jeremy Burgess/Science Photo Library, p 116tl Maksim Toome/Shutterstock, p 116tc courtesy of Apple, p 116tr Maria Gioberti/Shutterstock, p 116ct dardespot/iStockphoto, p 116cu HomeStudio/Shutterstock, p 116cl DNY59/iStockphoto, p 116cb Pamela Cowart-Rickman/iStockphoto, p 116b swinner/Shutterstock, p 117 Brad Mitchell/Alamy, p 118tl zuender/Shutterstock, p 118tc Dmitriy Shironosov/Shutterstock, p 118tr Stefanie Timmermann/iStockphoto, p 118bl vadim kozlovsky/Shutterstock, p 118bc yuris/Shutterstock, p 118br Mincemeat/Shutterstock, p 120t Angus McBride/The Bridgeman Art Library/Getty Images, p 120l PaulPaladin/Shutterstock, p 120r Joe Gough/Shutterstock, p 121tl Mau Horng/Shutterstock, p 121tr Pichugin Dmitry/Shutterstock, p 121cl andesign101/Shutterstock, p 121cr Ken Durden/Shutterstock, p 121b Dr Jeremy Burgess/Science Photo Library, p 122 Ferenc Szelepcsenyi/Shutterstock , p 123 stanislaff/Shutterstock, p 124tl Sandro Vannini/Corbis, p 124tr Shutterstock, p 124c Anna Gafiyatullina/iStockphoto, p 124b Myszka Brudnicka/Shutterstock, p 126l Lisa M. Robinson/Getty Images, p 126r Charles D Winters/Science Photo Library, p 128t Jean-Daniel Sudres/Corbis, p 128b Neale Cousland/Shutterstock, p 130l Martyn F Chillmaid/Science Photo Library, p 130r Valerie Loiseleux/iStockphoto, p 130b Cordelia Molloy/Science Photo Library, p 132 Andrew Lambert Photography/Science Photo Library, p 140t Jakez/iStockphoto, p 140u Andy Z/Shutterstock, p 140l Ferenc Cegledi/Shutterstock, p 140b Shawn Hempel/Shutterstock, p 141t Vulkanette/Shutterstock, p 141u Ria Novosti/Science Photo Library, p 141l Bjorn Svensson/Science Photo Library, p 141b Martyn F Chillmaid/Science Photo Library, p 142 Furchin/iStockphoto, p 144 Roger Ressmeyer/Corbis, p 146t Mariia Sats/Shutterstock, p 146l Shutterstock , p 146c yui/Shutterstock, p 146r Iain McGillivray/iStockphoto, p 146bl Andrew Longden/Shutterstock, p 146bc Ruslan Dashinsky/iStockphoto, p 146br Pete Tripp/iStockphoto, p 147 Oleg - F/Shutterstock, p 148 Martin Bond/Science Photo Library, p 149l Paul Morton/iStockphoto, p 149r Igorsky/Shutterstock, p 150t Gary Whitton/Shutterstock, p 150c Ria Novosti/Science Photo Library, p 150b Maximillian Stock Ltd/Science Photo Library, p 151t indianstockimages/Shutterstock , p 151b syagci/iStockphoto, p 152t Vuk Nenezic/iStockphoto, p 152c Gordon Heeley/iStockphoto, p 152b Nomad_Soul/Shutterstock, p 153l Larry MacDougal/Rex Features, p 153r Aaron Amat/Shutterstock, p 154t Zoran Mijatov/Shutterstock, p 154b Andrew Lambert Photography/Science Photo Library, p 156t Tek Image/Science Photo Library, p 156b Jeremy Walker/Science Photo Library, p 157 Dikiiy/Shutterstock, p 158 Arno Massee/Science Photo Library, p 160 Mike Dabell/iStockphoto, p 162t Nigel Cattlin/Alamy , p 162c Martyn F Chillmaid/Science Photo Library, p 162b Michael Utech/Shutterstock, p 164 Johanna Doorenbosch/iStockphoto, p 165 Andrew Lambert Photography/Science Photo Library, p 166 Sabine Kappel/iStockphoto, p 168t Uzi Tzur/iStockphoto, p 168b Martyn F Chillmaid/Science Photo Library, p 171 Leslie Garland Picture Library/Alamy, p 172t Aaron Amat/Shutterstock, p 172c Luke Daniek/iStockphoto, p 172b T.W. van Urk/iStockphoto, p 173t OlesiaRu&IvanRu/Shutterstock, p 173l goce risteski/iStockphoto, p 173r courtesy of Paul Hurley, p 177 kryczka/iStockphoto, p 180 Andrea Danti/Shutterstock, p 184t Ana Abejon/iStockphoto, p 184u Nancy Louie/iStockphoto, p 184l ALEAIMAGE/iStockphoto, p 184b Pete Saloutos/Shutterstock, p 185t Michael Rolands/Shutterstock, p 185u Tomaz Levstek/iStockphoto, p 185l Victor Polyakov/iStockphoto, p 185b yusuf anil akduygu/iStockphoto, p 186t Bettmann/Corbis, p 186b mangostock/Shutterstock, p 187t David Burton/Alamy, p 187b Tony McConnell/Science Photo Library, p 188 Andrew Lambert Photography/Science Photo Library, p 190t NASA/Science Photo Library, p 190l Picture Contact/Alamy, p 190cr John Mead/Science Photo Library, p 190br Vakhrushev Pavel/Shutterstock, p 192l Simon Krzic/Shutterstock, p 192tr National Insulation Association, p 192br victor zastol`skiy/iStockphoto, p 194t Doug Johnson, p 194b Gustoimages, p 195 Gerry Boughan/Shutterstock, p 196cl jo unruh/iStockphoto, p 196cr niknikon/iStockphoto, p 196bl Andrew Howe/iStockphoto, p 196bcl Maksym Kravtsov/iStockphoto, p 196bcr Jane norton/iStockphoto, p 196br Mark Richardson/iStockphoto, p 197t University of Oslo, p 197b ESO, p 198t David M Martin/Science Photo Library, p 198c Topical Press Agency/Stringer/Getty Images, p 198b Crown Copyright/MOD, p 199 Power and Syred/Science Photo Library, p 200 Tumarkin Igor Alekseevich/Shutterstock, p 202 courtesy of G. D. Freeman/Gallica, p 204t courtesy of www.nought.de, p 204c GK Hart/Vikki Hart/The Image Bank/Getty Images, p 204r Baris Simsek/iStockphoto, p 205 Joe Gough/Shutterstock, p 206 Michael Bodmann/iStockphoto, p 207r Monkey Business Images/Shutterstock, p 207t Martin Bond/Science Photo Library, p 207b David Cannings-Bushell/iStockphoto, p 208t Shout/Rex Features , p 208b ariadna de raadt/Shutterstock, p 209 Charles D Winters/Science Photo Library, p 211 Lawrence Lawry/Science Photo Library, p 212t Edyta Pawlowska/Shutterstock, p 215 Science Photo Library, p 216 Corbis, p 218t Dr. P Marazzi/Science Photo Library, p 218b CRNI/Science Photo Library, p 219 NASA/Science Photo Library, p 226 Jason Stitt/iStockphoto, p 228t Stephanie Swartz/Shutterstock, p 228u stephen mulcahey/Shutterstock, p 228l Tjanze/iStockphoto, p 228b NASA, p 229t TebNad/Shutterstock, p 229u Nick Hawkes/Shutterstock, p 229l Pavel Tomanec/iStockphoto, p 229b Marvin Dembinsky Photo Associates/Alamy, p 230t Manfred Konrad/iStockphoto, p 230c Osuleo/iStockphoto, p 230b NASA, p 231t egd/Shutterstock, p 231b OxfordSquare/iStockphoto, p 232t Kadir Barcin/iStockphoto, p 232b Rodion/Shutterstock, p 233t Kevin Britland/Shutterstock, p 233b J.D.S/Shutterstock, p 234 Seb Rogers/Alamy, p 235 Ivars Linards Zolnerovics/Shutterstock, p 238 Todd Winner/iStockphoto, p 240tl Jitalia17/iStockphoto, p 240tc Ralph125/iStockphoto, p 240tr esemelwe/iStockphoto, p 240bl jacus/iStockphoto, p 240br Johann Helgason/Shutterstock, p 241 Alaska Stock/Photolibrary, p 242 ericsphotography/iStockphoto, p 244t JuliusKielaitis/Shutterstock, p 244b TebNad/iStockphoto, p 245t Rob Wilkinson/Alamy, p 245b mrSarunas/Shutterstock, p 248 Skyscan/Science Photo Library, p 249l US Department of Energy/Science Photo Library, p 249r US Department of Energy/Science Photo Library, p 250t Alexander Tsiaras/Science Photo Library, p 250b Mark Kostich/iStockphoto, p 251t tanikewak/Shutterstock, p 251b ISM/Science Photo Library, p 252t NASA/Science Photo Library, p 252b Shutterstock, p 254t Adrio Communications Ltd/Shutterstock, p 254b NASA/Science Photo Library, p 255t NASA, p 255b NASA, p 256t Mark Garlick/Science Photo Library, p 256c NASA, p 256b Stephan Hoerold/iStockphoto, p 257 NASA/JPL-Caltech, p 258l MattJones/Shutterstock, p 258r John Foster/Science Photo Library, p 260 NASA/ESA/STSCl/J Bahcall, Princeton IAS/Science Photo Library, p 262t Royal Astronomical Society/Science Photo Library, p 262c Take 27 Ltd/Science Photo Library, p 262b NASA, p 263 Jeff Hester and Paul Scowen, Arizona State University/Science Photo Library, p 264t Markus Gann/Shutterstock, p 264c asonbild/Alamy, p 264b Andrew Buckin/Shutterstock, p 268 Chris Sherry, p 269t Vladimir Caplinskij/Shutterstock, p 269b Warren Goldswain/Shutterstock, p 272-273 Yuri Arcurs/Shutterstock, p 272bl Valua Vitaly/Shutterstock, p 272br Martina Ebel/Shutterstock, p 273r Photoroller/Shutterstock, p 274-275 image courtesy of Bravo, text courtesy of The Times/NI Syndication, p 283t Andrew Lambert Photography/Science Photo Library, p 283c Pedro Salaverría/Shutterstock, p 283b Shawn Hempel/Shutterstock, p 288 Martyn F. Chillmaid/Science Photo Library

Group

1	2	

1 1 H hydrogen

7 3 Li lithium	9 4 Be beryllium
23 11 Na sodium	24 12 Mg magnesium

Group

3	4	5	6	7	8	9	10
39 19 K potassium	40 20 Ca calcium	45 21 Sc scandium	48 22 Ti titanium	51 23 V vanadium	52 24 Cr chromium	55 25 Mn manganese	56 26 Fe iron
85 37 Rb rubidium	88 38 Sr strontium	89 39 Y yttrium	91 40 Zr zirconium	93 41 Nb niobium	96 42 Mo molybdenum	99 43 Tc technetium	101 44 Ru ruthenium
133 55 Cs caesium	137 56 Ba barium	139 57 La lanthanum	178 72 Hf hafnium	181 73 Ta tantalum	184 74 W tungsten	186 75 Re rhenium	190 76 Os osmium
223 87 Fr francium	226 88 Ra radium	227 89 Ac actinium					

(continued)

59 27 Co cobalt	59 28 Ni nickel	64 29 Cu copper	65 30 Zn zinc
103 45 Rh rhodium	106 46 Pd palladium	108 47 Ag silver	112 48 Cd cadmium
192 77 Ir iridium	195 78 Pt platinum	197 79 Au gold	201 80 Hg mercury

Group

3	4	5	6	7	0
					4 2 He helium
11 5 B boron	12 6 C carbon	14 7 N nitrogen	16 8 O oxygen	19 9 F fluorine	20 10 Ne neon
27 13 Al aluminium	28 14 Si silicon	31 15 P phosphorus	32 16 S sulfur	35 17 Cl chlorine	40 18 Ar argon
70 31 Ga gallium	73 32 Ge germanium	75 33 As arsenic	79 34 Se selenium	80 35 Br bromine	84 36 Kr krypton
115 49 In indium	119 50 Sn tin	122 51 Sb antimony	128 52 Te tellurium	127 53 I iodine	131 54 Xe xenon
204 81 Tl thallium	207 82 Pb lead	209 83 Bi bismuth	210 84 Po polonium	210 85 At astatine	222 86 Rn radon

Modern periodic table. You need to remember the symbols for the highlighted elements.